Istanbul

NEW DIRECTIONS IN INTERNATIONAL STUDIES

Patrice Petro, Series Editor

The New Directions in International Studies series focuses on transculturalism, technology, media, and representation, and features the innovative work of scholars who explore various components and consequences of globalization, such as the increasing flow of peoples, ideas, images, information, and capital across borders. Under the direction of Patrice Petro, the series is sponsored by the Center for International Education at the University of Wisconsin–Milwaukee. The center seeks to foster interdisciplinary and collaborative research that probes the political, economic, artistic, and social processes and practices of our time.

For a list of titles in the series, see the last page of the book.

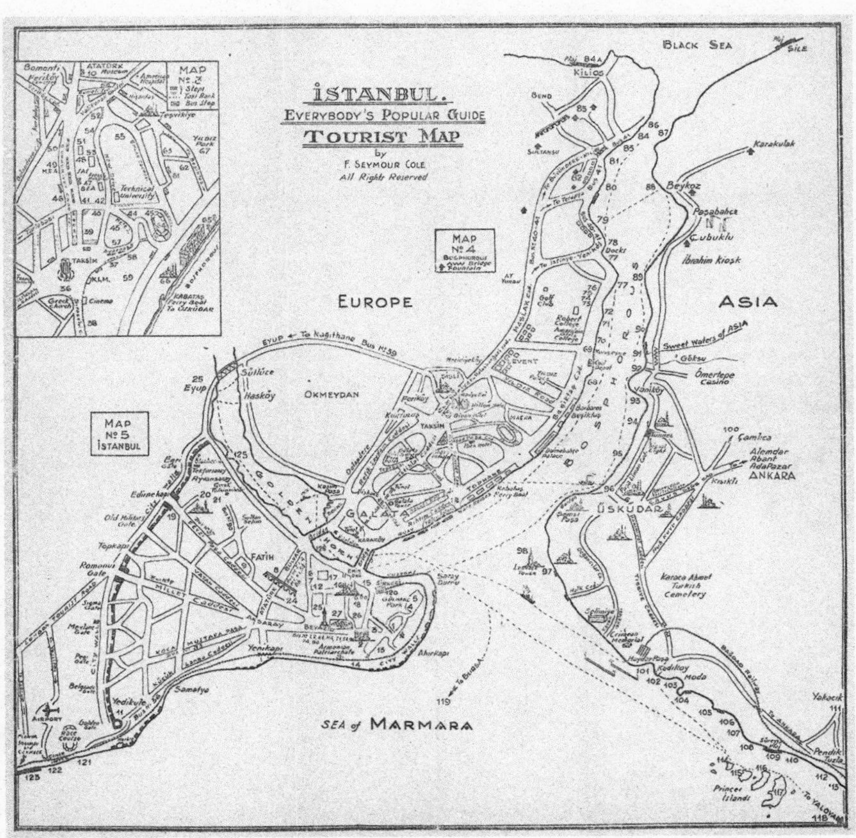

Courtesy of Nicholas Danforth.

Istanbul

Living with Difference in a Global City

EDITED BY
NORA FISHER-ONAR
SUSAN C. PEARCE
E. FUAT KEYMAN

RUTGERS UNIVERSITY PRESS
NEW BRUNSWICK, CAMDEN, AND NEWARK, NEW JERSEY, AND LONDON

Library of Congress Cataloging-in-Publication Data
Names: Fisher, Nora, 1976– editor. | Pearce, Susan C., editor. | Keyman, Emin Fuat, editor.
Title: Istanbul : living with difference in a global city / edited by Nora Fisher-Onar, Susan C. Pearce, and E. Fuat Keyman.
Description: New Brunswick : Rutgers University Press, 2018. | Series: New directions in international studies | Includes bibliographical references and index.
Identifiers: LCCN 2017016374 (print) | LCCN 2017021034 (ebook) | ISBN 9780813589114 (E-pub) | ISBN 9780813589121 (Web PDF) | ISBN 9780813589107 (cloth : alk. paper) | ISBN 9780813589091 (pbk. : alk. paper) | ISBN 9780813589114 (epub)
Subjects: LCSH: Cosmopolitanism—Turkey—Istanbul. | Istanbul (Turkey)—History. | Istanbul (Turkey)—Social conditions. | Cultural pluralism—Turkey—Istanbul.
Classification: LCC DR719 (ebook) | LCC DR719 .I78 2018 (print) | DDC 949.61/8—dc23
LC record available at https://lccn.loc.gov/2017016374

A British Cataloging-in-Publication record for this book is available from the British Library.

⊗ The paper used in this publication meets the requirements of the American National Standard for Information Sciences—Permanence of Paper for Printed Library Materials, ANSI Z39.48–1992.

www.rutgersuniversitypress.org

Manufactured in the United States of America

This book is dedicated to everyone across time and space who has known love for Istanbul in both its times of effervescence and its times of heartbreak.

Contents

PART II
Paradise Lost: Contested Memories of Cosmopolis

PART III
Actually Existing Conviviality: Sharing Space in a Globalizing City

FOREWORD

Istanbul

A SPACE OF UNTRANSLATABILITY, A CITY ALWAYS ARISING FROM ITS ASHES LIKE A PHOENIX

E. Fuat Keyman

In the book *Istanbul: Memories and the City* by 2006 Nobel laureate Orhan Pamuk, the term *hüzün* is used to explain the uniqueness and peculiarity of this city.[1] This emanates, in part, from its being the former capital of a world empire with a multiethnic, multireligious, and multicultural history, now lost. It is also due to Istanbul's location and image as straddling the West and East (sometimes being both, sometimes neither). The result is that one breathes and feels in Istanbul a sense of melancholy, sorrow, and longing. Yet none of these adjectives adequately describes Istanbul.

Orhan Pamuk finds that for this beautiful place where he was born, raised, and currently resides, the Turkish word *hüzün*, which encompasses all these adjectives, best describes the city. He writes "we might call this confused, hazy state melancholy, or perhaps we should call it by its Turkish name, *hüzün*, which denotes a melancholy that is communal rather than private."[2] It is, he observes, "a feeling that implicates us all not only in a spiritual state but a state of mind that is as life-affirming as it is negating."[3] A word of Arabic origin, *hüzün* resonates in Turkish at some levels that cannot be translated into other languages.

Engin Işın, in "The Soul of a City: Hüzün, Keyif, Longing,"[4] argues that *hüzün* alone cannot capture the soul of the city. Istanbul also involves a soul of enjoyment and another quasi-untranslatable term: *keyif*, or more precisely *şehrin keyfi*, which is the enjoyment of the city. Living and visiting Istanbul, siting in cafés, tea houses, bars, and *meyhane* (taverns), even wandering around neighborhoods and streets, one gets the feeling of *keyif*. Istanbul consists of both souls, *hüzün* and *keyif*, longing and enjoyment, and therein lies the specificity and peculiarity of Istanbul.

No doubt Istanbul is more than *hüzün* and *keyif*, carrying with it a number of characteristics. Istanbul is both a historical and a postmodern city. It carries history, tradition, modernity, and postmodernity at the same time. It is ancient with its significant and magnificent architecture, sites, and objects. One can stand at the intersection of a mosque, a church, and a synagogue. Yet it is postmodernity that shapes the identity of the city. There is no one Istanbul, but many Istanbuls, providing a living space for different cultural, ethnic, and religious identities and lifestyles, containing multiple modernities and offering a 24/7 life.

Istanbul is also a global city with an enormous economy that is bigger than many countries in the world in size and scale. It is a finance center. It is also more than a city, in that it constitutes an urban zone that includes a number of cities, a series of overlapping industrial, trade, service, and financial economies. Istanbul is of course Turkey's largest economic zone, providing 40 percent of the country's budget. By joining Marmara and the Black Sea, on the Bosphorus waterway, Istanbul connects two continents, Europe and Asia. Its geographical location and multilateral regional connections provide access to one-third of the total global population. Since the 1950s the population of the city has increased tenfold. As the most populous city of the country, its population is estimated at over 14.6 million, 18.6 percent of Turkey's total population.[5]

In economic terms Istanbul is one of the fastest-growing metropolitan economies in the world. The city creates US$250 billion total output by generating more than 50 percent of national exports and 43 percent of all budget revenues. This amounts to about 23 percent of Turkey's gross national product (GNP). After industry, trade is the second most important sector, contributing over 26.5 percent of provincial total added value.

However, Istanbul has recently been confronted by global terrorism. It has been subject to a series of deadly terror attacks that have taken many innocent lives. In recent years there has been a serious decline in the number of people coming to Istanbul. Terrorist attacks have given rise to an increasingly negative perception of the city. *Şehrin keyfi* seems to have been replaced by empty cafés, tea houses, restaurants, and bars. Nor is *hüzün*, as it is used by Pamuk, the soul of the city these days. Today, rather than *hüzün* or *keyif*, tears, fear, and anxiety increasingly define the soul of the city.

Yet Istanbul is not going to fall on its knees or surrender to terror; on the contrary, it has all the potential and power to resist these destructive forces. As has been the case many times throughout its history, it will arise from its ashes like a phoenix. I have no doubt that we will witness the resurrection of Istanbul as a global-historical city producing *keyif* and providing academics, researchers, and artists with a space for many souls, many identities, many modernities. It is with this conviction in the capability of Istanbul to rise from its own ashes that we seek through this book to make a humble contribution to advancing and enriching the existing interdisciplinary literature in the humanities and social sciences on this beautiful city.

NOTES

1. Orhan Pamuk, *Istanbul: Memories and the City* (New York: Vintage, 2006), 89.
2. Ibid.

3. Ibid., 91.

4. Engin Işın, "The Soul of a City: Hüzün, Keyif, Longing," in *Istanbul: Cultural Capital of Europe?*, ed. Deniz Göktürk, Levent Soysal, and İpek Türeli. (London: Routledge, 2010), 35–47.

5. These figures are from the Turkish Statistical Institute (TurkStat), accessed on December 19, 2016.

Historical Timeline

5000 B.C.E.	Significant human habitation of the site of present-day Istanbul.
13th–11th century B.C.E.	Thracian tribes begin to settle on the site of the present-day city.
approx. 657 B.C.E.	The Greek settlement of Byzantium is founded on the Thracian site by King Byzas.
196 C.E.	The Roman emperor Septimius Severus destroys Byzantium, massacring the population. He renames it Augusta Antonina, for his son, and begins to rebuild, adding Roman walls and building the city's first hippodrome.
330 C.E.	The Roman emperor Constantine designates the city as his capital, first as "New Rome" and then as Constantinople.
395 C.E.	The Roman Empire splits. Rome becomes the capital of the West and Constantinople the capital of the East.
536 C.E.	The Church of Saints Sergius and Bacchus is completed. Converted into a mosque (becoming Küçük, or "Little," Hagia Sophia) between 1506 and 1513, it is one of the city's oldest surviving Byzantine structures.
537 C.E.	The church of Hagia Sophia, built on the site of older places of worship, is completed in just six years.
1204 C.E.	Crusaders capture Constantinople and inflict major structural damage.
1261 C.E.	The city is recaptured by Greeks, who work to rebuild destroyed buildings.

13th century C.E.	Arabs begin to refer to the city as "Istinpolin," after hearing Greeks use the words *eis tēn polin* (meaning "to the city" or "in the city").
1349 C.E.	The Galata Tower is built by Genoese traders.
1453 C.E.	Sultan Mehmet II ("the Conqueror") captures the city, initiating Ottoman Muslim rule.
1461 C.E.	Mehmet II builds the first building of the Grand Bazaar, which becomes one of the world's largest covered markets.
1478 C.E.	Topkapı Palace is completed as a residential and administrative hub of the Ottoman dynasty.
1492 C.E.	The Sephardic Jews are expelled from Spain and migrate to Ottoman lands at the invitation of Sultan Beyazıt II, expanding the Jewish presence in Constantinople, Smyrna, Salonika, and other cities.
1520–1566 C.E.	Süleyman I ("the Magnificent") rules the Ottoman Empire. Flourishing cultural production, including works by the architect Sinan and his disciples, transforms the Golden Horn skyline.
1616 C.E.	The Sultan Ahmet Mosque, also known as the "Blue Mosque" for its interior lined with over 20,000 İznik tiles, is completed. Situated across from Hagia Sophia, the structure synthesizes elements of Byzantine and Seljuk/Ottoman architecture.
1703–1730 C.E.	Ahmet III rules the empire. During his reign, the latter part of which is often called the Tulip period, the empire begins to retrench militarily, but arts and culture thrive in Istanbul, with its hundreds of coffeehouses and population of circa 700,000.
1839 C.E.	The *Tanzimat* reforms are launched with the Edict of Gülhane, a park in the environs of Topkapı Palace. Culminating in the first Ottoman constitution in 1876, reform measures include elimination of the *millet* system and the institutionalization of Ottoman citizenship for all subjects irrespective of religious background.
1856 C.E.	The Treaty of Paris resolves the Crimean War, and the Ottoman Empire joins the Concert of Europe. Florence Nightingale returns to Great Britain, having revolutionized modern nursing through her treatment of war wounded in the Selimiye or Scutari barracks on the Asian side of the Bosphorus.

1908–1909 C.E.	The Constitution—first promulgated in 1876—is restored through the Young Turk revolution. When a counterrevolution, involving clashes near Taksim Military Barracks (Halil Paşa Topçu Kışlası–present-day site of Gezi Park), fails, the protonationalist Committee on Union and Progress deposes the sultan.
1914 C.E.	The Ottoman Empire enters World War I on the side of the Axis powers.
1919–1922 C.E.	The "War of Independence" (*Kurtuluş Savaşı*) is led by Mustafa Kemal Paşa (later Atatürk) against occupying Allied forces, in particular Greece. Istanbul is occupied by the British, and its straits are treated as international waters.
1923 C.E.	The Lausanne Treaty enables the foundation of the Republic of Turkey. It also leads to a mandatory population exchange of Muslims from Greece to Turkey and Greek Orthodox peoples to Greece. The Greek Orthodox community of Istanbul is exempted.
1920s C.E.	Kemalist reforms abolish the sultanate and caliphate and move the capital to Ankara, among other measures meant to sever institutional and cultural continuities with the Ottoman Empire.
1930 C.E.	The Turkish Post Office officially changes the name of the city to "Istanbul."
1955 C.E.	A pogrom perpetrated with state collusion against Greek Orthodox and other non-Muslim denizens of Istanbul on September 6–7 leads to a mass exodus.
1995 C.E.	Turkey, a NATO ally since 1952, enters a customs union with the then European Community (EC). The move bolsters Istanbul's role as the gateway to an economy that had undergone neoliberal restructuring under the leadership of Turgut Özal.
1999 C.E.	Major earthquakes strike near Istanbul and Athens. The Turkish tremor measures 7.4 on the Richter scale, leaving some 17,000 dead. The tragedy helps pave the way for Athens to lift its veto on Turkey becoming an official candidate for membership in the European Union.
2003 C.E.	Former Istanbul mayor Recep Tayyip Erdoğan becomes Turkey's prime minister, representing the Justice and Development Party (AKP).

2007 C.E. Liberal Armenian intellectual Hrant Dink is assassinated in front of his newspaper's office in Istanbul. Annual protests have been held on the anniversary of his death.

2010 C.E. Istanbul is designated the European Capital of Culture by the European Union.

2013 C.E. Mass protests are catalyzed by the planned reconstruction of Taksim Military Barracks at the location of Istanbul's Gezi Park.

2013 C.E. A train passage linking the European and Asian sides of Istanbul via a tunnel under the Bosphorus Strait opens.

2016 C.E. In commemoration of some 250 lives lost during a failed coup attempt, the first Bosphorus bridge is renamed "The 15 July Martyrs' Bridge."

Istanbul

INTRODUCTION

Between Neo-Ottomanism and Neoliberalism

THE POLITICS OF IMAGINING ISTANBUL

Nora Fisher-Onar

I am listening to Istanbul, my eyes closed.

—*Orhan Veli*

On an early summer day, in a year likely to be remembered for terrorist attacks, a coup attempt, and the aftermath of both, a seaside neighborhood in Istanbul prepared to memorialize a very different era. The May 29, 2016, celebration in Yenikapı's massive square brought together a million people, many arriving on 5,005 buses from thirty-eight provinces beyond the city. Their purpose was to honor the 1453 *fetih* or "conquest" of Istanbul by the Ottoman sultan Mehmet II.

The spectacle showcased poetry read by ax-wielding actors from an Ottoman-inspired soap opera. Audiences were also treated to an Ottoman-style marching band. Garbed in colorful period costume, the ensemble boasted 563 members in a gesture to the years that had passed since the conquest. Next on the program was a choreographed salute of "Turkish Stars" fighter planes, whose plumes of red-and-white smoke honored the national colors. Following a speech by Prime Minister Binali Yıldırım, President Recep Tayyip Erdoğan took the stage. In a rousing address to "sacred Istanbul," he linked the city's Ottoman-Islamic glories to a present political agenda: building a "New Turkey" with Erdoğan at the helm. Supporters were then dazzled by a 3D sound and light extravaganza featuring a 4,500-square-meter stage in the image of Istanbul's ancient ramparts. Boasting an LED screen of 450 square meters, over 500 period-costumed extras, and a life-sized replica of an Ottoman war galley, the spectacle was broadcast live in six world languages.[1]

A production befitting the globalized cultural industries, the scenario channeled a homegrown reading of Istanbul's history steeped in national-cum-religious pride. In keeping with the theme of "conquest," images like a massive sword inscribed in Arabic script were shown to overwhelm symbols of the city's earlier rulers: a crumbling cross and a bust of the Roman emperor Constantine, which spontaneously shattered. As the spectacle neared its climax, with Ottoman warriors breaching Byzantine ramparts, the crowd cheered as if at a rock concert finale. Affirming the sense of catharsis, a baritone narrator concluded by proclaiming that henceforth Ottoman "justice" (*adalet*) would rule a better world.[2]

The spectacle attested to how swiftly visions of a place's past—and future—can change. Only two decades earlier Erdoğan, whose star was rising as mayor of Istanbul, had complained that visiting tourists might not realize that they were in a Muslim country because of the lack of religious markers in public places, symbols that "allow you to make a statement to observers."[3] At that time Erdoğan's municipality had been a rival, not an ally, of the then prosecularist establishment in Ankara. His vision of Istanbul as once-and-future seat of Ottoman-Islamic glory accordingly was dismissed as a marginal project.

Ankara usurped Istanbul as the seat of government in the 1920s. The founders of the Republic of Turkey (1923) rejected the metropole's imperial mixing of waters and peoples. They were determined to build a brave new nation-state in arid Anatolia instead.[4] Like Venice, Istanbul became a fading if alluring hologram of an eclipsed world. This image of the city was immortalized in the melancholic ruminations of writers like Orhan Veli and Orhan Pamuk and in the gritty photography of Ara Güler.[5]

Economically and culturally, however, Istanbul proved "too big to fail."[6] Waves of rural to urban migration after the 1950s and economic liberalization beginning in the 1980s revitalized labor, capital, and trade flows. By the cusp of the twenty-first century, Istanbul was poised to reclaim its mantle as premier urban center of a vast region from the Balkans and Caucasus to the Levant.[7] Growing from a population of 1 million in 1940, to 3 million in 1970, to 7.3 million in 1990, Istanbul today is home to some 14 million souls.[8] The city further received almost one visitor per resident in 2015, making it the third most trafficked airport in Europe and—until a precipitous drop-off beginning in 2016 due to political upheavals—the world's fifth most popular tourist destination.[9]

In tempo with its mounting visibility, the contest for ownership of Istanbul's story intensified. Its position at the intersection of ancient and new histories[10] rendered the narrative possibilities vast. The menu of choices offered by Yenikapı alone, site of the *fetih* festivities, is illustrative. During the construction of the Bosphorus rail tunnel from 2004 to 2013, the terminus of which is at Yenikapı, Neolithic artifacts were discovered revealing 8,500 years of continuous habitation. Also uncovered were thirty-seven sunken ships, the oldest of which may date back 1,500 years. Like Yenikapı's original Byzantine-era walls, these maritime relics reveal the city's role as center of the Orthodox *oikumene* or "inhabited world" for almost a millennium. The enduring resonance of these finds is evident in their commodification for global audiences today. Plans are in place to build an "archeo-park" and a new museum to showcase the treasures for visitors. Yet neither the Stone Age nor the Byzantine legacy defines the city in the minds of its present owners.

A Tale of Two Cities: *Belle Époque* and Ottoman-Islamic Istanbul

Today it is the Ottoman era that has captured the collective imagination.[11] I argue that this period is widely read through two frames: *Belle Époque* Istanbul and Ottoman-Islamic Istanbul. They share many features, from neo-Ottoman nostalgia to function, social base, and normative thrust. These similarities belie simplistic readings of the city (and country) as torn between "liberalism" and a Western orientation and "Islam" and an Oriental character. Yet ultimately they offer, via Istanbul, rival answers to the driving questions of this volume and perhaps the outstanding challenge of our time: How do we live together in diversity? How can we share space, even thrive, with people whose hopes jostle against our own?

Neo-Ottoman Nostalgia

Belle Époque Istanbul is inspired by the city's role in nineteenth-century globalization, when many called it Constantinople. A major port whose commerce attracted 130,000 foreign residents, the city was embedded in a Mediterranean space and international system dominated by the European great powers.[12] Yet it was also an imperial hub in its own right—site of three millennia of continuous imperial government, and ruler of the Ottomans' Balkan, Caucasian, and Middle Eastern hinterlands.[13] The city's vibrancy was thus riddled with paradox: *Belle Époque* Istanbul was enlivened by the very economic, political, and cultural forces that were chipping away at the empire of which it was the capital.[14] This fraught interplay of internal and external imperial logics remains imprinted on the built spaces and syncretic vibe of neighborhoods like Beyoğlu, the old European embassy quarter.[15]

Beyoğlu and adjacent areas like the port of Karaköy also epitomize the *Belle Époque* emergence of Ottoman non-Muslim communities as the empire's first bourgeoisie. Comprising almost 20 percent of the Ottoman population in 1914, their legacy remains visible in apartment blocks, places of worship, schools, and place-names in the cityscape.[16] The people, however, are missing. Driven away by recurring waves of nationalism and persecution, among other forces,[17] Turkey's combined Greek, Armenian, Jewish, and Levantine population has declined from millions to under 100,000 today.[18] Nevertheless, as many of this volume's authors note, memorialization of the spaces that non-Muslim communities once filled in tribute to *Belle Époque* cosmopolitanism proceeds apace in the city's recreational districts.

A second widely invoked era is Istanbul's *Ottoman-Islamic* glory days. Increasingly salient across the cultural industries—advertising, design, architecture, fashion, television, and cinema production—Ottoman-Islamic Istanbul is the city of the *fetih* festivities. This neo-Ottoman imaginary begins in earnest with the life and times of Mehmet the Conqueror (1432–1481)—so named for his capture of the city—through the period of Süleyman the Magnificent (or "Lawgiver"; 1494–1566).[19] It was during this period that many of the minarets and domes of the Golden Horn's famed skyline were built. They served as a backdrop to the largest urban center in Europe, with some 700,000 inhabitants by the seventeenth century.[20] Renditions of its silhouette and other neo-Ottoman motifs in consumables from candelabras to kitchen tiles are a stamp of the Ottoman-Islamic imaginary today.

The glory days of Kostantiniyye, as it was called in the Islamicate world, are said to have continued through the Tulip period (1718–1730). Cultural and commercial life flourished in conversation with early modern Europe, but was not yet overtaken by Western forms and norms.[21] An often-cited example is the transmission of Ottoman high society's Tulip mania to Holland after the sultan gave bulbs and seeds to a Flemish ambassador. This Ottoman-centric reading of the flow of ideas, goods, and people legitimizes the claim today that the city embodies Turco-Muslim authenticity. This strand of nostalgia also can encompass later figures like the iron-fisted Sultan Abdülhamit II, whose reign from 1876 to 1909 is portrayed by some as a bulwark of Ottoman-Islamic integrity in the face of encroaching foreign powers.

Ottoman-Islamic Istanbul and its admirers are often associated with neighborhoods within the walls of the "old city." In Fatih, a quarter whose very name pays tribute to Mehmet's exploits, the historic mosque-market nexus of Islamicate urbanity is said to endure.[22] In the eyes of many an observer—local and outsider alike—the contrast between Fatih and Beyoğlu is suggestive of an Islamist versus Westernist divide.

Closer analysis, however, reveals entanglement. As a flourishing literature on the politics of space documents, rivalry between the *Belle Époque* and Ottoman-Islamic imaginaries is by no means binary. Both, after all, are products of the late modern, neoliberal order.[23] Their contestation entails overlap in substance, intersection in motives, and alliance building, as well as competitive behavior. In Fatih, as in Beyoğlu, Karaköy, and other historical neighborhoods like run-down Tarlabaşı—age-old sanctuary of the urban underclasses—multiple periods and protagonists clamor to be heard.

Istanbul's municipal headquarters is located in Fatih and has been run since 1994 by parties associated with Turkey's political Islamist tradition: the Welfare Party (RP) and its successor, the ruling Justice and Development Party (AKP).[24] Proreligious administrations have invested in the rehabilitation of both *Belle Époque* and Ottoman-Islamic Istanbul, while tending to privilege the latter. This is evident in commemorative activities employing the gamut of Ranger and Hobsbawm's tools of "invented tradition," in which historical memories are appropriated to legitimize present policies.[25] Examples include lavish events like the *fetih* extravaganza and an annual Tulip festival "to bring the once beloved flower home after centuries of neglect induced by Westernization."[26] Istanbul's Ottoman-era monuments are being restored and new structures evoke Ottoman-Islamic motifs. The pattern is especially evident in a boom of new mosques that gesture to the great, sixteenth-century architect Sinan. The massive Çamlıca mosque, for example, will redefine the Bosphorus skyline upon its completion. Municipal neo-Ottomanism and its inflection on ordinary lives attest, in turn, to the interplay of official and everyday "politics of piety."[27] By internalizing and demanding Ottoman-Islamic referents, the city's pious neoliberal subjects embrace and configure modernity in a Muslim-majority global city.[28]

Neoliberal Agenda

Belle Époque and Ottoman-Islamic Istanbul thus both display imperial nostalgia but attend to differentiated periods. Each also serves as a sort of municipal imaginary with national-level traction. That is, they enable selective assimilation of information about Istanbul's history to promote twenty-first-century agendas regarding the city, and the country more broadly. Politically, such interventions bestow material form and legitimacy on ideological projects while galvanizing supporters.[29] And analytically, as Charles King demonstrates in chapter 4 of this volume, they furnish a redolent site of analysis comparable across time and space. After all, just as *Belle Époque* and Ottoman-Islamic Istanbul share family resemblances, so do they display affinities with the brands that other rising cities across the global South are seeking to establish. As in Cape Town, Mumbai, Beirut, or Shanghai, in Istanbul-cum-Constantinople, neo-imperial nostalgia meshes happily with globalism.[30]

The touting of globally ascendant cities as microcosmic of their nation-states, moreover, underscores the degree to which these cities' rise remains bound to national projects. First, their very role as nexus between the neoliberal global economy and national or regional dynamics means that such cities rely on strategic investment from their states. Ankara's stake in Istanbul's status, for example, was evident at the *fetih* celebrations in the bussing in of audiences from the provinces, the national security symbolism of the fighter plane display, and the endorsement of the country's top leaders.

Second, as Çağlar Keyder observes in chapter 1 of this volume, national-level challenges can depress a city's prospects regardless of its intrinsic dynamism. For Istanbul, this truth came home after 2016 as tourists stayed away because of stormy national politics and spillover from the Syrian conflict. Attacks on strategic sites in Istanbul by Kurdish insurgents and radical jihadists underscore the intertwined fate of global cites with their nation-states. *Daesh* (the so-called Islamic State or ISIS) attacks on Istanbul's Atatürk airport on June 29, 2016, for

Figure I.1. Tram with Hagia Sophia in the background. Photo credit: Seray Pulluk.

example, attest to terrorists' cognizance that by sabotaging the gateway to Istanbul they would wound Ankara.

This climate dismays Istanbul's capitalists and intelligentsia, who as champions of the *Belle Époque* and Ottoman-Islamic narratives represent a second, overlapping feature of the two projects: their social base. The *Belle Époque* story appeals to liberal businesspeople and intellectuals, relatively influential offshoots of a prosecular ruling class that has been eclipsed during AKP rule. Rising pro-religious business interests and intellectuals, on the other hand, tend to endorse the Ottoman-Islamic narrative. Nevertheless, both camps are winners from

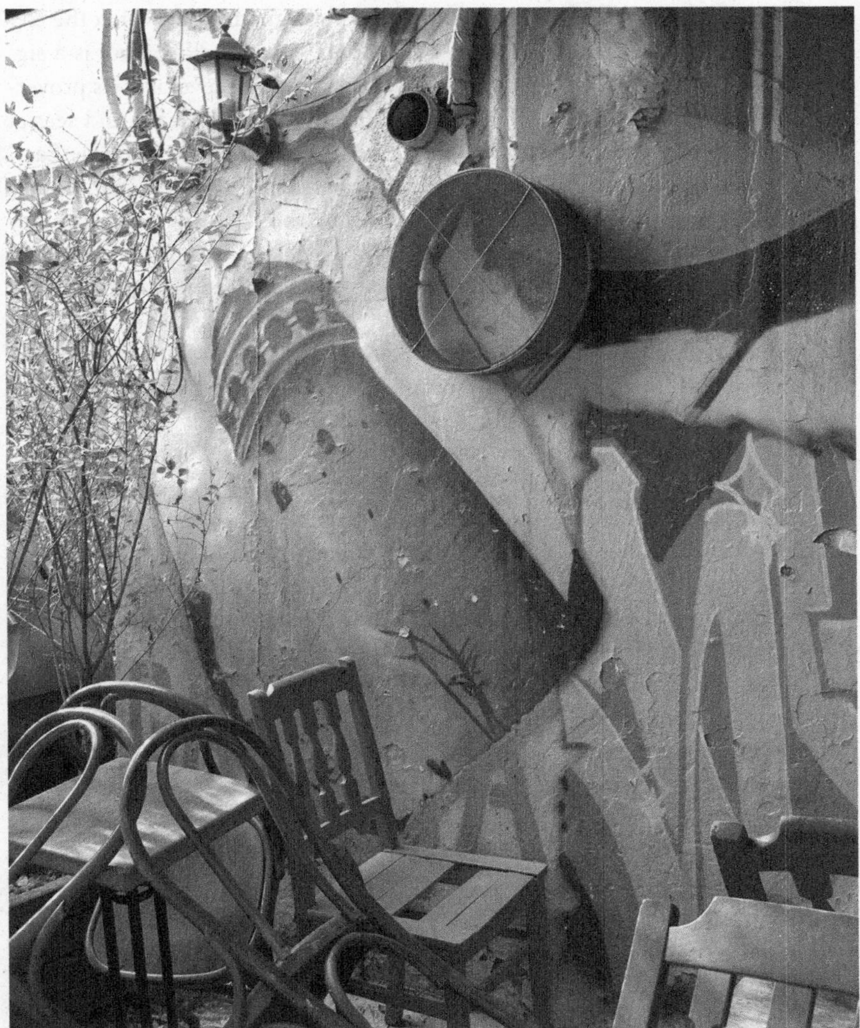

Figure I.2. Wall art backdrop in a café. Photo credit: Seray Pulluk.

globalization. They may cooperate or—given the paucity of conversation across epistemic communities—work independently toward the common goal of consolidating the city's status as a hub of global neoliberalism. Collusion is evident in the comparable themes of events that they sponsor. Among these are the symposia series from which this volume emanates as part of a 2010 Istanbul European City of Culture program that implicitly trumpeted both the *Belle Époque* and Ottoman-Islamic stories.

Over the course of the 2000s such efforts yielded dividends. Istanbul was ranked regularly among the world's top thirty cites in surveys like the Global

Cities Index. This performance is attributed to two functions at which the city excels. First, by virtue of its strategic "geocultural" location,[31] Istanbul is a significant facilitator of global policy conversations.[32] The role leverages its proverbial "bridge" status: linking geological formations like major straits and seas at one level, and political/civilizational blocs like "Europe" and the "Middle East" or the "West" and "Islam" at other levels.[33] This narrative of exceptional geocultural traction has lent the city clout since at least the late nineteenth century and especially after the onset of the Cold War.[34] A second, related source of strength according to global city indexes is that Istanbul's business-intelligentsia nexus, which included some forty public and private universities in 2015, fosters human capital.[35] Both roles are attested to by the high volume of business, civil society, and intergovernmental summits (e.g., NATO, OECD, UNDP) that Istanbul has hosted.[36]

These twin functions have been compromised by the current political climate, raising questions about Istanbul's ability to thrive in the short term. Both roles emanate, nonetheless, from structural rather than conjectural capacity.[37] As Sassen observes, it is Istanbul's inheritance at the intersection of North-South and East-West that makes it a natural arbiter in flows of trade, ideas, and people.[38] Istanbul combines, as Göktürk et al. observe, the transnational "global city" role of coordinator of markets with older, imperial "world city" service as arbiter of intellectual and aesthetic exchange. In both cases, the neo-Ottoman tale of two cities supplies "narrative[s]" for putting Istanbul on the map of "global media, the art world . . . investors, discerning tourists, curators of exhibits, real estate developers . . . [and] sundry consumers of culture."[39]

Pathways to Pluralism

Both *Belle Époque* and Ottoman-Islamic Istanbul furnish frameworks, at least in principle, with which to live with difference. The *Belle Époque* pathway to coexistence is liberal cosmopolitanism. By inviting individuals to rediscover late Ottoman Istanbul in all its multiculturalism, the narrative encourages transcendence of latter-day Turkish ethnonationalism. *Belle Époque* Istanbul thus opens a space for meeting, but also for mourning, its own protagonists, the lost Ottoman non-Muslim peoples. To be sure, nostalgia for an idealized past can serve to gloss over its grim realities, as İlay Romain Örs argues in chapter 5 of this volume. Her warning is all the more salient as pressure mounts in Turkey on those who challenge taboos. Nevertheless, in the mid-2000s there were notable openings like the initiative of faculty at private Istanbul universities to debate long-verboten topics like genocide and the fate of the Ottoman Armenians. In principle the pluralizing of mental and political space underwritten by *Belle Époque* nostalgia also can encompass heterodox and nonpracticing Muslim identities. That said, the aspirations of, say, Turkey's Alevi,[40] leftist, or lesbian, gay, bisexual, transgender, and queer (LGBTQ) communities, may not always align seamlessly with (neo) liberal pathways to pluralism.[41]

The *Belle Époque* frame further authorizes outreach to the pious Sunni elite and grassroots who arrived en masse in the city in recent decades. Engagement is based on treating Islamic observance as just one more expression of diversity to be governed by secular pluralism. This has been evident in liberal support for aspects of proreligious social movements since the 1980s. A case in point has been the search for acceptance of the headscarf in public spaces, a symbol of religiosity anathema to the Kemalist reading of secularism that until recently governed public life.[42] Despite such openings, the secular, liberal framework authorized by *Belle Époque* cosmopolitanism may mesh awkwardly with Ottoman-Islamic claims to normative primacy.[43]

Ottoman-Islamic Istanbul, after all combines affirmation of the neo-liberal subject with a faith-based and more communitarian orientation. A major inspiration is the *millet* system of hierarchal relationships between religious communities, which was used to manage diversity during the Ottoman golden era until its abrogation in the nineteenth century. In this framework, Sunni Muslims enjoyed preeminence regardless of their ethnic origin (e.g., Slav, Albanian, Laz, Circassian, Tatar, Kurdish, or Arab as well as Turkish).

At the same time non-Muslim groups were given communal autonomy maintained, as Feyzi Baban notes in chapter 3 of this volume, through intensive boundary-marking practices. As an approach to pluralism then, the *millet* system affirmed rather than ignored religious difference. Minorities thrived to the extent that the benign paternalism of the state—embodied in the person of the sultan—was indeed benign. By ensuring through differentiation that everyone knew their proper place, the framework was said to enable "harmonious relations in society."[44]

In today's Ottoman-Islamic imaginary of the city, the neo-*millet* formula for living with diversity erases divisions between (Sunni) Muslims. This furnishes a fragile space for reconciliation of, say, Turkish and Kurdish ethnic identities. Such an approach was used to frame a now defunct peace process with Kurdish militant, political, and civic organizations. Yet it problematically ignores some non-Sunni sensibilities. Alevi discomfort with neo-Ottomanism, for example, was attested to by outrage at the naming of a massive infrastructural project—the third Bosphorus bridge—after Selim I (1470–1520), whose expansion of Ottoman rule over the Middle East entailed suppression of Alevis as a potential "fifth column" for the Shi'a shah of Persia.[45]

At the same time, the Ottoman-Islamic approach acknowledges the difference of non-Muslim minorities in keeping with a neo-*millet* logic. Such recognition can lead to protection and the restoration of rights. During the 2000s, for example, an administration beholden to the Ottoman-Islamic narrative of Istanbul reinstituted numerous properties belonging to non-Muslim foundations (*vakıf; pl. evkâf*), which had been confiscated by hardline Turkish ethnonationalists in the 1970s.[46] Such policies may be why several prominent intellectuals of non-Muslim descent have thrown their weight behind the Ottoman-Islamic narrative.

Like any good story, the Ottoman-Islamic narrative of Istanbul can be interpreted in multiple ways. Its code of conduct, as evidenced by aspects of the *fetih* celebrations, also underwrites ethnoreligious nationalism. This can take the form of a bellicose and hegemonic rather than pluralistic and paternalistic Turkish-Islamist synthesis.[47] In this form, the approach raises flags for both non-Muslims and Muslim religious "minorities" like heterodox Alevis and many a secular Sunni. On the basis of national voting patterns, such groups comprise at least one-quarter of the national electorate[48] and dominate vital quarters of the Istanbul city center.[49] Their concern is that neo-Ottomanist trumpeting of Turco-Muslim primacy will spur vigilantes if not the authorities to purge rather than protect the religiously nonconformist.

Such fears were amplified when a leading liberal of Armenian heritage, Hrant Dink, was assassinated as he walked to work along a *fin de siècle* Istanbul boulevard in 2007. A decade later they were further exacerbated when a nationwide campaign castigating people who celebrate "culturally alien" New Year's Eve was followed by a *Daesh* attack on a cosmopolitan Istanbul nightclub in the early hours of January 1, 2017. Waking to the news of thirty-nine dead, citizens of secular orientation in particular began the new year with a sense of malaise.[50]

Kozmopolitical Acts

Belle Époque and Ottoman-Islamic Istanbul are nonetheless pluralistic and inclusive in principle if not always in practice. Many an Istanbulite will describe this condition as *kozmopolit* or "cosmopolitan." The term, as Amy Mills shows in chapter 6 of this volume, has an old and ambivalent local genealogy. Many who call Istanbul home have long seen it as both *cosmos*—the embodiment of the human condition—and the quintessential *polis*, a term used by Greek Orthodox inhabitants to describe not just any but "*the* City." This emic cosmopolitanism, as Örs puts it in chapter 5, is at once universalistic and particular, and remains a *leitmotif* in Istanbulites' self-understandings. The city, as such, offers a foil or "strategic space where our major challenges become acute and visible—a lens to see a larger world that remains difficult to grasp."[51] As Erdoğan, who grew up in the historic inner-city neighborhood of Kasımpaşa, expressed with a flourish: "If you try to write history without recognizing Istanbul your ink will dry, your pen will become blunt."[52] This native claim to embody the universal via the city's particularity—a paradoxical expression of cosmopolitanism that is fiercely local—is one that contributors to this volume critically engage as they explore modes of conviviality in the city.

Their findings speak, in turn, to a growing literature that grapples with "actually existing cosmopolitanism" via empirical research.[53] The goal is to move beyond the blithe assumption of mutual recognition that runs through much liberal cosmopolitan thought.[54] Instead, this volume's contributors draw on rich archival, literary, and ethnographic data to unpack multiple modes of grappling with difference in Istanbul. Authors hail from across the humanistic social sciences—history, religious studies, geography, anthropology, and sociology—as well as political theory, political science, and political economy. Their interventions offer emplaced rather than *a priori*, contingent rather than definitive, windows onto the dynamics that shape the sharing of space in the city.

What the chapters have in common is the Arendtian intuition that the act of occupying city space is both political and performative.[55] As Mumford wrote about New York in the 1930s, it is in "the city as theater" that our "more purposive activities are focused, and work out . . . into more significant culminations;" such outcomes are generated through the interactions of "conflicting and cooperating personalities, events, [and] groups."[56] Templates like *Belle Époque* and Ottoman-Islamic cosmopolitanism serve as scripts for these interactions. Yet they are open to improvisation by sundry actors on the city stage. Each performance, moreover, reinterprets the narrative generating "mixity"[57]—a "constellation of trajectories"[58]—which coalesces into new, often volatile ways of living with difference.

One such mode is that of the cosmopolitan subaltern who tenaciously fills the city's rougher spaces. If the bourgeoisie, enamored of *Belle Époque* or Ottoman-Islamic Istanbul, exemplifies the cosmopolitanism of "frequent fliers,"[59] Istanbul's "rootless underclasses," like de Certeau's urban walker, also "constantly cross symbolic boundaries" to "negotiate their ways through the cityscape."[60] Hailing from Anatolia are Turkish and Kurdish migrants, mostly pious Sunnis but also Alevis, who impress a heterodox stamp on core Istanbul neighborhoods like Okmeydanı.

These internal relocations rub against documented and surreptitious arrivals from abroad. Economic migrants and asylum seekers, they serve as day laborers and waiters, housecleaners and caregivers. Cohabitation can cause tensions but also, as Kristen Sarah Biehl argues in chapter 8 of this volume, pragmatic and transformative interconnections—a multidiasporic conviviality. Uzbek nannies from Central Asia and Georgian drivers from the Caucasus mingle with West African bouncers and Moldovan maids.[61] They are "acutely aware what different segments of the society [think] about them" but determined to "play with this difference in their own terms."[62] In so doing, they consume and produce the city's *kozmopolitik* energies. A fraught "sense of urbanity" becomes "essential to their lives" even as they grapple with the exile's nostalgia for a hometown or homeland left behind.[63]

A massive influx of Syrians, moreover, is making its mark on Istanbul, the latest in a long line of refugee movements into and out of the city. From Sephardic Jews in the fifteenth century and Polish officers in the nineteenth, to White Russians on the eve and German Jews at the apex of the world wars, Istanbul always has offered a port to weather storms, even as it generates its own.[64] As a 1922 pathfinder survey put it, "Constantinople, owing to its geographical situation and its political importance in the Near East, has been for many years and apparently always will be the great center for all refugees from political or religious upheaval in the Near East," conflicts "which render life difficult if not impossible where they occur."[65]

The management of intersecting identities that Istanbul requires is also inherently gendered. Decisions made every morning, like what a woman will wear, are governed by a visceral assessment of the cityscape to be traversed that day. On balance, more open attire is *de rigueur* in Beyoğlu or newer shopping districts like Bağdat Avenue, while conservative gear is appropriate to, say, Fatih. That said, the binary juxtaposition of veiled and unveiled women that so saturates media imagery of Istanbul belies the multiplicity of motives and audiences that women entertain. Mobilization over the past three decades by conservative women for the right to wear the veil in public universities, for example, was long pursued by invoking both liberal arguments for women's inclusion in public spaces and (Ottoman-)Islamic morality.[66]

Women's mobilization is microcosmic of the challenges faced in generating solidarities more broadly. For example, a study of self-proclaimed activists from multiple political, religious, and ethnic backgrounds found that it was possible to form common platforms around "thin" shared values like preventing violence against women. However, there was considerable culturally driven disparity in the strategies advocated.[67] So when mass protests unfurled in February 2015 to mourn the rape and murder of Özgecan Aslan, some organizers delighted in male allies' move to march along Istanbul thoroughfares in miniskirts. The tactic garnered ample media coverage for the cause. But some proreligious activists worried that by defying traditional gender roles the skirted men had undermined the platform's credibility in the eyes of other potential allies among conservatives. Nevertheless, advocates for women from across the identity spectrum repeatedly find ways to bring thousands onto the city's streets to pursue overlapping visions of empowerment.[68]

In recent years, such tense but creative encounters have shaped mobilizations of all colors and sizes. The liberal cosmopolitanism of *Belle Époque* nostalgia, for example, inflects demands—to date unrequited—to bring to justice the killers of Hrant Dink. Mustering thousands on the anniversary of his death, the movement also draws energy from contemporary symbols of transnational solidarity with the Other, such as black-and-white placards that read in multiple languages: "We are all Hrant; We are all Armenian."

Another annual performance pushes the envelope of the Ottoman-Islamic narrative: the mass prayer—galvanized by a Sunni youth movement—held before Hagia Sophia on the anniversary of the *fetih* of Istanbul in 1453. The goal of participants is restoration of the great monument as a mosque. The sixth-century edifice served as a church for over 900 years, and then as a mosque for almost 500, but it has been a museum since 1935. To date, as Anna Bigelow examines in chapter 7 of this volume, the AKP authorities have only paid lip service to such demands. Changing Hagia Sophia's status would outrage Christian interlocutors around the world. It could call into question, moreover, Turkey's commitment to the secular (neo)liberal order from which mainstream champions of Ottoman-Islamic nostalgia have benefited.

Appropriation of Istanbul's tale of two cities is also evident in the coalitions, often counterintuitive, that can form when actors claim space in the city to "gain freedoms."[69] Impromptu alliances crystallized, for example, during the Gezi Park protests of 2013. The uprising was catalyzed by Turkey's environmentalist movement, a cause mapped by Hande Paker in chapter 9 of this volume to a neoliberal Ottoman-Islamist project: the slated demolition of a city park. In its stead, the authorities planned to commemorate and commodify an earlier Ottoman site by building a replica to serve as a shopping mall. Opponents of the plan included an unexpected green-green alliance, as it were, for postmaterialist values, when anti-capitalist Islamic youth joined secular environmentalists to resist neoliberal urban transformation. Yet protestors also leveraged tongue-in-cheek Ottoman-Islamic referents to their cause. A striking case in point was the performance of gas-masked, gender-bending whirling dervishes during the occupation of the park.

Still other groups mobilized not for a cause but against the heavy-handed police response to the initial protests. This yielded unexpected acts of solidarity between, for example, football fans and LGBTQ activists. As Susan C. Pearce documents in chapter 10 of this volume, the latter ably channeled energies from Gezi Park toward the annual Pride parade, which coincided in timing and locale with the broader protests. For years the only Pride parade held in a Muslim country, events were banned in 2016 due to "security concerns" and are unlikely to be permitted again in the near future.

To be sure, most impromptu acts of recognizing the Other prove ephemeral, as Sami Zubaida cautions in chapter 2 of this volume. Yet Benhabib's work suggests that "iterative encounters" have the potential to transform political subjectivities.[70] New coalitions indeed helped to shift national political trajectories as political parties sought to appropriate—or contain—the energies unleashed by Gezi and its aftermath. Over the course of municipal (2014), presidential (2014), and parliamentary (2015) elections, old and new cleavages became inflamed across the country.

At the same time, unprecedented political alliances were forged. One form this took was the campaign of the pro-Kurdish Peoples' Democratic Party (*Halkların Demokratik Partisi*; HDP) to harness the post-Gezi oppositional coalition. The bold move thrust the HDP into parliament in national elections on June 7, 2015, an outcome that cost the AKP its parliamentary majority.[71] President Erdoğan responded by paving the way for snap elections less than five months later and peace talks with the Kurdish movement collapsed in a cycle of terrorism and reprisals.

The post-Gezi fallout within the proreligious camp between Erdoğan's supporters and followers of the US-based preacher Fethullah Gülen was just as dramatic. The feud led on July 15, 2016, to a coup attempt allegedly spearheaded by

Gülenist elements. The putsch failed in part due to concerted opposition from across the otherwise polarized society: the AKP grassroots defied tanks and live ammunition, as liberal journalists and the leadership of all the major political parties—right wing, center left, and pro-Kurdish—rallied behind the government. At the cost of some 250 lives, the events proved a watershed moment in the emergence of Erdoğan's New Turkey.

Within just three weeks, 50,000 passports were canceled;[72] 18,756 people were detained and 10,192 arrested, including soldiers, police officers, judges, and prosecutors, according to the state news agency.[73] In the months that followed, and under the auspices of emergency law, over 100,000 public employees were purged from the bureaucracy, especially from an education sector said to be a Gülenist stronghold. A significant number of those dismissed at the university level, moreover, had signed a petition protesting government policies toward Kurds.[74] In widening waves, opposition political and media figures and institutions came under siege. This was evident in the arrest, en masse, of the HDP municipal and national leadership in the fall of 2016, the shuttering of some 160 media outlets, and the imprisonment, according to watchdog reports, of over a hundred journalists.[75]

At the time of writing, the closing down of oppositional political space has been accompanied by co-optation of the ultranationalist right. These developments unfolded alongside a heated contest over a constitutional referendum that passed narrowly on April 16, 2017, and that may enable consolidation of President Erdoğan's new order.

In many ways, the outcome is a victory for the more combative strain of Ottoman-Islamic Istanbul as microcosmic of Turkey. What then will happen to the constituents of the *Belle Époque* and other visions of collective identity? Indeed, what will become of the Ottoman-Islamic narrative's inclusive thrust at a time when the frame is increasingly employed to champion an exclusionary ethnoreligious nationalism?

Whatever the answer to these questions, Istanbulites will prove resilient. If there is anything on which rival claimants to the city agree, it is that Istanbul—and the stage it supplies to enact diversity—is more enduring than efforts to eliminate it under any regime, imperial and national alike. After all, Istanbul's neo-Ottoman tale of two cities at the dawn of the twenty-first century entails its own omissions, highlighting some stories and eliding others. The chapters in this volume seek to recover still more. They are an attempt to close our eyes, like Orhan Veli, and listen to what Istanbul and its people have to say—for better and for worse—about living together.

Chapter Overview

Çağlar Keyder's contribution launches the volume with an overview of the platform for pluralism that the city has provided for centuries. At the intersection of historical sociology and political economy, he examines urban cosmopolitanism as an empirical description and normative category across Istanbul's nineteenth, twentieth, and twenty-first centuries. In the *fin de siècle* period, he argues, earlier multicommunitarian pluralism began to evolve into a more individualistic cosmopolitanism. Both forms of living with diversity, however, were eclipsed by the triumph of nationalism in the twentieth century. Examining Istanbul's subsequent bid to rise through the ranks of global cities, Keyder questions the prospect of consolidating recent cosmopolitan gains given Turkey's increasingly restrictive political environment.

Illuminating Keyder's story in rich historical and sociological detail, Sami Zubaida examines Istanbul as a meeting place of Middle Eastern cosmopolitanisms during the *Belle Époque.* A "promiscuous" cosmopolitanism, he shows, infused the city's subcultures but was eclipsed by the transition to Turkish ethnonationalism. Is this pattern, he asks, being repeated in Istanbul's recent cosmopolitan renaissance and its encounter with a resurgent Turkish-Islamist synthesis?

Feyzi Baban expands on the historical relationship between multiculturalism and prospects for living together today. He shows that despite today's romanticism about the city's pluralistic past, cohabitation in the nineteenth century did not mean empathy across communal divides. Baban demonstrates this via three literary pieces that evoke, in turn, the sensibilities of Ottoman Muslim elites whose moonlit entertainments along the Bosphorus rarely brought them into contact with counterparts among the *Belle Époque* Greek bourgeoisie. Wealthy Greeks, for their part, rarely mingled with the Orthodox working class in the city's shabbier districts. Baban argues that the self-contained nature of these communities—their dearth of mutually transformative interactions—makes Ottoman pluralism a historical artifact rather than a model for the present. It nonetheless spurs us to think about pluralism in refreshingly decentered ways.

Charles King moves us forward temporally and expands our perspective geographically by comparing cosmopolitanism, violence, and the state in Istanbul and Odessa. Noting that robust research indicates that while purveyors of violence seek to portray it as a natural outgrowth of incommensurable identities, large-scale social conflict—from riots to genocide—rarely takes place without state complicity. Examining the relationship between intercommunal relations and state policies in prewar Istanbul and Odessa, he surveys two urban environments in which diversity was decimated in the twentieth century. King's argument is that successful sustenance of diversity requires a constant effort to privilege the suffering of others over one's own. This demands embracing "one's own cultural discomfort" toward building "a set of social networks and institutions which make the fate of other communities an inextricable part of one's own destiny."

Engaging the fates of others, however, is challenging even for the well-intentioned. As İlay Romain Örs's exposé of "cosmopolitanist" nostalgia for *Belle Époque* Istanbul reveals, rosy-eyed portrayals of the period often gloss over its aftermath: the persecution and expulsion of the communities in question. Seeking via their exilic literature to recover the "actually lived" cosmopolitanism of the Greek Orthodox community of Istanbul (*Rum Polites*), Örs recovers an emic cosmopolitanism derived, as she puts it, from "their Istanbul roots, not from their world travels."

Amy Mills expands the search for "situated knowledge" of the Other in conversation with leading theorists. Her chapter offers a critique of renowned geographer David Harvey's curious elision of emplaced knowledge in his work on cosmopolitanism. In its stead, she invokes Doreen Massey's notion of "throwntogetherness" as a frame with which to capture both local particularity and its globally interconnected production—the ways that "here" is shaped by "there." She does so by surveying historical and nostalgic accounts of *Belle Époque* cosmopolitanism, culminating with an ethnography of "neighboring" practices among local women today. Such acts of mutual recognition, she affirms, are "contingent upon careful negotiation and are vulnerable to heightened moments of state nationalism or global crisis." The sharing of space, she concludes, is a negotiation "in process, always fluctuating, filled with promise as well as vulnerability."

Picking up these tensions, Anna Bigelow explores the perennial contest for Hagia Sophia: a church, a mosque, or a museum, depending on one's vantage point. The chapter draws on archival, textual, and ethnographic research to trace three moments of transition in the building's 1,400-year history: from church to mosque (in 1453), from mosque to museum (in 1934), to debates today driven by Ottoman-Islamist enthusiasm to reconvert Hagia Sophia into a mosque. Each moment, Bigelow argues, reveals the cosmopolitan power of the monument to absorb diverse worldviews. Yet each set of claims—Orthodox and Islamic as well as the secular, liberal UN Educational, Scientific, and Cultural Organization (UNESCO) regime for world heritage sites—also radiates a universality that is, paradoxically, exclusionary.

Turning from the grandeur of Hagia Sophia, Kristen Sarah Biehl addresses the granular realities of neighboring Kumkapı, a transitory home to migrants from across the country and globe. Based on ethnographic immersion, Biehl's chapter explores how housing practices engender a certain "conflicted openness": a form of conviviality that can be grudging but which nevertheless underwrites a pragmatic cosmopolitanism.

The generation and management of crosscutting solidarities is also examined in Hande Paker's account of opposition to Istanbul's third Bosphorus bridge. She argues that environmental struggles like the anti-bridge movement offer fruitful sites with which to ground the project of cosmopolitan citizenship in concrete relations of solidarity, conflict, and political action. Examining local and transnational sources of activism, she shows that the anti-bridge campaign generated referents that went on to inform the Gezi Park movement. Paker suggests that cosmopolitical encounters catalyzed by exigency and *ad hoc* solidarities can open the door to transformative fusions of "local" and "universal" values.

Susan Pearce wraps up the volume by exploring an explosive moment of urban performance during the summer of 2013: Istanbul's trans and LGBT Pride parades, which unfolded in tandem with the Gezi Park protests. She examines how activists' "presence—and the insistence on the right to be present—interacts with the ethnic and religious social identities of other urban denizens." Her findings suggest that political cross-fusions generated at least a "momentary intensity" that "forwarded the project of gender and sexuality inclusion." Closing with words resonant for the volume as a whole, Pearce argues that "far from a cosmopolitan patina over a canvas of historically entrenched ethnic divisions," Istanbul reveals plural, if volatile, paths to living in diversity.

NOTES

1. "Istanbul Marks 1453 Ottoman Conquest of Istanbul with Grandiose Ceremony," *Hürriyet*, July 1, 2016, http://www.hurriyetdailynews.com/istanbul-marks-1453-ottoman-conquest-of-istanbul-with-grandiose-ceremony.aspx?pageID=238&nID=99825&NewsCatID=341.

2. Notions like "conquest" (*fetih*), and "justice" or (*adalet*) are core elements of Turkish political Islam's revisionist lexicon of history and the will to achieve a culturally "authentic" modernity. The marriage of that tradition with a neoliberal economic agenda is inscribed in the very name of the Justice and Development Party or *Adalet ve Kalkınma Partisi* (AKP).

3. Cited in Alev Çınar, *Modernity, Islam, and Secularism in Turkey: Bodies, Places, and Time* (Minneapolis: University of Minnesota Press, 2005), 116.

4. Esra Özyürek, *Nostalgia for the Modern: State Secularism and Everyday Politics in Turkey* (Durham, NC: Duke University Press, 2006); and Zeynep Kezer, "Familiar Things in Strange Places: Ankara's Ethnography Museum and the Legacy of Islam in Republican Turkey," *Perspectives in Vernacular Architecture* 8 (2000): 101–116.

5. A productive way to read about Pamuk's Istanbul is through the eyes of his translators; see, for example, Erdağ M. Göknar, *Orhan Pamuk, Secularism and Blasphemy: The Politics of the Turkish Novel* (New York: Routledge, 2013).

6. Deyan Sudjic, "The City Too Big to Fail," in *Urban Age—Istanbul: City of Intersections* (London: London School of Economics & Alfred Herhausen Society, 2009–2010), 3–4.

7. Zeynep Merey Enlil, "The Neoliberal Agenda and the Changing Urban Form of Istanbul," *International Planning Studies* 16, no. 1 (2011): 5–25.

8. Istanbul Municipality statistics, http://www.ibb.istanbul/tr-TR/kurumsal/Pages/IlceveIlkKademe.aspx.

9. Mastercard Global Cities Index 2015, https://newsroom.mastercard.com/wp-content/uploads/2015/06/MasterCard-GDCI-2015-Final-Report1.pdf.

10. Saskia Sassen, *The Global City: New York, London, Tokyo* (Princeton, NJ: Princeton University Press, 2001).

11. In recent years a prosecularist strand of nostalgia has also emerged for early republican Istanbul as a site of Westernist modernity, early secularist leaders' preference for Ankara notwithstanding. As Orhan Pamuk's oeuvre suggests, such nostalgia—apparent in commodified imagery of beauty pageants and shopping boulevards, balls, and tramways—is nevertheless enmeshed in a melancholic sense of both the echoes and the erasure of the late Ottoman social fabric.

12. Çağlar Keyder, *İstanbul: Küresel İle Yerel Arasında* (İstanbul: Metis, 2000); and Dimitar Bechev and Kalypso Nicolaidis, eds., *Mediterranean Frontiers: Borders, Conflict and Memory in a Transnational World* (London: I. B. Tauris, 2009).

13. Enlil, "The Neoliberal Agenda."

14. See, for example, Zeynep Çelik, *The Remaking of Istanbul: Portrait of an Ottoman City in the Nineteenth Century* (Berkeley: University of California Press, 1993).

15. Keyder, *Istanbul.*

16. Amy Mills, *Streets of Memory: Landscape, Tolerance, and National Identity in Istanbul* (Athens: University of Georgia Press, 2010).

17. For detailed accounts see, for example, Samim Akgönül, *The Minority Concept in the Turkish Context: Practices and Perceptions in Turkey, Greece, and France, Muslim Minorities* (Leiden: Brill, 2013); Ayhan Aktar, "Homogenising the Nation, Turkifying the Economy," in *Crossing the Aegean*, ed. Renee Hirschon (Oxford: Berghan Books, 2003), 79–95; Rıfat N. Bali, "The Politics of Turkification During the Single Party Period," in *Turkey Beyond Nationalism: Towards Post-Nationalist Identities*, ed. Hans-Lukas Kaiser (London: I. B. Tauris, 2006), 43–49; Dilek Güven, "Riots Against the Non-Muslims of Turkey: 6/7 September 1955 in the Context of Demographic Engineering," *European Journal of Turkish Studies. Social Sciences on Contemporary Turkey* 12 (2011): 1–17; Soner Çağaptay, "Race, Assimilation and Kemalism: Turkish Nationalism and the Minorities in the 1930s," *Middle Eastern Studies* 40, no. 3 (2004): 86–101; and Kerem Öktem, *Angry Nation Turkey Since 1989* (London: Zed, 2011).

18. Precise figures are difficult to ascertain, but a widely cited source for the Ottoman period is Kemal Karpat, *Ottoman Population 1830–1914: Demographic and Social Characteristics* (Madison: University of Wisconsin Press, 1985). Contemporary non-Muslim numbers are taken from the US State Department website (https://www.state.gov/j/drl/rls/irf/2004/35489.htm), which cites 65,000 Armenians, 25,000 Jews, and 3,000 Greek Orthodox for officially recognized minorities, and an estimated 10,000 Baha'is, 15,000 Syriac Christians, 5,000 Yezidis, and 3,000 Protestants, among other tiny denominations.

19. For strands of neo-Ottomanism across the national political spectrum see Nora Fisher-Onar, "Echoes of a Universalism Lost: Rival Representations of the Ottomans in Today's Turkey," *Middle East Studies* 45, no. 2 (2009): 229–241. For a historical overview of the genesis of these strands since 1923 see Fisher-Onar, "Between Memory, History, and Historiography: Contesting Ottoman Legacies in Turkey, 1923–2012," in *Echoes of Empire: Memory, Identity and Colonial Legacies*, ed. Kalypso Nicolaïdis, Berny Sèbe, and Gabrielle Maas (London: I. B. Tauris, 2014), 139–152.

20. Said Amir Arjomand, "Coffeehouses, Guilds and Oriental Despotism: Government and Civil Society in Late 17th to Early 18th Century Istanbul and Isfahan, and as Seen from Paris and London," *European Journal of Sociology* 45, no. 2004: 23–42.

21. John-Paul A. Ghobrial, *The Whispers of Cities: Information Flows in Istanbul, London, and Paris in the Age of William Trumbull* (Oxford: Oxford University Press, 2013).

22. Heiko Henkel, "The Location of Islam: Inhabiting Istanbul in a Muslim Way," *American Ethnologist* 34, no. 1 (2007): 57–70.

23. Çınar, *Modernity, Islam and Secularism.*

24. For a genealogy of the AKP's emergence from Turkey's political Islamist tradition see Ümit Cizre, ed., *Secular and Islamic Politics in Turkey: The Making of the Justice and Development Party* (London: Routledge, 2008).

25. Terence O. Ranger and Eric J. Hobsbawm, eds., *The Invention of Tradition* (Cambridge, UK: Cambridge University Press, 1983).

26. Explanation offered in municipal brochure. Fisher-Onar, "Echoes of a Universalism Lost."

27. Saba Mahmood, *Politics of Piety: The Islamic Revival and the Feminist Subject* (Princeton, NJ: Princeton University Press, 2011).

28. See, for example, Banu Gökarıksel and Anna J. Secor, "New Transnational Geographies of Islamism, Capitalism and Subjectivity: The Veiling-Fashion Industry in Turkey," *Area* 41, no. 1 (2009): 6–18; Yael Navaro-Yashin, *Faces of the State: Secularism and Public Life in Turkey* (Princeton, NJ: Princeton University Press, 2002).

29. Çınar, *Modernity, Islam and Secularism.*

30. See, for example Xuefei Ren's study of Chinese cities in *Building Globalization: Transnational Architecture Production in Urban China* (Chicago: University of Chicago Press, 2011).

31. Nora Fisher-Onar, "Neo-Ottomanism, Historical Legacies, and Turkish Foreign Policy," Centre for Economic and Foreign Policy Studies, EDAM/GMF Discussion Paper Series (2009), http://trends.gmfus.org/doc/Discussion%20Paper%20Series_Fisher.pdf.

32. Nora Fisher-Onar, "Historical Legacies in Rising Powers: Toward a (Eur) Asian Approach," *Critical Asian Studies* 45, no. 3 (2013): 411–430.

33. For a genealogy of such representations see Paul Levin, *Turkey and the European Union: Christian and Secular Images of Islam* (New York: Palgrave Macmillan, 2011).

34. See, for example, Pınar Bilgin, "'Only Strong States Can Survive in Turkey's Geography': The Uses of 'Geopolitical Truths' in Turkey," *Political Geography* 26, no. 7 (2007): 740–756; and Lerna K. Yanık, "The Metamorphosis of Metaphors of Vision: 'Bridging' Turkey's Location, Role and Identity after the End of the Cold War," *Geopolitics* 14, no. 3 (2009): 531–549.

35. In the Global Cities Index 2016, Istanbul ranked 25, up from 29 the prior year. https://www.atkearney.com/documents/10192/8178456/Global+Cities+2016.pdf/8139cd44-c760-4a93-ad7d-11c5d347451a.

36. North Atlantic Treaty Organization (NATO), Organisation for Economic Co-operation and Development (OECD), and United Nations Development Programme (UNDP).

37. The Global Cities Index (2011; http://documents.mx/education/global-city-index.html) suggests that to establish and maintain global financial traction a city must be able to draw and keep a well-educated population, provide infrastructure for the circulation of information, foster social openness to debate and criticism, project "soft" cultural power, and contribute to policy dialogues.

38. Saskia Sassen, "The Immutable Intersection of Vast Mobilities," in *Urban Age—Istanbul: City of Intersections* (London: London School of Economics & Alfred Herhausen Society, 2009), 5–6.

39. Çağlar Keyder, "Istanbul into the Twenty-first Century," in *Orienting Istanbul: Cultural Capital of Europe?*, ed. Deniz Göktürk, Levent Soysal, and İpek Türeli (London: Routledge, 2010), 25–34.

40. See, for example, Jeremy F. Walton, "Confessional Pluralism and the Civil Society Effect: Liberal Mediations of Islam and Secularism in Contemporary Turkey," *American Ethnologist* 40, no. 1 (2013): 182–200.; Kabir Tambar, *The Reckoning of Pluralism: Political Belonging and the Demands of History in Turkey* (Palo Alto, CA: Stanford University Press, 2014); and Élise Massicard, *The Alevis in Turkey and Europe: Identity and Managing Territorial Diversity* (London: Routledge, 2013).

41. For a fascinating investigation of neo-Ottomanism as "queer self-making" see Rüstem Ertuğ Altınay, "The Queer Archivist as Political Dissident: Rereading the Ottoman Empire in the Works of Reşad Ekrem Koçu," *Radical History Review*, no. 122 (2015): 89–102.

42. Yeşim Arat, *Rethinking Islam and Liberal Democracy: Islamist Women in Turkish Politics* (Albany: State University of New York Press, 2012).

43. For more on variations of pious neoliberal nostalgia for the Ottoman era, see Jeremy F. Walton, *Muslim Civil Society and the Politics of Religious Freedom in Turkey* (New York: Oxford University Press, 2017); and more broadly, Bruce B. Lawrence, "Competing Genealogies of Muslim Cosmopolitanism," in *Rethinking Islamic Studies: From Orientalism to Cosmopolitanism*, ed. Carl W. Ernst and Richard C. Martin (Columbia: University of South Carolina Press, 2012), 302–323.

44. Betül İpşirli Argıt, "Clothing Habits, Regulations and Non-Muslims in the Ottoman Empire," *Journal of Academic Studies* 6, no. 24 (2005): 79–96. See also Lawrence, "Competing Genealogies."

45. Rasim Ozan Kütahyalı, "Syria Crisis Prompts Turkey's New Openings to Its Alevis," *Al-Monitor*, September 15, 2013, http://www.al-monitor.com/pulse/originals/2013/09/syria-crisis-turkey-open.html#ixzz4Vx7GKNYZ.

46. For an overview, see Nora Fisher-Onar and Meriç Özgüneş, "How Deep a Transformation? Europeanization of Greek and Turkish Minority Policies," *International Journal on Minority and Group Rights* 17, no. 1 (2010): 111–136.

47. For variants of religious nationalism see Jenny White, *Muslim Nationalism and the New Turks* (Princeton, NJ: Princeton University Press, 2014); and Ayşe Kadıoğlu and E. Fuat Keyman, *Symbiotic Antagonisms* (Salt Lake City: University of Utah Press, 2011).

48. This figure is based on the assumption that the 20–25 percent of the national vote typically garnered by the CHP in the past decade is cast by prosecularist Sunni and heterodox Alevi voters, though such groups also vote for other parties (the Nationalist Movement Party [MHP] and the pro-Kurdish HDP, and in some instances the AKP). Also, far from all prosecularist CHP voters are concerned with religious minorities' rights.

49. Electorally: Beşiktaş, Şişli, and Kadıköy.

50. See Ezgi Başaran, "Secular Citizens of Turkey Have Never Felt So Alone," Washington Post, January 3, 2017, https://www.washingtonpost.com/posteverything/wp/2017/01/03/secular-citizens-of-turkey-have-never-felt-so-alone/?utm_term=.0c53d42ef1c0.

51. Saskia Sassen, *Cities in a World Economy* (Los Angeles: Sage Publications, 2011), ix.

52. "İstanbul'un Fethinin 563: Yıldönümü Nedeniyle Cumhurbaşkanı Erdoğan ve Başbakan Yıldırım'ın da Katıldığı Kutlama Töreni Düzenlendi," May 29, 2016, http://www.ntv.com.tr/turkiye/istanbulun-fethinin-563-yili-kutlandi,lc8TTCLwukGoIBGQA6Jrjw.

53. The theoretical call for "bottom-up" approaches was championed by figures like Pheng Cheah and Bruce Robbins, eds., *Cosmopolitics: Thinking and Feeling Beyond the Nation* (Minneapolis: University of Minnesota Press, 1998); Ulrich Beck and Natan Sznaider, "Unpacking Cosmopolitanism for the Social Sciences: A Research Agenda," *British Journal of Sociology* 61, no. 1 (2010): 381–403; David Harvey, *Cosmopolitanism and the Geographies of Freedom* (New York: Columbia University Press, 2009); and Pnina Werbner, *Anthropology and the New Cosmopolitanism: Rooted, Feminist and Vernacular Perspectives* (Oxford: Berg, 2008). Empirically grounded studies of emplaced cosmopolitanisms include, for example, Nora Fisher-Onar and Hande Paker, "Towards Cosmopolitan Citizenship? Women's Rights in Divided Turkey," *Theory and Society* 41, no. 4 (2012): 375–394; and Mica Nava, *Visceral Cosmopolitanism: Gender, Culture and the Normalisation of Difference* (New York: Berg, 2007).

54. Prominent exponents include Martha Nussbaum, David Held, and Daniel Archibuigi, among others showcased in Garrett W. Brown and David Held, *The Cosmopolitanism Reader* (London: Polity, 2010). For a critique and window onto non-Western genealogies of local cosmopolitanisms see, for example, Engseng Ho, "Names Beyond Nations," *Études Rurales* 3 (2002): 215–232.

55. For a discussion of Arendt's insights into performative spaces see Mustafa Dikeç. "Space as a Mode of Political Thinking," *Geoforum* 43, no. 4 (2012): 669–676.

56. Lewis Mumford, cited in Paul Makeham, "Performing the City," *Theatre Research International* 30, no. 2 (2005): 151.

57. Gita Saghal and Nira Yuval-Davis, eds., *Refusing Holy Orders: Women and Fundamentalism in Britain* (London: Virago Press, 1992).

58. Doreen Massey, *World City* (Cambridge, UK: Polity, 2007).

59. Craig Calhoun, "The Class Consciousness of Frequent Travelers: Toward a Critique of Actually Existing Cosmopolitanism," *South Atlantic Quarterly* 101, no. 4 (2002): 869–897.

60. Pekka Tuominen, "The Clash of Values Across Symbolic Boundaries: Claims of Urban Space in Contemporary Istanbul," *Contemporary Islam* 7, no. 1 (2013): 41. See also Michel de Certeau's seminal "Walking in the City," in *The Certeau Reader*, ed. Graham Ward (Oxford: Blackwell, 2000), 101–118.

61. For a study of the gendered nature of migrant labor to Turkey see Mine Eder, "Turkey's Neoliberal Transformation and Changing Migration Regime: The Case of Female Migrant Workers," in *Social Transformation and Migration: National and Local Experiences in South Korea, Turkey, Mexico and Australia*, ed. Stephen Castles, Derya Özkul, and Magdalena Cubas (London: Palgrave Macmillan, 2015), 133–150.

62. Tuominen, "Clash of Values," 44.

63. Ibid.

64. For a compulsively readable account of Istanbul in this period see Charles King, *Midnight at the Pera Palace: The Birth of Modern Istanbul* (New York: W. W. Norton, 2014).

65. Clarence R. Johnson, *Constantinople Today; or, The Pathfinder Survey of Constantinople: A Study in Oriental Life* (London: Macmillan, 1922), 203.

66. Nora Fisher-Onar and Meltem Müftüler-Baç, "The Adultery and Headscarf Debates in Turkey: Fusing 'EU-niversal' and 'Alternative' Modernities?," *Women's Studies International Forum* 34, no. 5 (2011): 378–399.

67. Fisher-Onar and Paker, "Towards Cosmopolitan Citizenship."

68. Cases in point include joint strategizing and advocacy regarding proposed penal code reform, such as joint action against a bill that would have pardoned child rapists if they married the girls in question. See "Turkey Withdraws Child Rape Bill after Protests," *BBCNews*, November 22, 2016, http://www.bbc.com/news/world-europe-38061785.

69. Berna Turam, *Gaining Freedoms: Claiming Space in Istanbul and Berlin* (Palo Alto, CA: Stanford University Press, 2015).

70. Seyla Benhabib, *Another Cosmopolitanism,* The Berkeley Tanner Lectures (Oxford: Oxford University Press, 2006).

71. Previously, the HDP had fielded its candidates as independents to circumvent Turkey's high, 10 percent electoral threshold.

72. Lizzie Dearden, "Turkey Coup Attempt: Government Cancels 50,000 Passports as Global Concern Grows Over Crackdown." *Independent*, July 30, 2016. Available at: http://www.independent.co.uk/news/world/europe/turkey-coup-attempt-erdogan-news-latest-government-cancels-50000-passports-amid-international-a7163961.html.

73. Ankara: Anatolia Agency, "Feto's Coup Attempt in Turkey: A Timeline," August 2016, http://aa.com.tr/uploads/TempUserFiles/pdf%2Ffeto_en_sn.pdf.

74. Human Rights Watch, "Turkey: Events of 2016," World Report 2017, https://www.hrw.org/world-report/2017/country-chapters/turkey.

75. Amnesty International gives a figure of 120+ since the crackdown. Amnesty International, "Turkey: Journalism Is Not a Crime," n.d., https://www.amnesty.org/en/latest/campaigns/2017/02/free-turkey-media/.

PART I

The Past of Istanbul's Present

CHAPTER 1

Imperial, National, and Global Istanbul

THREE ISTANBUL "MOMENTS" FROM THE NINETEENTH TO TWENTY-FIRST CENTURIES

Çağlar Keyder

Cosmopolitanism is not a project but an effect; it is the reality and the consequence of the coexistence of groups whose diversity is sufficiently great that their interaction entails mutual reshaping and redefinition. It implies a common commitment to public openness in a society, to make a society on whatever scale—a city, a country, the world—work through communication, debate, and interaction between projects. Cosmopolitanism is a stance against assimilation into homogeneity, but also an attempt to overcome the mutually isolated existence of multiple communities and cultures. It presupposes the communicability of desires and objectives, of competing meanings attached to components of the social. It implies the ability of individuals to switch codes, to employ diverse sociolects, and to recognize the different grammars that provide structure to different groupings. In this way, communication among a multiplicity of populations is possible.

One premise of any discussion of cosmopolitanism is that there are cosmopolitan individuals who are indispensable to its existence. Cosmopolitanism creates the consciousness necessary for the emergence of such individuals. Such individual dispositions do not arise out of personal preference or as an option exercised in favor of a cosmopolitan orientation. The choice is simply not available unless there is an environment in which the cosmopolitan is socially produced and politically accommodated. A cosmopolitan social imaginary may emerge only when the state can be persuaded to allow the institutions within which a cosmopolitan arena may flourish. These institutions include the norms guiding the economy and the cultural and political practices that shape the contours of the universe within which individuals interact. A cosmopolitan disposition may be nourished under these conditions, but whether it will be tolerated by the guardians of the "natural" normative boundaries of the society will be determined by multiple factors.

In this chapter I analyze the opportunities for cosmopolitan orientation in Istanbul's history over the last century and the degree to which cosmopolitanism was able (or not) to become a reality in distinct periods characterizing the city's evolution. These periods are familiar ones: the imperial city of the turn of the last century, the national city of the republic, and the global city of the last two decades.[1] However, before describing Istanbul's adaptation to and accommodation of—cosmopolitan and otherwise—the political, economic, and cultural environments in each of these periods, some general comments about the defining features of the city in each epoch are in order.

Periodization of Cosmopolitan Affinities

To talk about the degree of cosmopolitanism of a city is difficult, for the population of a city is always diverse and heterogeneous. In a great city, heterogeneity and the mixing of diverse populations is unavoidable. The question for cosmopolitanism is whether this mixture becomes organic through interaction. If diversity leads to the definition of boundaries in such a way as to equate difference with mutual exclusion, we will be talking about coexistence and tolerance (or, to use a more contemporary concept, multiculturalism) but not cosmopolitanism. Diversity will be contained and channeled, expressible only in predetermined ways. In this sense, the counterpart (and the opposite) of cosmopolitanism that is most familiar in historical experience is nationalism. Within the national society, difference is reluctantly tolerated, but certainly not celebrated. We know that cosmopolitanism and nationalism have been historically, and currently are, counterposed, irrespective of the political orientation of national regimes (both the Left and the Right, have, with equal vehemence, condemned cosmopolitan consciousness). The very premise of nation building has excluded considerations of cosmopolitan orientation from our analytical agenda.[2]

Empires, by way of contrast, have been identified as possessing a framework for the comfortable existence of cosmopolitan individuals and cosmopolitanism. Empires are made up of disparate communities typically brought together under conquest, not in line with a preexisting project of unity as in the case of the nation-state, but through expediency. Empires generally do not seek to develop homogenizing projects. They do not aim to make reality conform to some presumed imperative of ethnic coherence. They simply become a collection of communities through a series of contingencies unfolding in military conquest and interstate accommodation. Under the framework of empire, communities continue to exist relatively undisturbed, allowing heterogeneity to survive. Different communities, relatively intact, carry the potential for interaction, for mutual influence, and for transforming the imperial framework under which they have to exist. In other words, empires may accommodate a cosmopolitan orientation but also may govern by compartmentalizing communities into their respective lifeworlds. Mutual exclusion of religious communities has been prevalent historically, especially when imperial institutions adopt a confessional idiom.

In rare cases, especially during the final stage of empires before World War I, it has been possible to detect more of a commitment to the sharing of urban social space by diverse communities and hence grounds for a political orientation that was more rational and associative than nationalism. This commitment may be termed "civic," something akin to a constitutional engagement that invites deliberation, exchange, and competition over projects and mutual transformation of the actors. There is much room in such an arena for cosmopolitans: those who are at home in various ethnolects and sociolects, who are adept at switching codes and at translation. Whether the promise of cosmopolitanism is actually realized (as it perhaps was in Vienna or London) is a different matter and requires concrete historical analysis of the location in question.[3]

The nineteenth-century expansion of the world economy in terms of flows of goods, capital, and especially people, imbued what have been termed "port cities" with clear-cut examples of cosmopolitan potential. From the Pacific and Latin America to the Mediterranean and Asia, port cities such as İzmir, Alexandria, Bombay, Hong Kong, and Buenos Aires became the face of the global extension of trade, investment, and migration. Given their loose relationship with the states to which they were attached, port cities were prone to develop forms of local governance that privileged their relationship with imperial centers in Europe. Given their orientation to trade and their heterogeneous business population, these cities also were inclined to be "liberal" in their governance. Because they were not circumscribed by any geographically bounded project, the potential for a cosmopolitan dialectic among their ethnically and socially diverse communities was greater even than in great seats of empire like Istanbul, which in fact was a seat of power and therefore subject to a much stricter administrative logic than port cities. Port city populations were oriented to a global modernity, made concrete in the extension of European modes of material and intellectual life. Their physical aspects matched this orientation, especially in their marketplaces, which showcased multiple worlds.[4]

Twentieth-century nationalism, especially the variety adopted by newly independent states, was the opposite of imperial orientation in its embrace of the parochial. In arguing for the particular virtues of the chosen ethnic or religious group, it upheld the desirability of a homogeneous population base. Attributes of race, religion, and language could be foregrounded alternately according to immediate needs, but the underlying assumption remained the same: to establish a strong state, alien elements should be expunged and the nation should be constituted as a community with as much apparent unity as possible. In

Turkey, Egypt, India, and China (among many other new nation-states), the creation of such homogeneity required various forms of exclusion and socialization. These efforts at ethnic engineering sought to fit existing populations into procrustean blueprints and attempted to mold future generations according to design. Cosmopolitan consciousness was considered a threat, signifying an active challenge to the national project because it admitted to and cherished the existence of diverse allegiances. Cosmopolitanism was castigated for positing an overly sophisticated social architecture, with layers of belonging entailing divided commitments and loyalty. It thus was regarded with suspicion and was often equated with betrayal. Nationalism emerged as a project of carefully directed modernity negotiated among the educated elites within an exclusionary national space. This presented an alternative to the globalizing modernity of the nineteenth century.

Hostility to cosmopolitan dispositions in national projects can be seen concretely in the attitude of the new nations of the twentieth century toward their port cities. These cities had housed the feared cosmopolitan societies connected through material and cultural flows to the imperial world. By ousting diverse ethnic and religious groups, nation builders sought to secure the desired demographic composition of the new nation. Postcolonial or new nation-states, whether after World War I, as in the case of Turkey, or after World War II, as in Egypt or China, all waged war against the memory of colonial mentalities, including the cosmopolitan nature of their port cities: İzmir, Alexandria, or Shanghai. These cities were symbolically (and sometimes literally) cordoned off from the national entity and conquered by the true owners of the country: the natives whom nationalist regimes sought to turn into nationals. Such conquests culminated in plunder: foreign or "non-national" properties were nationalized, the very spaces reminiscent of cosmopolitan coexistence seized by locals. Old mansions were turned into government offices, parks and gardens were occupied for informal housing, and banks and trading houses were left to decay. The old, imperial, and interconnected world cities with large "non-national" populations were transformed into the megacities of the global South, receiving migration from the modernizing countryside with the promise of urban employment. The newcomers were the former peasantry, often ideologically glorified as the soul of the nation. Their essentialized appearance on the historical stage contributed to the formation of the often xenophobic and developmentalist regimes of the post–World War II period.

In this world of national construction, homogeneity of the population became the ideal, pursued through policies that were legitimated on the basis of building monolithic, nonfissured communities. States claimed to embody and represent the popular ideal and opted for the uncomplicated simplicity of excluding the messy realities of the cosmopolitan. Such conceits, however, increasingly after the 1980s, came under the pressure of real-world developments. The insularity of the national was breached by economic, cultural, and technological developments, forcing political authorities reluctantly to adjust their focus as the world began to change under globalization.

Globalization, however defined, signified an end to attempts at isolated capitalist development by "third world" countries. Modernization projects directed from above were surrendered to the vagaries of global flows of capital, commodities, and culture. In this context the national megalopolises of the previous era began to give in to sweeping new connections, new economies, new social groups, and new divisions in the society. Those cities that succeeded in attracting larger shares of the global flow of capital, migration, and cultural flows did so by developing spaces that accommodated residents who considered themselves to be global citizens, based on criteria of occupation, lifestyle, and cultural orientation. Once again, those great cities had to accommodate diversity and difference within the urban space. As global cities became places for a more footloose population, ranging from short-term tourists to longer-term expatriates, migrant workers, and refugees, the earlier ideal of homogeneity had to be reconsidered, compelling municipal administrations and national residents and governments alike to accept the rights of others to the city. The exclusionary nationalist sentiments of the interwar and post–World War II period began to change in the 1980s, albeit slowly.[5]

It is not the case, of course, that in global cities nationalist exclusion will smoothly give way to cosmopolitan interaction among diverse communities and lead to civic engagement and shared commitment to the polis. In fact, globalization is often accompanied by social segregation with class divisions, creating a supranational consciousness in the top strata of transnational globalizers, while inciting localist reactions in those who remain outside of the new order.[6] Despite (or because of) this dividedness of global cities, urban entrepreneurs urge citizens to buy into notions of city-belonging and urban citizenship. They do so to boost the city's global competitive advantage, ignoring any potential divergence of interests. These pitches are reinforced by advertising copy issuing from urban growth coalitions of global cities as well as governments.[7] Such exhortations and the overall rhetoric surrounding world cities entails a much more deliberate evocation of cosmopolitan consciousness than in imperial times. Global cities are supposed to enjoy an advantage of scale over imperial diversity, serving as the crucible for the creation of a new order in the world as a whole.[8]

When Was Istanbul Cosmopolitan?

The history of Istanbul neatly fits in with this periodization. Istanbul served as imperial capital for over one and one-half millennia and accumulated numerous layers of diverse populations. Most of these populations, like the Celts during the Byzantine period, as well as Arabs, Albanians, and various exiles and fortune seekers from Europe during the Ottoman Empire, lost their distinctive characteristics. They tended to assimilate into the major groups of Muslims, Greeks, and Armenians or leave the city. Some managed to retain a recognized communal identity. In Ottoman times there was a legal identification attached to the more recognized communities, in the form of *millets* defined by confession. (The *millet* system has a long history in the empire, reaching back to the conquest of Istanbul, although its political significance increased after the eighteenth century.) In tandem with the globalization of the nineteenth century, an influx of foreigners increased the urban population, designating a new quarter of the city (Pera) as their own.[9] These new settlers were confident enough to claim a right to the city, as they did in many port cities around the world, going so far as to establish a municipality in the chosen district in an attempt to exercise a degree of self-governance.[10] In addition to port city foreigners, the population of Istanbul came to constitute a sample of all the ethnic constituents of the empire—Turks, Greeks, Armenians, Jews, Arabs, Albanians, Kurds, Bosniaks, Tatars, Circassians, and Bulgarians, among others—with all the languages spoken in true imperial style. To this *potpourri* were added the foreign elements of merchants, masons, sailors, prostitutes, and various fortune hunters who hailed from points west.

Did all these elements interact in the sense of creating a cosmopolitan dialectic? The answer is probably more than is commonly assumed, although barriers to such aspects as marriage across religious lines remained insurmountable. Nonetheless, within confessional confines, imperial currents mixed and flowed together; ethnic affiliations were easily ignored. This is how on the Muslim side Istanbul absorbed exiles from the Russian empire, refugees from all over the Balkans, enslaved peoples from the Caucasus and Africa, and children from Kurdish and Arabic lands who came to complete their education and become imperial bureaucrats, not to mention merchants from Central Asia and other fortune seekers. They intermarried to become the city's "Muslim element" and were later (in the nation-state to follow) denominated as Turks. Similarly, among the Christians or the Jews, locals married newcomers, conversions were common, churches proliferated, and the boundaries of the so-called Levantine population (mostly Catholic Christians who had settled in Ottoman lands) under embassy protection remained blurry and porous in their lines of demarcation. Ottoman Greeks and Armenians could gain access to embassy protection and also marry European Christians. Intermarriage between Muslims and Christians or Jews, however, was almost nonexistent, except under duress. Around the turn of the century, with 15 percent of the population recorded as "foreign" and Greeks and Armenians making up close to half of the city, the Muslim population in Istanbul had likely become a minority.[11]

How might we characterize the dominant tenor of the production of social space in this period? And how did the particularity of this space accommodate or discourage cosmopolitan interaction? The most important physical change in the city was the emergence of a new section, Pera, on the opposite side of the Golden Horn from the old city. This newly developing space was defined by apartment buildings, paved pedestrian streets, shops, cafés, and entertainment venues—the amenities of nineteenth-century bourgeois life in imitation of Paris—which had not until this juncture been part of the urban scene in Istanbul. The new district brought together the *évolués* of the city, providing venues for dialogue (in French) and interaction and a degree of anonymity to those who ventured to the new quarter (see chapter 2 in this volume). Down the hill from the more sophisticated streets of Beyoğlu were interaction and entertainment of a more raunchy sort, in the public houses and narrow streets of Galata and Karaköy, where the working and lumpen population of the entire Mediterranean mixed. Today, as Istanbul is gripped by the cosmopolitan aspirations of the global city, tribute is being paid to this earlier era: the old Grande Rue de Pera, the principal axis of Beyoğlu, has regained its earlier status, with apartment buildings and public spaces lovingly restored, and side streets and the lower neighborhoods are being gentrified to serve the demands of a younger, prosperous, but bohemian crowd.

The period from the mid-nineteenth century to the end of World War I was a time of cosmopolitanization, in that the diverse aforementioned ethnic and religious groups lived and formulated political projects in awareness of each other. Through this process the city became an arena of conflict, for it figured differently in each group's project. Some sought to have Istanbul remain the capital of a multiethnic empire, albeit one in transformation. For others, it was becoming a national center for "Turks." Still others, subscribing to the Greek irredentist *Megali Idea*—the aspiration to reconstitute the Byzantine world—believed it might become the seat of the Greek Orthodox Church for a greater Greece. By way of contrast, the fact that Ottoman sultans like Abdülhamit II had reinvigorated the title Muslim Caliph led some believers to envisage Istanbul as the holy city of a revitalized Islamic caliphate. For still others it might even evolve into a self-governing port city dominated by settlers and operating as an extension of a world economy under European hegemony. In this line of thinking was a project (ultimately rejected) of the British and French occupying authorities (after the Ottoman defeat in World War I) to turn the city and its environs into an "international" zone that would serve as home to the future League of Nations. All such projects evolved in competition and conjunction with the others and were shaped by the changing parameters and aftermath of the world war.

The 1922 victory of Turkish resistance to the Greek occupation of Anatolia signaled an end to political competition over the future of the city. As Allied occupation forces left at the end of 1922, the fate of the city was sealed; henceforth it would be defined by a national project. Temporary wartime populations such as the community of Russians escaping the Bolshevik Revolution quickly found ways to move westward. Most settled foreigners likewise felt that the nineteenth-century liberal experiment was over and chose to leave. Soon thereafter Greece and the new Ankara government agreed to a compulsory exchange of populations brokered by the League of Nations. The move authorized the departure of all remaining Greek Orthodox peoples from Turkey except those who could demonstrate resident status within the city limits of Istanbul (and Turkey's two remaining Aegean islands). This formal agreement was only the beginning of a wave of departures of the historic Greek Orthodox community, which culminated in the city indeed becoming "national." A quarter century after the victory of the Turkish Republic, non-Muslims made up 10 percent of the city's population, as recorded in national censuses; by 1980, after the mass departure of Greeks between 1955 and 1975, they had declined to less than 2 percent.

The national government proceeded to abandon Istanbul in favor of the new capital in Ankara, symbolically located in the center of Anatolia. The economic center of the developmentalist project that Istanbul became during the 1950s reflected the concerns of a regime of state-dominated capital accumulation, with the industrialists in Istanbul in tow. This was a politically driven, militantly national endeavor, third-worldist in inspiration and suspicious of outsiders. It was an attempt to establish state control over economic processes to achieve national integration.

As Istanbul's population expanded from one million in 1950 to five million in the 1980s, newcomers from the Anatolian countryside were too timid to challenge the role accorded to them in the developmentalist model as actual and potential workers. They remained in new neighborhoods and continued to live near other migrants from their village or hometown communities. The *gecekondu* (shantytown; literally "placed overnight") areas they built informally came to be marked by their affiliation with the province of origin. Their populations collectively strove to raise the value of their land and housing stock through obtaining municipal services and eventually titles for their squatter property.

The *Belle Époque* urban spaces that had accommodated Istanbul's cosmopolitan opening suffered neglect and loss of status during the national period. While middle-class residential districts were developed in newly expanding districts of the city (mostly along the Marmara coast and the highlands beyond Beyoğlu), the spaces of the developmentalist era tended to replicate in social and cultural makeup the places of origin of the new inhabitants. In other words, these new settlements were insular and segregated, reproducing the mores of the traditional village community while actively seeking to reject any "foreign" impurity. In this period of physical and spatial expansion of the city, there was hardly any attempt by the authorities to develop "public space" to provide for and accommodate any potential dynamics of urban interaction.

It was only in the decade of the 1980s, when national developmentalism was challenged by neoliberal globalization, state guarantees for populist subsidies were withdrawn, and the market was established as the unchallenged arbiter of life chances, that other voices demanding full participation in urban politics were heard. After the span of a generation, immigrants to the city became urban citizens asking for their rights to the city.[12] The assumptions of national development had to be revised at the same time that the *gecekondu* population began to ask for political and cultural recognition by the elites.

The conjunction among globalization, market liberalization, and political opening asserted itself in Istanbul's urban politics as Turkey emerged from the dark days of the 1980 coup. The 1980s was a decade of urban awakening in which diverse ethnic, political, and cultural groups in the city gained the courage to go into the streets to voice their claims. As more independent media developed, Istanbulites were forced to become aware of the heretofore "hidden" communities sharing the urban space. Kurdish groups, Alevis, Christian sects, transvestites, various "tribes" defined by their cultural affiliation, hipsters, Goths, vegetarians, and all forms of political activists from Islamist to anarchist asserted their rights to the city. For the first time since the foundation of the republic in 1923, Istanbul emerged as a privileged locale for a variety of voices and movements. In the subsequent period these voices were amplified and were characterized by increasingly clear links to emerging global networks.[13]

In the early 1990s the new links with global networks were predominantly those of trade. These were driven by petty merchants from the ex-Soviet lands who engaged in unrecorded "suitcase" commerce. Soon, however, larger-scale buyers of manufactured goods arrived, followed by foreign banks and then global brand-name stores. Importantly, this period also coincided with the opening of airwaves to TV and radio channels that were not under strict government control. European political networks, the Helsinki process, human rights organizations, and most notably various agencies of the European Union began to take an interest in Turkish nongovernmental organizations (NGOs), ethnic and political struggles, and freedom of expression. These networks emboldened Istanbul's claimants, and the city gradually became an arena like other global cities, in which global issues, albeit refracted in the local mirror, were continuously on the agenda. As the new millennium approached, Istanbul found itself on the global map due to its attraction to foreign visitors and its denizens' participation in the economic, political, and cultural transnational networks that make up our globalized world's new cartography.

It was a gradual path from this initial period of informal globalization, when processes unfolded without much formal regulation, to a new phase of deliberate management by transnational capital, willingly regulated by the state. In the new millennium, and with the political victory of the moderate Islamic Justice and Development Party (AKP), the globalization of the city became an active policy pursued as a concerted project. The new prime minister, Recep Tayyip Erdoğan, was the former mayor of Istanbul and a proponent of neoliberal development. Under his supervision, local politicians and entrepreneurs of space embarked on a more deliberate course to exploit fully the imperial capital's potential as a global city. Deindustrialization had already been completed in the 1990s; now foreign investment was invited to upgrade services, developing regionally significant banking, media, business services, and construction sectors. Tourism was actively encouraged, with old Ottoman edifices converted into luxury hotels and pedestrian zones established around the showcased cultural heritage sites. The government, the city, and business circles embarked on infrastructure projects to build the framework for accelerated exchanges with the world economy. As the global city project seemed on course to succeed, cultural investment accelerated in the form of museums, festivals, concerts, and conferences undertaken by public-private partnerships of national and global organizations.[14]

Istanbul, moreover, was made into an attractive city. It was trumpeted to advertise a high quality of life for foreign populations. One consequence of this renewed attractiveness has been the long-term settlement of new populations, from refugees and undocumented immigrant workers on one end of the spectrum to corporate expatriates, artists, and students on the other. Migration to the city, however, has been moderate compared to any other city in the top ranks of global cities.[15] The migrant situation gained a new salience with the massive inflow of Syrians to Turkey after 2013—a subject meriting a chapter on its own. Of about 2.7 million Syrians in Turkey, more than 400,000 are estimated to have settled in Istanbul to date.

The presence of the migrants and long-term visitors, as well as eight million tourists every year, is a factor in Istanbul's increasing display of global city dynamics. These include the growing visibility of cultural industries, a thriving art scene, a large variety of cultural and entertainment venues, and an accelerated process of gentrification. This cosmopolitan potential binds the city to a range of other global cities in networks, cooperation, and competition. Istanbul's growing cosmopolitanism, moreover, estranges it, in varying degrees, from the projects, concerns, and material habits of the rest of the country.

The current period has dialectically reversed the course of spatial transformation as well. Now both public institutions and private enterprise endeavor to create spaces of consumption, culture, and leisure. Most of these, such as pedestrian zones, malls, waterfront promenades, public parks, museums, and refurbished city squares, which facilitate encounters and exchange, are readily accessible to everyone. There are also, of course, the familiar privatized spaces of gated communities and socially stratified neighborhoods with their shopping centers. That said, spatial segregation in Istanbul based on class does not seem to be as acute as in India or Brazil. Public spaces have also become much more prominent; there was never this degree of use of public space in Istanbul's past incarnations.

Is the Global City Cosmopolitan?

How much of Istanbul's transformation can be characterized as realization of cosmopolitan potential? In the sense that the new visage of the city driven by a project of urban revitalization in a global context explicitly aims to invite foreign populations and promote global awareness, there is a positive sway in the cosmopolitan direction. When middle-class Istanbulites visit the new spaces, stroll in the pedestrian zones that replicate global urban districts elsewhere, visit exhibits that are on global tour, or shop in European-origin chain stores, they cannot escape the feeling of partaking in a global experience.[16] A postnational awareness is also engendered by the pervasive discourse about "global city-hood." It is this transmutation of global meanings to local citizens that is the foundation of a cosmopolitan consciousness.

Yet the crucial question remains: Does the emergence of a global city guarantee a cosmopolitan ethos? Istanbul's turn-of-the-century cosmopolitanism before World War I, after all, proved fleeting at a time of great political uncertainty. It was contingent upon British regional hegemony and ability to underwrite new forms of governance, especially in geographies where local powers did not seem able to contain challenges from various ethnic and religious movements. Today's global cities are quite different. After an initial period of naive optimism about globalization and cognate tools of governance, the state has reasserted its mode of governance. Since at least September 11, 2001 (9/11), states have resorted to the national security argument to exercise fuller control over the political arena than ever before. Economic insecurities and social dislocation brought in by neoliberal globalization have led, moreover, to Polanyian movements seeking social justice via a statist remedy. This is especially the case in countries like Turkey, where there is a trend toward populist authoritarianism. The consequences for cities like Istanbul are clear: Turkey's leadership is prone to interpret any political platform permitting communication, let alone negotiation, between players in the urban cosmopolitan space as a challenge to popular sovereignty and autocracy.

This potential for confrontation was highlighted in the summer of 2013, when the authorities responded in a heavy-handed fashion to a wave of protests in Istanbul. The demonstrations had started as a challenge to a top-down decision to demolish a park and build a shopping mall in the main *meydan* or square of Istanbul. The initial protesters were middle-class university students and young graduates and professionals in precisely the corporate sectors that are the motors of globalization: finance, law, advertising, consulting, and the like. They were joined by foreign students, noncorporate expats, journalists, and itinerant artists, and were applauded by the "cosmopolitan" population of the city.

This early protest took the form of defending Gezi Park, but it was clearly also an expression of frustration in the face of growing authoritarian rule in which decisions, especially those pertaining to the use of urban space, were closed to discussion and the global aspirations of this rather small segment of the population were stifled. Subsequently many other groups who felt excluded from the growing nativism of the ruling party joined the protests, which turned into an uprising venting the accumulated anger of the opposition against the increasingly high-handed rule of Erdoğan. For two weeks, street fighting continued in all the larger cities, and the *meydan* came under the control of the protestors. Erdoğan, however, mobilized the security forces to suppress the insurgency, which he saw as a challenge to the popular sovereignty that had brought him to power. A lesson from Gezi then is that the nation-state and its nativist base are well entrenched. Its legitimacy is based on the popular vote, and state agencies wield powers that may be deployed to shut down the arena that cosmopolitanism requires for intercourse among groups with diverse orientations, projects, and dispositions. In short, a city's cosmopolitan potential can be smothered easily.

Istanbul's story is also suggestive of another dimension of the cosmopolitan venture: the location of class politics in relation to cosmopolitanism. The denizens of port cities a century ago were divided along lines of ethnicity; there were locals and foreigners (and those among the locals who dealt with foreigners). Each category was characterized by a different level of access to the very globalization that created the port cities. Ethnic categories, in turn, could be mapped onto these class differentials; it was the merchants and the bankers who were members of the clubs and masonic lodges, attended dances, shopped in department stores, and strolled on the corniche who took an interest in local government. In our time too, the new populations of global cities are divided. Those who are able to reap the benefits of the global economy and participate in global culture are the managers of transnationals and financial professionals, architects and software engineers, publishers, writers, and academics. They have language skills and knowledge of the world; they have histories and cultural preferences similar to those of their counterparts in other countries. Globalization valorizes their assets.

On the other side, however, are the relative losers. These are groups that lack the cultural capital and resources to be able to participate in cosmopolitan politics. They watch as the city in which they live is transformed, its economic life is dominated by the globalizers, and its desirable neighborhoods are gentrified even as the new cosmopolitans argue for a politics that could make this transformation permanent. The frustration of those sidelined by such projects is a resource for savvy politicians like Erdoğan, who when it is expedient can rally such grievances against the cultural-capital rich middle class with global aspirations. The resentment of the excluded is harnessed to a platform of localism.

Therefore, the prospects for cosmopolitanism are not great in Turkey or in any other country where the lexicon of the nation-state continues to carry sanctity and which authoritarian rulers can manipulate. There will certainly be more social movements mobilizing the new middle classes in the future. But while movements such as the Gezi uprising of 2013 may seek to counter the hegemony of authoritarian nationalism, their class base is too narrow and their ability to form cross-class coalitions is too weak to pose an enduring challenge. Their chances of success arguably diminish further as the world political and economic climate grows less accommodating. Because, as this chapter has argued, cosmopolitanism requires an accommodating environment, the prospects of a cosmopolitan ethos flourishing in Istanbul at present remain limited. When the global political and economic climate reaffirms the powers of the nation-state, populist politicians ready to mobilize nationalist resentment present an insurmountable barrier against cosmopolitans and cosmopolitan ventures.

NOTES

1. Çağlar Keyder, "Port-cities in the Mediterranean During the Belle Epoque," in *Cities of the Mediterranean*, ed. Biray Kolluoğlu and Meltem Toksöz (London: I. B.Tauris, 2010), 14–23.

2. Ulrich Beck and Natan Sznaider, "Unpacking Cosmopolitanism for the Social Sciences: A Research Agenda," *British Journal of Sociology* 61, no. 1 (2010): 381–403.

3. Cf. Acbar Abbas, "Cosmopolitan De-scriptions: Shanghai and Hong Kong," *Public Culture* 12, no. 3 (2000): 769–786.

4. Çağlar Keyder, "Istanbul into the Twenty-first Century," in *Orienting Istanbul: Cultural Capital of Europe?*, ed. Deniz Göktürk, Levent Soysal, and İpek Türeli (London: Routledge, 2010), 25–34; and Biray Kolluoğlu and Meltem Toksöz, eds., *Cities of the Mediterranean: From the Ottomans to the Present Day* (London: I. B.Tauris, 2010).

5. Verena Andermatt Conley, "Chaosmopolis," *Theory, Culture and Society* 19, nos. 1–2 (2002): 127–138.

6. Çağlar Keyder, "Globalization and Social Exclusion in Istanbul," *International Journal of Urban and Regional Research* 29, no. 1 (2005): 124–134.

7. Cf. John Logan and Harvey L. Molotch, *Urban Fortunes: The Political Economy of Place* (Berkeley: University of California Press, 1987); Keyder, "Istanbul into the Twenty-first Century."

8. Allen J. Scott, "Resurgent Metropolis: Economy, Society and Urbanization in an Interconnected World," *International Journal of Urban and Regional Research* 12, no. 3 (2008): 548–564.

9. Edhem Eldem, "Istanbul as a Cosmopolitan City: Myths and Realities," in *A Companion to Diaspora and Transnationalism*, ed. Ato Quayson and Girish Daswani (Oxford: Blackwell Publishing, 2013), 212–230.

10. Stephen T. Rosenthal, *The Politics of Dependency: Urban Reform in Istanbul* (Westport, CT: Greenwood Press, 1980).

11. Stanford Shaw, "The Population of Istanbul in the Nineteenth Century," *International Journal of Middle East Studies* 10, no. 2 (1979): 265–277.

12. Anna Secor, "'There Is an Istanbul That Belongs to Me': Citizenship, Space and Identity in the City," *Annals of the Association of American Geographers* 94, no. 2 (2004): 352–368.

13. Nurdan Gürbilek, *The New Cultural Climate in Turkey, Living in a Shop Window* (London: Zed Books, 1998).; see also chapter 10 in this volume.

14. Cf. Benton Jay Komins, "Depopulated Cosmopolitanism: The Cultures of Integration, Concealment, and Evacuation in Istanbul," *Comparative Literature Studies* 39, no. 4 (2002): 360–385.

15. Lisa Benton-Short, Marie D. Price, and Samantha Friedman, "Globalization from Below: The Ranking of Global Immigrant Cities," *International Journal of Urban and Regional Research* 29, no. 4 (2005): 945–959.

16. Cf. Conley, "Chaosmopolis."

CHAPTER 2

Promiscuous Places

COSMOPOLITAN MILIEUS BETWEEN EMPIRE AND NATION

Sami Zubaida

Cosmopolitanism is not a precise concept. The term has many ideological, historical, and cultural connotations. In the case of Istanbul and other major cities in the Middle East, the notion is currently overlaid with nostalgia for an imagined recent past, a flourishing culture in which diverse ethnicities, languages, and styles mingled in public spaces like salons, cafés, art venues, and educational institutions, as well as in media such as newspapers and magazines. This chapter traces the waxing and waning of such promiscuous cosmopolitanisms in the late Ottoman period through to the turn of the twentieth century. It shows that at this juncture the cosmopolitan ethos was eclipsed by Istanbul's and Turkey's transformation from pluralistic empire to homogenized nation-state, with consequences for Istanbul's prospects as a global city.

As Keyder (see chapter 1 in this volume) has illuminated, the phenomena we characterize as cosmopolitan are the products of empires. This association with imperialism is one reason cited by nationalists and fundamentalists for denouncing cosmopolitanism. Empires pertinent to the modern history of the Middle East (since the mid-nineteenth century), namely the Ottoman, the British, and the French, were all cosmopolitan entities influenced by contemporary currents in French language and culture and notions of nationalism emanating from Germany.

In this context, the Ottoman *millet* system for managing the diverse population, which is often cited as a model of tolerance and harmony, was eclipsed. The reality was that the non-Muslim *millet* (and non-Sunni Muslims, not classified as a separate *millet*) were legally inferior and burdened with restrictions on residence, dress and comportment, and worship. They were subject to extortion by rapacious governors and soldiers. And in any case, the copresence of diverse peoples does not necessarily entail social and cultural mixing (see, for example, chapters 3, 5, and 6 in this volume). For the most part, individuals were confined within their own social boundaries—and often the topographical locations of their communities—under the authority of religious chiefs, whose status in turn was maintained by the power of the sultan.

Even when diverse peoples are "free" under a liberal regime, the coexistence of different ethnicities and cultures does not constitute what typically is connoted by cosmopolitanism, namely transformative mutual engagement. For example, the diverse ethnic and religious populations (dubbed "communities") who now inhabit many global cities often lead separate lives centered on family, neighborhood, and workplace, having little mixing with or exposure to others. Multiculturalism, the term used to describe these situations, entails contested policy initiatives in many Western countries. Yet as many have pointed out, multiculturalism in practice is often a situation of "multi-uni-culturalism": the coexistence of separate and bounded communal units with little in-depth interaction across the units.[1] One also might question the notion of "culture" as a separate and distinct unit over time.

Cosmopolitanism, on the other hand, has connotations of the mixing of individuals from diverse backgrounds, operating in milieus of social promiscuity: individuals liberated from communal belonging and cultural boundaries. One of the essential conditions for this mixing is the existence of venues and institutions as cosmopolitan spaces (see chapter 1 in this volume). In the case of Istanbul, these conditions were brought about in historical moments in the later nineteenth and early twentieth centuries, including the modernization and reform of empire, the dominant presence of European powers and institutions, and the socioeconomic transformations of capitalism and modernity.

It was only over the course of this period that communal barriers became more permeable, especially in the empire's main centers of power, commerce, and culture. This was due to the combined processes of modernity and capitalism under the growing influence of European powers, especially Britain, and the reforms that the Ottomans undertook in response. The new print media, the creation of "public opinion," the spread of literacy to wider sectors of society, and attractive European models of public and cultural life all combined to bring about new social strata and associations. Many of these new formations cut across communal barriers, at least among elites. The result was the emergence of cosmopolitan milieus.

Cosmopolitan Milieus

In the latter part of the nineteenth century, Istanbul, Cairo, Alexandria, and Beirut became places where economic and cultural modernity flourished. While some intellectuals and statesmen were ideologically attached to older Islamic and Ottoman formulas, many adopted new lifestyles and associations, stimulated partly by the painful realization of European superiority in wealth and arms.

Such figures included intellectuals from the various *millet* communities, who cited the ideas and aspirations of the Enlightenment to reject "backward" religious and communal authority. This was further stimulated among the Christian *millet* by the attractions of Anglo-Saxon Protestant missions and their educational and cultural activities.[2] Such missions played an important part in the revival of Arabic language and culture in Syria and Lebanon and are credited with stimulating the beginnings of Arab nationalism among Ottoman Christian Arabs. The Alliance Israélite Universelle played a similar role for the Jewish communities of the empire. The human products of these educational institutions cultivated notions of citizenship and active participation in public life, which were partly satisfied by the emergence of the modern sectors of state bureaucracy, education, and commerce.[3] The railways and telegraphy were crucial not only in facilitating this opening up of isolated regions and integrating them into the capitalist market, but also in providing employment for the literate.[4]

One enclave of cultural as well as political endeavor was the Young Ottomans, a group of intellectuals versed in European languages and ideas who sought a renaissance of Islamic-Ottoman civilization.[5] A prominent member, Namık Kemal (1840–1888), was a poet, essayist, and liberal political philosopher who was deeply influenced by European currents. He translated the philosophers Charles de Secondat and Baron de Montesquieu, debated Voltaire and Nicolas de Condorcet, analyzed the French Revolution and its aftermath, and followed the nationalist models of Giuseppe Garibaldi and Giuseppe Mazzini. (The Young Ottomans had personal and political connections with Italian nationalists and the secret revolutionary Carbonari societies.) Kemal and many of his contemporaries spent periods of exile in Paris, London, and Geneva, where they published journals that were prohibited in Istanbul, intriguing with patrons and factions in and out of government. Intellectually and politically, they were cosmopolitans.

Yet Kemal was firmly attached to the idea that a revived Islam must form the basis of society and government. He tried to find Islamic idioms for expressing the main ideas and concepts of the Enlightenment: those of Jean-Jacques Rousseau, Montesquieu, and the natural law tradition. He also was highly critical of the ruling functionaries of the Porte (the Ottoman government) for their blind imitation of Europe. He denounced the *Tanzimat* reforms not for their intention—to introduce modern modes of governance—but for failing to culminate in a liberal constitution that empowered the people as citizens. Kemal's goal was to secure liberties he believed to be granted by God, as opposed to reforms imposed from above by an autocratic government. For these Young Ottoman intellectuals and reformers, Islam became an ideology of national authenticity rather than of ritual observance and its disciplines, a kind of cultural nationalism that persists to the present day.[6]

In this era Kemal, as writer, poet, and publicist, also campaigned for a new, direct style and vocabulary in Turkish writing, rejecting old, ornate, Persianized forms of rhyming prose and fanciful allusions. This transformation in language was an important feature of a public sphere that depended on wider circles of literacy and participation and more utilitarian and direct forms of communication. Such endeavors gave groups beyond the elite access to current ideas.

What were the social and geographical locations of Ottoman cosmopolitanism? Clearly the vast rural and provincial hinterlands of the empire were home to highly bounded communities, dominated by kinship, localism, and religious authority, including hierarchical orders within Sufism (Islamic mysticism). These populations of peasants, artisans, and traders were disadvantaged by the empire's inclusion in capitalist world markets and processes of reform. Non-Muslim groups—who were associated in the popular mind with Christian Europe and did indeed benefit to some degree from Ottoman reforms and proclamations of equality—were particularly resented by the Muslims. This occasionally led to violence, such as attacks on Christians in Syria and the communal wars in Lebanon in the mid-nineteenth century.

In the major cities, including Istanbul, the lives of the great majority revolved around family; community; and religious/communal calendars of holidays, feasts, fasts, and rituals. Yet the boundaries between these groups were becoming more permeable, and individual members participated, more or less, in the milieus of social mixing and cultural hybridity, whether through work or voluntary associations. Such interactions were not confined to the upper classes and the elites, but included groups of workers and entrepreneurs: the docks, the railways, and the incipient tourist trade were also sites of social mixing.

The height of these reforms, modernization, and Ottoman cosmopolitanism is widely regarded to have occurred under Ottoman Sultan Abdülmecit (reigned 1839–1861). It was the age of the *Tanzimat*, of the proclamation of equality between subjects of different religions, and of cultural flourishing and mixing. The sultan himself was a notable painter in the European style. As historian Philip Mansel has explained, this was a time of population diversity, social and cultural encounters, and hybridity between the elements of the empire and the European presence.[7]

At the same time, however, this was a period of multiple conflicts and wars, socioeconomic transformations, and contests between classes and nationalities. Conservative and religious forces—rightly recognizing their ebbing power—sought to defend their world against the encroachment of reform and European-flavored modernity.

New forms of transportation and communication nonetheless facilitated movement, mixing, and innovation. These included the steamship, urban tramways (horse-drawn, on rails), telegraphy and faster postal services, and ultimately railways. The Galata Bridge, crossing the Golden Horn, was built in 1845 and became the hub of commerce and entertainment. These activities were conducted by and enjoyed by individuals of many nationalities—Arabs, Kurds, Albanians, and Greeks, as well as Europeans—all in their distinctive modes of dress and behavior. A Japanese visitor is reported to have called it the "Bridge of Ten Thousand Nations."[8]

During this era the embassies of the great powers, especially the British, held their own magnificent courts, with many officials, agents, servants, and hangers-on. Together with the imperial court and the higher echelons of the Porte, as well as the rich merchants and financiers, the city formed a glittering society of multiple nationalities and hybrid cultures, in which European, especially French, elements predominated. Love affairs were common, but it must be emphasized that intermarriage remained within confessional boundaries, with Greek beauties marrying into European aristocracy. The sultan himself put in an appearance at one British embassy ball in 1856 celebrating a national occasion, a notable departure from traditional court etiquette, under which the sovereign was not even to preside at official court banquets. This elevated milieu featured rivalries, conflicts, and conspiracies to do with great power interests, overlaid by intrigues between men and offices of state, clients, or allies of one or the other embassy.

As noted, the decree of equality for non-Muslim Ottomans of 1856 (Hatt-ı Hümayun) also exacerbated tensions among the different *millets*. Not only was there resentment within the Sunni majority at the loss of their formal predominance, but conflicts arose between Greek and Bulgarian Orthodox prelates (high-ranking church dignitaries) over predominance in various dioceses and control of assets. Greek notables similarly resented equality with Jews. Such rivalries were themselves products of the reforms and the intensified interaction among the various sectors of the population: a defense of boundaries that were being breached.

The liberality of the empire at this juncture, together with the ascendancy, even the arrogance, of the great powers made Istanbul a destination for entrepreneurs, adventurers, writers, and "flaneurs"(casual strollers) from Europe and the Levant. Business communities, such as the British, founded their own chambers of commerce. Trade and finance, as well as the nascent tourist industries, expanded with the arrival of steamships and, ultimately, railways from Europe. These brought together diverse elements, including agents of Europeans, Greeks, Armenians, Jews, and Ottoman grandees. Muslims constituted a small proportion of this modern business community, challenged to compete in linguistic skills and networks that favored foreigners and the now-liberated non-Muslim *millet* communities.

Galata and Pera, the European quarters, offered avenues of entertainment and the pleasures of cafés, bars, brothels, and salons with Parisian aspirations. They stood in contrast to the quarters of the old city across the Golden Horn. Adding to the city's global mix was Istanbul's position as a major outpost for the troops and hospitals of the Crimean War (1853–1856), in which the Ottomans participated as part of the European anti-Russian alliance. Soldiers from the European armies stationed in the city added to the mix and chaos. Entertainment and services sprang up to cater to these foreign soldiers, accompanied by much drink and disorder.

In trying to characterize this state of affairs as "cosmopolitanism," let us contrast it with another model of social diversity, that of the "plural society," advanced by anthropologists in the middle decades of the twentieth century to describe some colonial encounters.[9] An example is the colonial Caribbean, where the European powers brought enslaved Africans, indentured workers from India, and bosses and governors from Europe. The descendants of these diverse groups kept to their own bounded communities and only encountered others in the marketplace and official bureaus. Features of Istanbul society in the nineteenth century could be similarly characterized. Greek tourist guides and hoteliers, Kurdish porters, Albanian peddlers, and Armenian caterers would mix in the marketplace and employ limited vocabularies in several languages, but remained socially bounded within their ethnic milieus.

For the mixing of minds and cultures, we have to look to another social location that persists to the present time, that of the new middle and upper classes, the personnel of government bureaucracies and legal and educational institutions, journalists and writers, artists and musicians, and some modern entrepreneurs. While many of these individuals kept a foot in their communal milieus through family and the ritual cycles of their religious communities (e.g., feasts and fasts), they also escaped from these bonds into crosscutting cultural, intellectual, and political universes. In these new public spheres they found identity and kinship with the other inhabitants. Within these spheres notions of common citizenship were upheld (which proved fragile in the ensuing nationalist conflicts), as were ideas of liberty and equality, if not always fraternity.

Freemasonry

Freemasonry featured prominently in the cultural and political life of the Ottoman world in the nineteenth and early twentieth centuries and constituted an important aspect of the cosmopolitan milieu. Branches of British, then French and other continental lodges were established in Istanbul from the early nineteenth century, often by diplomats, including ambassadors from these countries.[10] Initially their membership was confined to Europeans, officials, and merchants, but was then opened to non-Muslim Ottomans. Beginning in the 1860s it was fully opened to Muslim Ottomans, especially statesmen, intellectuals, and other public figures. Istanbul, İzmir, Salonica, Cairo, and Alexandria were prominent centers for Masonic lodges, but they also spread to Syrian and even Iraqi cities.

Masons included some of the main reformers and intellectuals, including Reşit Paşa (1800–1858) and Mithat Paşa (1822–1884), and the aforementioned writer and intellectual Namık Kemal. Masonic lodges, especially the French ones, came to foster Ottoman reforms, liberalism, and constitutionalism.[11] Sultan Murat V, who ruled briefly in 1876 before being deposed and imprisoned by his brother Abdülhamit II, was a patron of the liberal constitutionalists and a Freemason himself.[12]

A failed conspiracy to liberate and restore Murad emerged from Masonic networks and incurred the wrath of Abdülhamit.[13] Thus commenced the long reign of Sultan Abdülhamit II (r. 1876–1909), a period of reaction against liberalism, suspension of the nascent constitution, and the exile of prominent reformers and liberals, notably Mithat and Kemal. Abdülhamit's reign was marked by repressive measures, censorship, and strict regulation of associative life. Freemason lodges came under scrutiny and occasional interdiction. The sultan, it transpired, had been correct in distrusting the lodges, as the Young Turk conspiracy that deposed him in 1909 was partly hatched in an Italian lodge in Salonica.

According to the scholar Thierry Zarcone, these Masonic lodges—as secret brotherhoods with elaborate rituals and hierarchies of promotion—had close affinities with Sufi orders and lodges as a form of sociability and brotherhood. One of those orders, the Bektaşi, had originated in Turkish Anatolia within Sunni Islam and incorporated some Shi'ite beliefs. They were associated with a core Ottoman military corps, the Janissaries, which Sultan Mahmut II abolished in 1826. The Bektaşi orders nevertheless flourished clandestinely, generating secret organizations that attracted intellectuals who combined modern Enlightenment ideas with heterodox mysticism. This amounted to an "enlightened Sufism," a combination also salient in the case of Iranian secret societies of the time. Zarcone argues that there was an overlap of personnel, institutions, and ideas between the Masonic and Sufi forms of association. He shows that many of the people involved in the politics of and after the Young Turk period were adepts of both Sufi orders (mainly Bektaşi and Melami) and Masonic lodges.[14]

Rıza Tevfik was among those hybrid thinkers. A prominent intellectual, philosopher, teacher, and politician of the Young Turk era, he wrote, among other things, a dictionary of philosophy. Tevfik declared himself a follower of both Ibn Arabi, the source of much Sufi philosophy and mysticism, and Herbert Spencer, the English evolutionist philosopher and social theorist. Tevfik's outlook was not uncommon among modernist Turkish and Iranian intellectuals of the nineteenth and early twentieth centuries. Such figures combined subscription to European Enlightenment currents that were mainly positivist, rationalist, evolutionist, and skeptical of religious dogma with adherence to mystical philosophies of Muslim and Greek provenance. They also formed and affiliated with secret societies, including Freemasonry.

In the Ottoman context, these diverse currents seem to have shared a rejection of the verities and disciplines of orthodox Islam and the authority of its *ulema* (clergy) and institutions. Above all, it was the idea of the Shari'a as the basis of social order—buttressed by the authority of *ulema* and *müçtehit* (jurists) and enforced by absolute rulers—that was rejected and seen as the cause and hallmark of the stagnation and backwardness of their societies and polities.

Another commonly held view was that religious orthodoxy had forbidden free philosophical enquiry, an avenue, intellectuals were finding, to exciting truths and programs for renewed conceptions of social and political life. Montesquieu,

Rousseau, Spencer, Darwin, and John Stuart Mill were the inspiration for an aspirational modernity of liberty and rationality. Many of the intellectuals from the *Tanzimat* generation onward stopped at that, rejecting the religious baggage of their Ottoman heritage to embrace an unencumbered positivism and scientism. Many others, however, attempted to find a link between the European Enlightenment and elements of their philosophical heritage. Such attempts were linked mostly to heterodox Sufism, which evolved in nineteenth-century intellectual and political contexts into Bektaşi practices (the aforementioned Sufi order). All these currents—indeed torrents—of ideas were socially embedded into the secret societies of and traffic between Freemasonry and Sufi lodges.

Drinking Cultures

If masonic lodges, cafés, and salons represented cosmopolitanism in nineteenth-century Istanbul, a further site was taverns and the drinking culture that they enabled. The prohibition against alcohol is for orthodox and political Islam a marker of authenticity and distinction from the dissolute other—that is, "the West." Yet its proscription has also contributed to the intrigue and romance of drink throughout the history of Middle Eastern societies, as evidenced by poetry, mysticism, and *belles lettres*. There were high and low drinking cultures: the sumptuous wine tables of the rich and the taverns of the soldiery and *ayak takımı* (rabble). The janissaries, for one, were well-known drinkers. Many janissary entertainments, as well as intrigues and conspiracies, were conducted in taverns. For example, dancing boys, dressed as girls and offering sexual favors, were a regular item of entertainment.[15] The disorder and violence perpetrated by the janissaries in their years of decadence in the late eighteenth century, until their elimination in the early nineteenth, were fueled by drink.

In some Middle Eastern cities in the nineteenth and twentieth centuries public male drinking cultures became respectable and open—a sign of modernity and "civilization" or *medeniyet*. For the most part, however, the respectable classes drank in private within their own circles of companions. Soldiers and the lower orders, however, were not the only patrons of taverns. One Nihali, a sixteenth-century kadı (Shari'a court judge or magistrate) of Galata and a celebrated poet under the pen name Jaafar, boasted of frequenting the taverns of that famous neighborhood, which even then was "cosmopolitan."[16]

According to historian François Georgeon, alcohol was symbolic of modernity and civilization in Turkey from the nineteenth century.[17] Sultan Mahmud II (r. 1808–1839) was the first reforming ruler who had a serious impact when it came to drink. He modeled himself on other European rulers and included alcohol as a feature of public occasions such as official dinners and receptions. Champagne—which was not new to the Ottoman court—was poured in public. Over the course of the century, and among the modern elites and the official classes, drink came to be associated with being modern and civilized.

Georgeon adds that the disappearance of the janissaries and their association with alcohol from the public scene after 1826 "permitted a shift to civilian, and by extension "civilized" consumption of alcohol." Later in the century, the new bureaucrats of the expanded and reformed state became the vanguard of the drinking classes. To cater to them, a new type of refined and opulent tavern or *meyhane* came into existence, with a professional guild of tavern keepers and their assistants trained in the arts of serving drink and its accompaniment of meze (appetizers) and in the skills of nursing a *nargile* (water pipe). Among the consumers, a new *adap*—etiquette and lore of drink—emerged.

Much of this new culture of drinking revolved around the newly fashionable *rakı*, as distinct from wine and *boza* (a fermented wheat beverage with low alcohol content). *Rakı*, the clear, anise-flavored brandy made from grapes and raisins, became an identity marker as a specifically native drink, in contrast to the more cosmopolitan and European wine.[18] It acquired the honorific description of lion's milk (*aslan sütü* in Turkish; *halibsba'* in Iraqi Arabic). It became the drink of choice in the cafés, clubs, and salons of intellectuals and reformers, which included the poet Namık Kemal and the statesman Mithat Paşa. Later in the century, under the more religious and authoritarian reign of Abdülhamit II, there was a backlash, both religious and medical, against this drinking culture, but with little effect. *Rakı* was to feature again as part of the culture of the Turkish Republic under Atatürk, himself a noted devotee of the beverage.

Cosmopolitanism under Nationalist and Religious Regimes

The persistence of such dynamics raises suggestive historical questions: Was Istanbul's cosmopolitanism impeded by the Islamic conservative ethos during the 1876–1909 reign of Abdülhamit II? What was the impact of the nationalist regimes that followed the coup that removed him? And what about ensuing religious revivals and contests with secularism?

Abdülhamit instituted an authoritarian conservative regime, with wide surveillance and censorship of political and associational life and cultural production. Despite the salience of religious and traditionalist propaganda, however, the underlying processes of reform and secularization continued under the exigencies of socioeconomic pressures and the transformations of class, occupational structure, and education. As Berkes remarked, "while Abdul-Hamid's reign was boasting of the superiority of Arab civilization over that of Europe, the economy of Turkey was settling more firmly into the hands of European bankers."[19] The ranks of the modern educated middle class were expanding. The literate strata constituted a market for print products: newspapers, magazines, novels, and plays, many translated from French. While censorship curtailed political contest and undesirable news, it did not stop the fascination with science and literature, such as the translated science fiction of Jules Verne, as well as pertinent histories and biographies of key figures in the European Enlightenment.[20] The expansion of mental horizons, modernist trends toward secular positivism, and venues for its propagation continued with the flourishing of the social strata by which secular positivism was upheld. If anything, repressive measures intensified the ferment of ideas and associations, many of them clandestine. Some of this energy fed into the Young Turk conspiracy that toppled the regime in the 1908 constitutionalist coup, then removed Abdülhamit in 1909.

The constitution of 1908 and the representation of all corners, nationalities, and religions of the empire in the first parliament inspired great optimism and celebrations of liberty and unity. The object was to institute common citizenship, with the empire conceived as a vast (multi)nation-state. In this milieu, Istanbul's cosmopolitanism flourished and expanded, with delegates, activists, journalists, and hangers-on congregating around the new regime and its parliament from across the Arab world, Caucasus, and Balkans. The Iraqi poet Ma'ruf al-Rusafi, in Istanbul first as a journalist in 1909, then as a member of parliament for an Iraqi constituency, recalled frequenting the bars and nightspots of Beyoğlu wearing his traditional robe and turban. He had no inhibitions about celebrating with drink and carousing.[21] The regime expanded and modernized educational institutions and facilitated the education of girls. It also made tangible advances in the life of backward provinces such as Baghdad. This optimism and fraternization were short lived, however, with the forces of ethnic nationalism rampant across the empire and regional wars imminent. These subsequent nationalist struggles and wars involving the European powers proved more powerful than Istanbul's cosmopolitanism. But did they end it?

The War Years, Cosmopolitanism, and Nationalism

The Balkan Wars of 1912–1913, then the Great War of 1914–1918 (World War I), and the ensuing occupation of Turkey by the Allies, in turn, followed by the war of independence (1919–1923), brought devastation and penury. Between the fighting, the country experienced an intensification of European presence and domination, travel and tourism, and literary and artistic representation by such figures as Pierre Loti and André Gide. The increasing dominance of European powers over a crumbling empire meant more officials, soldiers, merchants, and financiers, as well as tourists and pleasure seekers from across Europe, their travel facilitated by the ever-advancing transport links of railways and ships.[22] As François Georgeon reveals in a fascinating analysis of the *Guide Joanne to Turkey*, with its Eurocentric accounts of the city, European preponderance was reflected in the many legal and fiscal privileges allowed to foreigners, which included some non-Muslim native individuals.[23] Many layers of the urban population were exposed in various ways to this European presence, especially the non-Muslim populations who made up at least half of Istanbul's inhabitants at that point. Members of the rising Ottoman bourgeoisie benefited from the European presence and participated in venues and activities created by the penetration of

European actors, from business opportunities to avenues of entertainment and pleasure. This expression of "cosmopolitanism" in the capital of an enfeebled empire could only be viewed with ambivalence, if not outright hostility, by the native population. As Mills (see chapter 6 in this volume) shows, it indeed served as a stimulus to heightened nationalist and nativist sentiments—conservative and religious in some quarters, modernist and positivist among other elements of the intelligentsia.

World War I and the Occupation

The Great War saw the sharpening of nationalist sentiment and hostility toward non-Muslim Ottomans, many of whom were sympathetic to one or another of the enemy powers. The Armenians, some of whose members saw the war as an opportunity for obtaining their own independent territory in Anatolia, were the main victims of the forced migrations and massacres in 1915. Then came the defeat of the Ottomans, alongside their German allies, and the occupation of Ottoman territories, including Istanbul, by the armies of the victorious powers. This devastation ushered in another brief era of "cosmopolitanism" for the capital under the occupation authorities, especially the British, their multinational personnel, and establishments catering to such a clientele. Stephan Yerasimos conjures up this milieu in his account of the inhabitants of one building on the Grand Rue de Pera (now İstiklal Caddesi) in Istanbul at the time of the British occupation. On the fourth floor were officers engaged in a conspiracy to save Turkey; the second and third floors were a brothel as well as the headquarters of a committee for the liberation of a Caucasian nation; the first floor housed a federalist Ottoman party; and the ground floor was the shop of a Greek tailor ornamented by a large portrait of Venezelos, the nationalist leader of Greece. The street outside was patrolled by a Sikh of the British army, a Senegalese soldier, a member of the Italian *carabinieri*, and a Greek *evzone*.[24]

As noted by Charles King (see chapter 4 in this volume), the Bolshevik Revolution in Russia likewise had consequences for Istanbul cosmopolitanism. One was the influx of White Russian refugees, anticommunists who fought the Bolsheviks, often with claims to aristocracy and a Francophile culture. Many became the patrons and personnel of bars, restaurants, brothels, and other entertainment venues. Some also pursued paths of political organization and publication. Traces of this influx persist into recent times in the form of a handful of restaurants. Russian commerce and entertainments also resurfaced in Istanbul in the 1990s after the fall of the Soviet Union brought to Istanbul a new breed of Russian and Ukrainian "merchant-prostitutes" trading goods and sex in Istanbul markets, often in nightclubs.

Another effect of the Bolshevik Revolution was to incite labor and socialist activism, including a tram strike in 1920.[25] Was this internationalism of the organized working class an expression of cosmopolitanism? While remaining a minority current in Turkey, an internationalist socialist sensibility with cosmopolitan inflections did infuse an important strain of Turkish intellectual production in the years that followed, epitomized in the works of iconic Istanbul poet Nazim Hikmet.

After World War I, İzmir and Western Thrace were occupied by the Greek army, with the agreement of the Allies in 1921. A counter-campaign by the resurgent Turkish nationalist army under the command of Mustafa Kemal Paşa (later Atatürk), reversed the Greek gains and ended in the expulsion of the Greek army from all of Anatolia and Thrace. Part of the settlement was an agreement to "exchange" populations, leading to the forced migration of most of the Greeks of Anatolia to Greece.

The Turkish Republic, as such, ended the empire. The capital was transferred from Istanbul to Ankara. The Armenian massacres and the Greek migrations rendered the population of Turkey much more homogeneously Muslim, Turkish-speaking (with a notable Kurdish-speaking component), and Sunni (with a considerable Alevi community, Turkey's largest religious minority, which has affinities with Shi'ism). The Turkish Republic was declared to be "secular." The ideal citizen of this republic, however, was a Sunni Muslim.

Did the republic definitively end Istanbul's cosmopolitanism? In terms of population, diversity was much diminished. Turkish Muslims predominated, though the city retained considerable numbers of Greeks, Armenians, Jews, and some Russians, now firmly subordinated and cautious. The 1930s and the Nazi persecutions were to bring some notable refugees from Germany to the city: scientists and intellectuals expelled from their universities by the Nazis. Such figures often were sponsored by their former Turkish students at German universities. Among them was Erich Auerbach, who wrote his influential *Nimesis: The Representation of Reality in Western Literature* (1946) while a professor at Istanbul University. The welcome shown to these Jewish refugees contrasted with the harsh treatment of native Jews and other non-Muslims in the republic under a special wealth tax that expropriated many into penury and condemned those who could not pay to forced labor.[26] In the 1950s nationalist riots in the city over the Cyprus conflict between the island's ethnic Turkish and Greek residents were directed against the remaining Greeks of Istanbul, precipitating an exodus. Nationalism, wars, and persecutions thus rendered the city more homogeneous, a trend later reinforced by migration from rural and provincial Anatolia. But that is not the whole story.

The ideology of the republic envisaged the Turkish essence as European and sought to distance the national character from Islamic connections with Arabs and Persians. Leading intellectuals Ziya Gökalp and Fuat Koprülü, writing in the early years of the twentieth century, traced the Turkish nation to pre-Islamic Asian and Anatolian civilizations, overlaid in later centuries by Arab and Persian Islam.[27] The national renaissance of Turkey was intended to revive those cultural essences that seemed to agree with modern civilization, rationality, positivism, and the liberation of women. These themes were taken up actively by Atatürk, who saw Turkey's destiny as oriented toward Europe and rejected Ottoman imperial history and culture, including its multiethnic composition, in favor of Turkish purity. Secularism, namely the subordination of religion to the state, and his radical language and script reforms all pointed in such a direction. The republican elite pursued European lifestyles, including dancing the tango at the balls they held, with men in European formal suits with tails and women in décolleté ball gowns. Paradoxically then, a Western-inflected cosmopolitan veneer was adopted as an ideological performance, while the population and the culture of the republic, including Istanbul, was being driven toward a pure vision of national uniformity.

Return to Cosmopolitan Istanbul?

In the last two decades of the twentieth century and into the twenty-first century Istanbul rose to prominence as a global city, a cultural and emerging economic capital. It has become a European city with a Middle Eastern heritage that is playing an ever more important part in world affairs. International corporations, NGOs, and institutions have multiplied and brought ever more diverse residents in their wake. Istanbul, in short, has become a nodal point of the ever-accelerating process of globalization, reinforced by the end of the Cold War after 1989.

At the same time Istanbul, alongside other major Turkish cities, has been host to massive migration from rural and provincial Anatolia, expanding the population and the surface extension of the city and complicating urban problems of housing and transport, as well as ethnic tensions.[28] Tied to these population movements has been the spread of religious sentiment and its manifestation in social life, culture, and politics: a politics of ethnoreligious nationalism and insularity. The cosmopolitan, secular bourgeoisie are viewed, within this perspective, as alien and are portrayed as inauthentic "white Turks"—a colloquial term for upper-middle-class urban cohorts who embrace open lifestyles.

This cultural clash has crystallized in a debate over alcohol. When the Islamic Welfare Party (*Refah Partisi*) won the Istanbul municipality in 1994, one of the first contests to arise between the Islamic mayors and the Kemalist bourgeoisie was over drink. The bars and restaurants of Beyoğlu, the cosmopolitan center of the city, were targeted by the mayor, who did not dare to ban alcohol but made rules restricting its visibility; establishments were requested not to allow drinking on terraces and at street tables and to hide their drinkers behind curtains. An outcry from the city's bourgeoisie, however, with demonstrations of street drinking, soon forced the withdrawal of the order. This spirit infuses today's romantic nostalgia for old Istanbul, including the naming of bars in recent decades. One—Victor Cohen Şaraphanesi (wine bar)—was named in a conspicuous gesture to the city's Jewish heritage, and another employed the equally typical Greek name of Stavros Şaraphanesi. On inquiry, it seemed that both were run by Turkish Muslim entrepreneurs who had used the old names to re-create the atmosphere and associations of old "cosmopolitan" Beyoğlu. Another disco bar in the same quarter carried the potentially blasphemous name Abdul-JabBAR.

Under the rule of the Refah-rooted Justice and Development Party (AKP) since 2002, there have been growing interventions against alcohol consumption in both Istanbul and other cities, especially in Anatolia. Dissatisfaction with such measures was widely cited as among the catalysts of the Gezi Park protests by groups who do not embrace conservatism. As such, alcohol consumption in today's Turkey remains a potent identity marker in the political and cultural struggles between secularism and religiosity and their corresponding readings of cosmopolitanism. (Note: This point was underscored by the attack on a posh Istanbul nightclub in the early hours of January 1, 2017, when an ISIS militant gunned down thirty-nine revelers. The attack took place on the heels of a campaign by ultrareligious activists and a sermon by the country's top religious official condemning New Year's Eve celebrations as "culturally alien".)

Conclusion

How does this transformed situation relate to "cosmopolitanism" in a globalized world? In short, does cultural globalization amount to heightened cosmopolitanism? I argue that manifestations of cultural globalism have transcended the problematic of cosmopolitanism. The cosmopolitanisms of the first half of the twentieth century were the networks and milieus of intellectuals, artists, dilettantes, and flaneurs in urban centers—daring and experimenting figures who were deracinated, transcending then impermeable communal and religious boundaries. At least that was the projected image. These kinds of networks and milieus persist and are probably more extensive than ever before. In the age of cultural globalism, however, they have been routinized and have lost their charismatic character.

Also in the global context, international business creates its own uniform milieus, with executives and personnel travelling the world and residing in diverse centers but staying in similar hotel rooms or apartments and mingling in networks of similarly socialized colleagues. Tourism likewise creates its own milieus: at the cheaper levels, resorts, hotels, entertainment, and food strive for standardization in tourist-magnet cities from Benidorm to Bodrum. Upmarket tourists pay for a touch of exoticism and local color, such as strong tea in tulip-shaped cups and whirling dervish performances, offered within the safe and hygienic confines of their hotels.

Cosmopolitanism in the Middle East—in the old-fashioned sense of communally deracinated and culturally promiscuous groups and milieus—continues to exist in corners of such urban spaces. These pockets, however, are submerged by the two major forces of the metropolis today: the urbanized masses and their transformation of the city and its politics; and the forces of international capital and tourism, with their towering hotels and offices, media, and promotion of goods and images that sell, cosmopolitan or otherwise.

NOTES

1. See Sami Zubaida, *Beyond Islam: A New Understanding of the Middle East* (London: I. B. Tauris, 2011), 9–12.

2. See Albert Hourani, *Arabic Thought in the Liberal Age, 1798–1939* (Cambridge, UK: Cambridge University Press, 1983), 245–259.

3. Nora Seni, "Combien de Raisins dans Votre The?," in *Istanbul 1914–1923: Capitale d'un Monde Illusoire, ou L'agonie des Vieux Empires*, ed. Yerasimos Stephane (Paris: Editions Autrement, 1992), 171–183.

4. Donald Quataert, *The Ottoman Empire, 1700–1922*, New Approaches to European History (Cambridge, UK: Cambridge University Press, 2000), 110–139.

5. See Serif Mardin, *The Genesis of Young Ottoman Thought: A Study in the Modernization of Turkish Political Ideas* (Princeton, NJ: Princeton University Press, 1962).

6. For an exposition of Namık Kemal's ideological formulations, see Niyazi Berkes, *The Development of Secularism in Turkey* (London: Hurst, [1964] 1998), 208–222.

7. Philip Mansel, *Constantinople: City of the World's Desire, 1453–1924* (London: John Murray, 2006).

8. Ibid., 263.

9. M. G. Smith, *The Plural Society in the British West Indies* (Berkeley: University of California Press, 1965).

10. The most comprehensive work on Freemasonry in the Ottoman Empire is Thierry Zarcone, *Mystiques, Philosophes, et Franc-Macon en Islam: Reza Tevfik, Penseur Ottoman 1868–1949* (Paris: Maisonneuve, 1993), esp. 177–300.

11. Ibid., 98–99.

12. Ibid., 208–210.

13. Ibid., 209.

14. Ibid., 301–326.

15. Godfrey Goodwin, *The Janissaries* (London: Saqi, 2006), 87–89.

16. Cemal Kafadar, *Between Two Worlds: The Construction of the Ottoman State* (Berkeley: University of California Press, 1995), 150.

17. François Georgeon, "Ottomans and Drinkers: The Consumption of Alcohol in Istanbul in the Nineteenth Century," in *Outside In: On the Margins of the Modern Middle East*, ed. Eugene Rogan (London: I. B. Tauris, 2002), 7–30.

18. Ibid., 19–23.

19. *Berkes, Development of Secularism in Turkey*, 271.

20. Ibid., 278.

21. Zubaida, *Beyond Islam.*

22. Much of the material in this section is drawn from the contributions to Stephane Yerasimos, ed., *Istanbul 1914–1923: Capitale d'un Monde Illusoire, ou L'agonie des Vieux Empires* (Paris: Editions Autrement, 1992).

23. François Georgeon, "A la Veille de la Guerre, des Voyageurs," in *Istanbul 1914–1923: Capitale d'un Monde Illusoire, ou L'agonie des Vieux Empires*, ed. Stephane Yerasimos (Paris: Editions Autrement, 1992), 25–40.

24. Yerasimos, *Istanbul 1914–1923*, 20.

25. Ibid., 21.

26. Ayhan Aktar, *Varlik Vergasive "Turklestime" Politikalari* (Istanbul: Iletisim, 2002).

27. TahaParla, *The Social and Political Thought of Ziya Gökalp: 1876–1924*, vol. 35 (Leiden, The Netherlands: Brill, 1985); and Andrew Davison, "Secularization and Modernization in Turkey: The Ideas of Ziya Gökalp," *International Journal of Human Resource Management* 24, no. 2 (1995): 189–224.

28. Çağlar Keyder, ed., *Istanbul: Between the Global and the Local* (Boulder, CO: Rowman and Littlefield, 1999).

CHAPTER 3

The Past Is a Different City

ISTANBUL, MEMOIRS, AND MULTICULTURALISM

Feyzi Baban

Istanbul's Ottoman past as a cosmopolitan city is often contrasted with the homogeneous social fabric of the city during the republican period (see chapters 1 and 2 in this volume). Istanbul is not alone in this temporal dissonance. Across the Mediterranean, the centuries-old pluralistic composition of cities like Alexandria, Beirut, Thessaloniki, and İzmir unraveled over the course of the nineteenth and early twentieth centuries due to growing nationalisms.[1] The rise of singular national identities proved catastrophic for these great cities of the Levant. Thessaloniki, for one, had been known for its prominent Jewish community since the fourteenth century, but by the end of World War II that community had been erased.[2] As nationalism became the dominant form of social organization, Istanbul too lost its cultural plurality while becoming politically and economically irrelevant as the political center of gravity of the new Turkish nation-state shifted to Ankara.

Countering these currents is present-day nostalgia for Levantine cities' pluralism (see chapters 5 and 6 this volume). Such sentiments were captured by Egyptian-born French singer-songwriter Georges Moustaki: "The Alexandria of my childhood was the world in miniature with all races and all religions. I was rarely a foreigner anywhere because I always found some reference to Alexandria in the languages I heard, the smells I breathed or the colors."[3] Moustaki's nostalgia evokes a lost cosmopolitan world, which is cited in recent debates that contrast premodern societies' presumed ability to facilitate cultural diversity with the perceived inability of national projects to accommodate plurality. To be sure, national communities in the Eastern Mediterranean have proved rather inept at providing peaceful living arrangements for their populations, which are again becoming diverse, dynamic, and mobile due to globalization and related developments.

In response to the shortcomings of national projects in the region, many observers are turning to cities as likely places where cosmopolitan solidarity might emerge. Cities derive energy from the multiple identities of their citizens and usually develop intricate mechanisms that enable communities to cohabit. In contrast, nationalist discourses attempt to neutralize, control, and mold differences into singular identities. As a result, ever since the inception of the nation-state, there has been an ongoing tension between the multiethnic and multicultural nature of cities and the larger national projects within which cities are located.

This tension between the cosmopolitanism of cities and the monism of nation-states is as temporal as it is geographic, given that pluralistic urban arrangements often predate the emergence of national narratives. As receptacles of historical memory, large cities in particular defy the logic of national consolidation; collective memories of cosmopolitan pasts refuse to fade, experiences linger, and traditions are transferred from generation to generation.

This chapter asks whether a history of urban plurality indeed provides a basis for cosmopolitan solidarity in the contemporary world. A related question with which I also engage is whether the historical past of cities like Istanbul offers insights for thinking about the parameters of cosmopolitan solidarity in a globalized world. I argue that the cosmopolitan past of Levantine cities does not fit the bill for a global era. This is because Istanbul in particular, and Levantine cities in general, were not cosmopolitan places as we understand the term "cosmopolitanism" today. They did not enable conditions in which various groups and identities share a common set of values while maintaining what is unique to each group. Rather, Levantine cities entailed multicultural social structures that were hierarchical and segregated. Istanbul under Ottoman rule is a clear example of such an arrangement.

Therefore, the historical memory of Istanbul offers not a formula for reconstructing cosmopolitan living arrangements in contemporary modern societies but rather a corrective to contemporary cosmopolitan propositions, which still have difficulty accommodating difference and otherness. To demonstrate this, I outline the origins of the cosmopolitan tradition in Istanbul. Next, I examine the institutional dimensions of multicultural social arrangements in Ottoman Istanbul. I then use three historical examples to demonstrate the multicultural but segregated social fabric of Ottoman Istanbul. Finally, I reflect on how the Ottoman past of Istanbul can shed light on contemporary debates over cosmopolitanism.

Istanbul as a Cosmopolitan City

Throughout its history Istanbul has been hospitable to many cultural traditions, allowing people with varied backgrounds to live in and remake the city with endless energy. Neither European nor Asian, neither entirely Christian nor completely Muslim, Istanbul has never been ordered fully in a fashion considered to be modern. In this regard it is egalitarian; notably, the city has never been equated with a single ethnicity. Dynamic but also traditional, Istanbul, as Spanish writer Juan Goytisolo argues, has always been a perplexing city that has shocked, surprised, and influenced its visitors and inhabitants.[4] Istanbul's flourishing cultural plurality itself emanates from a multifaceted geography that enables movement from east to west and north to south over water and land. This position has allowed diverse multitudes to pass through and settle, blending into what has already been there while continually redefining the city.

This absorbent capacity of Istanbul accounts for the episode of the White Russians who flocked to the city following the Bolshevik Revolution (see chapter 4 in this volume). Arriving in large numbers in a very short span of time, they created a lively culture at the heart of Istanbul, replete with vibrant music halls, publishing houses, and literary societies. A particularly interesting aspect of the White Russians' experience was that due to their numbers and sudden appearance, they were able to graft onto the city and its culture very quickly, only to disappear as swiftly as they came.[5] This attests to a key feature of Istanbul, namely that it is not a city of records, deep memories, and firmly grounded lives, but rather a place of moments that come and go, more or less noisily, leaving a residue. These echoes are something one feels, but one is never quite sure of their source. Today, for example, there is hardly any physical evidence of the presence of a large Russian community, which existed with a distinctive culture in the city center only a hundred years ago. Nevertheless, quiet remnants of this presence appear in unexpected names on buildings, in life stories in books, in restaurants, and in other venues whose only connection to the vanished Russians are names whose stories nobody remembers. The Russians' appearance and near disappearance also helps to illustrate the haphazard physical organization of the city, which has resisted carefully planned boulevards like those in Baron Haussmann's Paris, where built structures are zoned and planned.

Housing many cultural traditions at once, Istanbul has long been a global and local city simultaneously. Historically, its restless energy, creativity, and ever-changing nature have been possible due to its openness to borderless flows of people, culture, and trade. Orhan Pamuk, in *Istanbul: Memories of a City*, described a post-Ottoman republican city full of *hüzün* (nostalgia/melancholy), a city looking inward, cut off from the global flows that had fed Istanbul's identity over the course of centuries. In Pamuk's republican Istanbul, ethnic diversity was long gone, and neighborhoods had lost their cultural contexts with the departure of Greek, Armenian, and other Levantine groups. He described the city as a place of amnesia where the past lingered but was disconnected from current residents' lives, its architecture delinked from a delicate social fabric that had developed over centuries.[6] This portrayal of a depressive Istanbul captures the sense of loss in a city that was no longer cosmopolitan but also not comfortable with the constraints of the nationalist era. Perhaps, for the first time in its long history, post-1923 Istanbul was neither connected to the global flow of goods, ideas, and people nor hospitable to multiculturalism.

Yet contrary to the republican elite's claim that Ottoman Istanbul was a chaotic aggregate of distinct groups who never came together as a coherent community, Ottoman Istanbul operated through sophisticated social arrangements maintained through elaborate legal and normative codes. Far from lacking any social and legal order, the social fabric of Ottoman Istanbul evolved over centuries by maintaining the autonomy of its segregated communities. I now address the social organization of Ottoman Istanbul that enabled this relatively peaceful coexistence.

Multicultural Social Fabric in Ottoman Istanbul

Istanbul's social fabric evolved during Ottoman times and was based on three distinct pillars: (1) communitarian social organization, (2) segregation of identities, and (3) management of cultural plurality.

In Ottoman Istanbul under the *millet* system, or system of nations, each religious group (Muslims, Orthodox and Catholic Christians, and Jews) was given communal autonomy to govern its internal affairs.[7] While the term *nation* eventually came to refer to nations in the modern sense, it was originally used to designate religious communities. These autonomous religious groups were arranged hierarchically. The system was based on the principle that Muslims constituted the dominant religious community of the empire, while non-Muslims were given protection to exercise their religion and govern themselves in exchange for special taxation.[8] To enforce this arrangement, an extensive set of codes regulated the sections of the city in which each group could live, the color of their clothing, and the style and height of their buildings. For example, Armenians were directed to wear red and violet, Greeks to wear black, and Jews to wear blue, while Muslims wore green.[9] In some instances, the regulations were so detailed as to designate the number of stairs that should extend up to each house.[10]

The neighborhoods of each *millet* had distinct traditions, norms, and social networks that were enforced formally and informally through elders' councils, security guards, and neighborhood clerks.[11] These autonomous communities also had internal hierarchies that began with religious institutions and extended to the level of neighborhood leadership. Each religious community constituted a universe of its own, just as each neighborhood was self-contained, with clearly demarcated physical and social boundaries.[12] The autonomous nature of these communities enabled the long-term sustenance of communal traditions, the control of entry, and the enforcement of internal norms and rules.

Ottoman pluralism then, as Nora Şeni rightly points out, was based on regulation and the rendering visible of ethnic and religious differences to maintain strict segregation.[13] The Ottoman social fabric thus accommodated multiplicity but prevented mingling, ensuring the purity of group identities. As Edmondo D'amicis describes the culturally fragmented topography of Istanbul: "While you were in a poor neighborhood of Marseille, you turn right and find yourself in a small Asian town. Turn left and you find yourself in a Black Sea town. Looking at languages spoken, faces and buildings you may think that you are in different countries. [Aspects] from France, light from England, other elements from Russia."[14]

This segregated system remained the dominant form of social organization in Istanbul until the collapse of the empire. The provision of municipal services, for example, was first initiated by bankers such as the Commondos and the Zogrofos around the 1860s in the Pera district, a district of non-Muslims and Levantines. The city's central administration remained indifferent to this urban development and disengaged from it, as it was regarded as an internal matter of non-Muslim communities.[15] Similarly, Jewish and Greek communities organized their own charitable organizations and schools at the beginning of the eighteenth century, with very little interference from the central administration. However much the administration took great pains to regulate and mark boundaries between communities, it showed no interest in applying similar levels of regulation to their inner workings.[16] Contrary to the unifying logic of modern nationalism, the Ottoman administrative structure discouraged the consolidation of separate identities into a single coherent one. This autonomous and segregated arrangement, in turn, created conditions in which communal identities not only were sustained but also coexisted with other groups with relative peace.

Finally, this fairly stable mode of cohabitation was reinforced by specific administrative practices that were geared toward managing cultural plurality. In other words, in addition to maintaining autonomy and segregation, city officials actively and effectively managed cultural and religious diversity. They did so by establishing rules governing interaction vis-à-vis the central administration that applied to all communities. These rules might be ethical or purely administrative, concentrating around three key areas: noninterference with cultural and religious practices, respect for property rights, and respect for dignity of the individual and the household. In his eighteenth-century travelogue, French traveler de La Motraye described the administration-community relationship as one of moral responsibility in which the central administration paid maximum respect to protect individual and household integrity.[17] According to de La Motraye, this particular attention to ethical principles, which was absent in the rest of Europe during this same period, provided the main pillar of orderly social organization of the empire. In several places he expresses astonishment that Christian subjects preferred Ottoman rule to Christian rule; he attributed this attitude to the Ottoman administration's strict adherence to respect for individual integrity and protection of personal property.[18]

Apart from the ethical and moral framework, the city employed administrative mechanisms to regulate relations between communities and preserve order. Such institutional and administrative networks covered security, food supply, and economic matters. The Kadı of Istanbul (the supreme judge), for example, was responsible for the overall administration of the city, while there were Kadıs within each district who were responsible for judicial, municipal, and financial administration. As a result, each religious community was only very loosely subject to the rule of the Istanbul Kadı.[19]

As such, the multicultural social fabric of Ottoman Istanbul was not accidental but fostered through intricate normative, legal, and social practices. The administration both guaranteed the survival of these communities and ensured that they remained visible and segregated from one another. The result was the coexistence of solitudes, of people sharing the same geography without much interaction. In the following section I briefly discuss three of these solitudes to demonstrate in more detail the nature of the segregated and separate lives of the inhabitants of Ottoman Istanbul.

Contrapuntal Reading of Solitudes in Cosmopolitan Istanbul

Its cultural plurality notwithstanding, the social fabric of the Ottoman Istanbul was also one of isolation. What sort of sensibilities did these arrangements create in practice? To address this question, I propose a contrapuntal reading of the city. A contrapuntal approach, as developed by Edward Said, considers the intertwined histories and divergent experiences of people and communities. It involves the simultaneous interpretation of divergent experiences to reveal the omissions and silences within different narratives; this enables us to better understand how divergent experiences narrate seemingly similar situations.[20] This methodology is particularly useful because it reveals moments of contact, discrepant experiences, spaces of absence, and the dynamics of living together in a city of cultural plurality. I apply a contrapuntal method to three texts that describe lived experiences of late Ottoman Istanbul of 1890s. The first one is *Boğaziçi* or *Bosphorus* by Abdülhak Şinasi Hisar, the second is *My Memoirs* by Yorgo Zarifi, and the last is *Loksandra—An Istanbul Dream* by Maria Yordanidu. All three tomes depict Istanbul's distinct communities at around the same time period that simultaneously coexist and have very little connection with one another.

In *Boğaziçi*, the writer and poet Abdülhak Şinasi Hisar depicts the neighborhoods of Boğaziçi during the 1890s as evincing a distinct combination of Muslim and Turkish cultures, manifest in a mélange of smells, colors, and sounds that create serenity and tranquility.[21] This distinctly Muslim and Turkish culture is evident in the architecture of the wooden *yalı* (traditional Ottoman houses built on the edge of the water), and gender-segregated rituals of social life, and food culture.[22]

One particular cultural practice Hisar describes in great detail is the "Mehtap" ritual, which brought the inhabitants of Boğaziçi together during the summer months. During the full moon period on summer evenings, wealthy residents paid for events in which prominent musicians and singers performed music as they sailed in large boats, accompanied by a procession of hundreds of smaller boats populated by Boğaziçi residents.[23] The procession slowly moved along the

Figure 3.1. Bosphorus mansions (*yalı*). Photo credit: Susan C. Pearce.

waters of Boğaziçi, occasionally pausing in front of a *yalı*. Prior to each Mehtap event, residents made extensive preparations about what to wear and who would be seated in which boat. During the event everybody tried to stay near the musicians. As the boats sailed side by side in close proximity, young men and women were able to flirt with one another, and the whole event usually lasted until dawn.[24] Hisar poetically describes the social scene, at which hundreds of boats sailed slowly in great harmony from cove to cove, following and accompanying the music, during which residents of Boğaziçi not only listened to music and sailed, but gossiped, made arrangements for engagements and marriages, flirted, and discussed current issues. Beyond being musical events, Mehtap rituals reflected social hierarchies, norms, and roles. They acted as conduits of social life through which the latest news was whispered from ear to ear, in which secret intimacies were exchanged, often with the help of rowers, but where the participants also strictly observed proper attire and etiquette.

In Hisar's *Boğaziçi*, there is almost no reference to non-Muslims. If you read the text for a deeper understanding of neighborhood life along Boğaziçi, you would not realize that these neighborhoods contained large non-Muslim populations, especially Greek and Armenian. From time to time Hisar refers to the multiplicity of cultures in passing while mentioning Albanians, Circassians, and Arab merchants and tradesmen of the city, but there is no mention of non-Muslims as being included in Boğaziçi culture. Although Christian residents of

Boğaziçi were mainly concentrated on the European shore, the neighborhoods described by Hisar on the Anatolian side of the Boğaziçi also contained a significant proportion of non-Muslim residents, who had distinctive everyday rituals and built houses and places of worship along the shore. Hisar's description of the spiritual existence of Boğaziçi culture is devoid of these inhabitants.

Yorgo Zarifi's *My Memoirs* portrays Boğaziçi culture in the late 1890s and early 1900s quite differently. Yorgo Zarifi was a wealthy Greek banker and the confidant and personal banker of Sultan Abdülhamit II. His memoirs offer a detailed picture of the upper-class Greek community's life in Istanbul in the late eighteenth century. In Zarifi's portrayal, elements of modern life such as the elimination of gender segregation, European style of architecture, and new forms of consumption were in full force. Certain neighborhoods where Christian residents of the city lived, such as Büyükdere and Tarabya, appear to be no different than their counterparts in other European cities, with European-style promenades, intellectual salons, ballrooms, and classical music concerts.[25]

In these Boğaziçi neighborhoods, the traditional wooden houses were replaced by European-style stone and brick mansions with large gardens. The traditional private social life gained a public character in public places such as coffeehouses and modern restaurants. The mystical nature of the Muslim Boğaziçi that is poetically described by Hisar is absent in Zarifi's Boğaziçi, and Zarifi barely mentions Muslims. There are occasional passing references to Zarifi's Muslim friends, but no trace of Muslim life (Zarifi 2005, 306–320). And even though Boğaziçi occupies a significant place in Zarifi's memoirs, there is no mention of the Mehtap rituals. One cannot but wonder how Zarifi omits an event during which hundreds and sometimes thousands of boats sailed down the Boğaziçi with music at least monthly in the summer. We do not have an answer to this question, but it is possible that in Zarifi's narrative the Mehtap rituals, which were strictly enjoyed by Muslim Ottomans, especially Turks, did not occupy any place whatsoever in his self-contained Boğaziçi. As a result, even though he might have known of the practice, it was not a significant enough part of the non-Muslim social fabric to be mentioned in his memoirs, in contrast with Hisar, who devoted an entire section of his book to the Mehtap viewings as one of the most characteristic social events of Boğaziçi life. While Hisar's Boğaziçi appears to be a spiritual place with a distinctive Turkish and Islamic identity, the same Boğaziçi in Zarifi's account is a modern, European space in which new gender roles are prevalent, high society organizes elaborate parties, and full-fledged public life is on display.

Finally, in Maria Yordanidu's novel *Loksandra: An Istanbul Dream*, we observe a completely different Istanbul of the 1890s through a portrait of a modest Greek household in the relatively poor neighborhood of Samatya.[26] This is neither the European Istanbul depicted by Zarifi nor the spiritual Turkish and Islamic Istanbul portrayed by Hisar, but a traditional Greek neighborhood closed and steeped in tradition. The main character of the novel, Loksandra, does not speak Turkish, and her occasional interaction with Turks is limited to the milkman, who passes through the neighborhood. Loksandra's husband Dimitro is quite content living in a neighborhood where there is little change and time moves slowly, without interaction with other parts of the city.[27] He is saddened, for example, every time he sees the minarets around Hagia Sophia (formerly the patriarchal basilica for Eastern Christian Orthodoxy and the world's largest cathedral in the Byzantine era; see chapter 7 in this volume).

Loksandra neither is aware of the surrounding Turkish culture nor feels a need to establish connections with people outside of her immediate neighborhood. Her very limited interaction with people outside her neighborhood occurs when periodic fires bring together residents of the city and the street sellers who pass by her house.[28] From time to time she hears news about the city and the sultan as if it is coming from a foreign territory rather than the city in which she lives.[29] Her depiction of life in the neighborhood of Samatya, defined by the local and historical rituals associated with her immediate surroundings, illustrates well the closed universe of neighborhood life. In Loksandra's Istanbul, there is a trace of neither Şinasi Hisar's mystical and transcendental Muslim Istanbul nor Zarifi's European and modern Istanbul. Instead, we witness a modest Greek Orthodox life, confined, moreover, by the values and norms of a poor neighborhood.

While reading these three works in a contrapuntal fashion provides us with a picture of multiple and colorful lives in Istanbul, the absences and omissions in each work tell a story of a multicultural but not precisely cosmopolitan Istanbul. Sharing the same urban space, three distinct lifeworlds are imbued with cultural and normative fullness that can only be observed in social settings in which there is a high level of cultural and administrative cohesion but also segregation. Ottoman Istanbul was, in short, communitarian. Coupled with a rather weak central administration, Ottoman Istanbul showcased a premodern form of multiculturalism in which group rights and logics were the dominant form of social cohesion. Individuals in this context lived within the borders of their respective communities without significant interaction with members of other communities. Ottoman Istanbul was a city defined by a distinctive multiplicity of cultural and social spaces.

From Multicultural to Cosmopolitan Istanbul

The multicultural past of Istanbul suggests that when it comes to the possibility of cosmopolitan living in late modern cities, it is important not to romanticize the Ottoman past of Istanbul as a period of tolerance and peaceful coexistence, an often committed fallacy.[30] Istanbul's past nevertheless stands as testimony to what is lost in national narratives and to a historical record of living with cultural plurality in relative peace. In this way, it helps us to rethink cosmopolitanism's uneasy relationship with cultural plurality. The nostalgia for a lost cosmopolitan city is as much about yearning for plurality as it is a critique of the way the social fabric of the city was reimagined through modern nationalism. As noted, the decline of Levantine cities such as Istanbul and Alexandria was part and parcel of the rise of nationalism and its rejection of social pluralism. Cultural plurality, which had been a natural condition of human societies for centuries, became the principal obstacle to government's ability to create a single homogeneous national culture within the confines of nation-states.

Istanbul's history as grounded in plurality—however checkered—is thus of some relevance to its aspirations as a global city. Istanbul today anchors growing transnational linkages (see chapters 9 and 10 in this volume) while remaining—and reaffirming—the imprint of a century of nationalism. As globalization reveals the limits and pitfalls of nationalist thinking, however, the past experience of Levantine cities like Istanbul has attracted attention as a cosmopolitan model.

It should be remembered, however, that such cities, like Ottoman Istanbul, were not cosmopolitan in the traditional sense of the word as a political project that seeks to transcend particular cultural identities. Since the time of the Stoics, advocates of cosmopolitanism have imagined a social order in which the particularities of individuals and separate human communities are replaced by a single universal framework that unites all humanity.[31] Suspicious of individual differences as divisive and detrimental to achieving human solidarity, cosmopolitans imagined a world where everybody feels at home without attachment to any singular particular identity or belonging.[32]

This strand of cosmopolitan theory and its goal of human solidarity through the rejection of particular cultural attachments found its strongest manifestation in the Enlightenment tradition. From Marquis de Condorcet to Immanuel Kant, Enlightenment thinkers imagined a modern world in which traditional and religious worldviews would be replaced by universal reason, uniting diverse societies around a universal framework.[33] The role of reason in creating such a universal framework was emphasized, as the Enlightenment thinkers viewed reason as the only characteristic common to all human beings, which would enable them to overcome particularistic differences.

Yet reason was also a guiding principle in the attempts to engineer national communities in the modern world, with disastrous outcomes for cultural difference. Rather than unifying humanity around a common framework, reason all too often has been applied as an essentialized category with which to assess the level of civility of human societies.[34] In this respect, Ottoman multicultural Istanbul provides a corrective to traditional cosmopolitan thinking, as its social fabric did not rest on universalizing logic or cultural reference points; instead the very existence of cultural plurality was ensured with segregated coexistence of cultural and religious communities.

Since the time of the Stoics, traditional cosmopolitan thinking has failed to recognize that the universal against which particulars are judged is nothing but another form of cultural particularity. Enlightenment reason is no exception to this. While Enlightenment thinkers thought that the universality of reason derived from its essential quality of being free from cultural particularities, they failed to recognize that this very understanding was a cultural product of seventeenth-century Europe.[35] By extension, this assumption helped propel a colonial rationale to bring those still gripped by religion and tradition into the fold of universal reason. This impulse has resulted in a painful history of subjugation of human communities, the physical destruction of the natural environment, a debasing of cultural practices, and endless human suffering.[36] Today, postcolonial intellectuals seek to rewrite colonial history, uncovering previously suppressed voices and restoring the dignity and ability of agents to articulate local reason(s). This in turn has further called into question the universality of Enlightenment notions of reason.[37] Yet the postcolonial movement has not yet provided new alternatives.

This problematic articulation of universality finds its political manifestation in national narratives' desire to create geographically segregated homogeneous communities out of diverse human populations. The multicultural Ottoman Istanbul, however, depicts an alternative picture in which social cohesion is achieved through recognition of cultural plurality instead of trying to create a singular community out of diversity. Despite its problematic past, if the cosmopolitan ideal retains the potential to offer alternative ways of thinking about how to live with cultural difference because it is built on the assumptions that human beings are unavoidably related to one another and that it is this relationality that forms the very basis of our living together, what does the multicultural Istanbul offer to rethink about the cosmopolitan condition? The cosmopolitan ideal is a condition that needs to be created and nurtured, not from above by invoking some sort of universal category, but painstakingly from below, through everyday human actions and solidarities. While multicultural Istanbul cannot be a model for cosmopolitan living arrangements in modern national societies, it provides an important corrective, reminding us that any form of cosmopolitan condition should start with acknowledging cultural plurality rather than creating a singular community.

Conclusion

One can nevertheless conclude that if the precondition of a bottom-up form of cosmopolitanism is for culturally diverse populations to live peacefully in one community, the historical memory of Istanbul, along with that of other similar cities across the Levant, provides a corrective to the preoccupation with homogeneity in most national narratives. Despite its relatively short existence, modern nationalism has successfully established an artificial link between territory and society with the argument that every nation-state should be identified with a single all-encompassing identity. Precisely because of this, the history of modern nationalism is the history of forgetting histories, cultures, and peoples that coexisted in the same geographies, erasing memories and suppressing the expression of nonprivileged identities. Present-day Istanbul stands in testimony to this process, as the culturally diverse history of the city has almost completely been erased, and current residents have few ways of relating to those who preceded them. Furthermore, the vocabulary, norms, traditions, and everyday life practices that emerged over centuries as a result of cultural diversity have been forgotten. Invoking the cosmopolitan past of the city is a first move toward resisting homogenizing thinking and can be a political strategy to counter nationalist historical discourses.

In fact, Istanbul's multicultural past reveals the anomalous nature of its republican history. Istanbul's story also provides a corrective to traditional forms of cosmopolitan thinking that insist on an essentialized universal, given that community coexistence did not jeopardize cultural particularity. However, the absence of solidarities across differences in Ottoman Istanbul attenuates the relevance of its experience as a model for the present. Similarly, bottom-up cosmopolitan thinking today must confront the challenge of how to convert cultural plurality into experiences of solidarity as a basis upon which to build a cosmopolitan ideal.

NOTES

1. Robert Ilbert, Illios Yannakakis, and Jacques Hassoun, eds., *İskenderiye 1860–1960: Geçici Bir Hoşgörü Modeli Cemaatler ve Kozmopolit Kimlik* (Istanbul: İletişim Yayınları, 2006); Selim İleri, *İstanbul Seni Unutmadım* (Istanbul: Oğlak Yayıncılık, 2001); Serhat Öztürk, *Selanik* (Istanbul: Can Yayınları, 2012); and Leon Sciaky, *Elveda Selanik* (Istanbul: Varlık Yayınları, 2006).

2. Sciaky, *Elveda Selanik*; and Kim Willsher, "George Moustaki Obituary," *Guardian*, May 24, 2013, http://www.guardian.co.uk/music/2013/may/24/georges-moustaki-obituary?INTCMP=SRCH.

3. Willsher, "George Moustaki Obituary."

4. Juan Goytisolo, *Osmanlı'nın İstanbul'u* (Istanbul: Yapı Kredi Yayınları, 2000).

5. Jack Deleon, *Beyoğlu'nda Beyaz Ruslar* (Istanbul: Remzi Kitabevi, 2003).

6. Orhan Pamuk, *Istanbul* (New York: Vintage, 2006).

7. Bilal Eryılmaz, *Osmanlı Devleti'nde Millet Sistemi* (Istanbul: Ağaç Yayınları, 1992).

8. Bilal Eryılmaz, "Birlikte Yaşama Düzeni: Osmanlı Millet Sistemi" [System of living together], *Bilgi ve Hikmet Dergisi* 5 (Winter 1994): 91–97.

9. Nora Şeni, *Seni Unutursam İstanbul* (Istanbul: Kitap Yayınevi,, 2008).

10. Ibid.

11. Eryılmaz,"Birlikte Yaşama Düzeni."

12. Pinelopi Stathis, *Yüzyıl İstanbul'unda Gayrimüslimler* (Istanbul: Tarih Vakfı Yurt Yaymları, 1999), 19.

13. Şeni, *Seni Unutursam İstanbul*, 74.

14. Cited in ibid., 156.

15. Ibid., 120.

16. Balıkhane Nazırı Ali Rıza Bey, *Eski Zamanlarda İstanbul Hayatı* (Istanbul: Kitabevi Yayınları, 2001).

17. Aubry de La Motraye, *La Motraye Seyahatnamesi* (Istanbul: İstiklal Kitabevi, 2007), 140 and 192.

18. Ibid., 140.

19. İlber Ortaylı, *İstanbul'dan Sayfalar* (Istanbul: Alkım Yayınevi, 2007), 83.

20. Edward W. Said, *Culture and Imperialism* (New York: Vintage Books, 1994).

21. Abdülhak Şinasi Hisar, *Boğaziçi Yalıları* (Istanbul: Yapı Kredi Yayınları, 2006), 9–12.

22. Ibid.

23. Abdülhak Şinasi Hisar, *Boğaziçi Mehtapları* (Istanbul: Yapı Kredi Yayınları, 2006), 45–60).

24. Ibid.

25. Yorgo L. Zarifi, *Hatıralarım: Kaybolan Bir Dünya İstanbul 1800–1920* (Istanbul: Literatür Yayıncılık, 2005), 352.

26. Maria Yordanidu, *Loksandra: İstanbul Düşü* (Istanbul: Marenostrum, 1995).

27. Ibid., 13.

28. Ibid., 37.

29. Ibid., 64.

30. Selim İleri, *Yıldızlar Altında İstanbul* (Istanbul: Oğlak Yayınları, 1998); and İleri, *İstanbul Seni Unutmadım.*

31. Martha Nussbaum, "Patriotism and Cosmopolitanism," in *For Love of Country*, ed. Martha Nussbaum and Joshua Cohen (Boston: Beacon Press, 1996), 3–19.

32. Michael Walzer, "Spheres of Affection," in *For Love of Country*, ed. Martha Nussbaum and Joshua Cohen (Boston: Beacon Press, 1996), 125–126.

33. Lisa Hill, "The Two Republicae of the Roman Stoics: Can a Cosmopolite be a Patriot?," *Citizenship Studies* 4, no. 1 (2000): 65–79.

34. David Harvey, "Cosmopolitanism and the Banality of Geographical Evils," *Public Culture* 12, no. 2 (2000): 529–564.

35. Ernesto Laclau, "Universalism, Particularism and the Question of Identity," in *The Identity in Question*, ed. J. Rajchman (New York: Routledge, 1995), 93–110.

36. Harvey, "Cosmopolitanism and the Banality."

37. Gayatri Chakravorty Spivak and Sarah Harasym, *The Post-Colonial Critic: Interviews, Strategies, Dialogues* (New York: Routledge, 1990).

CHAPTER 4

Cosmopolitanism, Violence, and the State in Istanbul and Odessa

Charles King

What does cosmopolitanism look like in practice? As an ideal, cosmopolitanism stresses the sense of thriving as a citizen of the world and being comfortable in multiple cultural contexts, with the additional—perhaps negative—connotation of never being truly at home anywhere. But as a practical feature of late modern life in an age of immigration, easy travel, and multilingual cities, how has cosmopolitanism actually been practiced? And given the persistence of nationalizing states—countries that seek to define themselves as, at base, the legitimate homeland of a single cultural group—what is its fate?

As theorists such as Kwame Anthony Appiah have realized, cosmopolitanism is not so much a single thing as a collective name for a persistent set of tensions: between the tug of fellow feeling for humanity and the specific sense of attachment to some smaller community, between the ethical obligations to other people and to one's own people, and between what one owes strangers and what one owes friends.[1] But cosmopolitanism can also be a set of practical ethics—a lived behavior—especially when geography forces people of different backgrounds, traditions, and abilities to live in proximity to one another. Cosmopolitanism as a concept stresses universality, but it has been most often experienced in a specific context: cities. Being in a city and being civilized, being urban as a route to being urbane, are assumptions that wind throughout the history of cosmopolitan thought and theory.

In practice one might even say that living together—rubbing shoulders with people who talk differently, eat differently, and clothe themselves differently—is the normal state of affairs in urban societies. These multifarious communities, in turn, seem remarkably capable of working out their own informal mechanisms of reducing all-out conflict, getting beyond episodes of violence, and crafting a workable form of "pragmatic pluralism."[2] The failures of these methods usually have little to do with the imagined difficulties of cooperating across cultural lines. Indeed, being multilingual and assuming different identities depending on the social and economic incentives for doing so have been commonplace in human history. As political scientists James Fearon and David Laitin pointed out in game-theoretic terms more than a decade ago, interethnic cooperation is actually far more common than ethnic conflict, even though the latter usually attracts the most attention from theorists.[3] Rather, what unbuilds practical cosmopolitanism seems to be not so much an ethical lapse on the part of individuals as a systematic attempt by modern states to untangle the diverse communities that cities naturally produce.

This chapter examines how the two most important cities on the Black Sea dealt with the transition to modernity in the late nineteenth and early twentieth centuries, as well as the contrasting approaches each exhibited with respect to order, civility, and cosmopolitanism. It highlights the central role of states in fomenting violence and in unbuilding cosmopolitan urban centers. Both cities saw their relative status change vis-à-vis their own (in a sense, new) metropoles: Moscow and Ankara. Both experienced, by the middle of the century, the forced removal of key minority populations—Jews, Greeks, and Armenians—as a result of state policies of national purification, social distrust, and various forms of intervention by external actors.

"Crooks learn their profession in Pera," went a nineteenth-century saying, "but practice it in Odessa." From the late 1700s forward, the fates of Odessa and Istanbul were inextricably linked. An outbreak of the plague in Istanbul raised the quarantine flag in Odessa. The fall in wheat prices in Odessa depleted transit revenues in Istanbul. But the two cities reflected each other in more profound ways as well. Both were multicultural spaces struggling with modernity. Odessa was a self-consciously modern city and a product of Enlightenment-era town planning, yet it was also an urban space that depended almost entirely on the produce of Russia's serf-bound economy. Istanbul was the capital of an ancient empire whose workable multiculturalism was confronted by the challenges of nationalism, minority rights, and political reform.

Both cities have recently engaged in a rediscovery of their own cosmopolitan heritage. A walk down İstiklal Avenue or Deribasovskaia Street—the places where inhabitants come to engage in the universal Mediterranean institution of the early evening stroll—offers a picture of urban centers that may be becoming more comfortable with their raucous and variegated identities. But the present is not the past. Both cities are today more ethnically homogeneous than at any point in their histories (even though Istanbul continues to be a major destination for Kurdish migrants from Anatolia). How things got that way, and what the contrasting experiences of Odessa and Istanbul might reveal about the possible threats to cosmopolitanism, are the subjects of this chapter.

Odessa from "Southern Capital" to Soviet Periphery

Odessa was, by almost any measure, a city for which cosmopolitanism was part of its birthright. Its truest founding father was José de Ribas, a Neapolitan adventurer of Spanish Irish heritage who scouted the site of the future city during his service in Catherine the Great's navy. Its early administrators were often French nobles on the run from the revolutionary crowds of Paris. When Aleksandr Pushkin arrived in the city in the 1820s—as part of his internal exile on the western frontier of the Russian Empire—he divided his time between socializing with Greek revolutionaries and wooing the multicultural denizens of the port's ballrooms and brothels. Over the course of the nineteenth century the early dominance of French and Italians in the city gave way to the arrival of Jews. By the end of the century Jews were more than a quarter of the city's total population. The booming trade in grain from the Ukrainian heartland, a well-developed shipping industry, and a speculative market in commodity futures drew a wide variety of immigrant groups to the expanding port city.

In 1894 Odessans celebrated their city's centennial, and a snapshot of that era reveals the cultural, linguistic, and religious diversity that had come to define a port routinely labeled the "southern capital" of the Russian Empire, yielding only to St. Petersburg and Moscow in imperial grandeur. Commemorative albums hailed the city's rapid development and European mores. Speeches and solemn masses extolled the city's bright future. The opera house at the top of Rishelevskaia Street, with its wedding-cake façade modeled on the latest Viennese styles, hosted grand concerts. Citizens with the right combination of interests and connections might join the Black Sea Yacht Club, the New Russian Society for the Encouragement of Horse Breeding, the New Russian Society of Hunting Enthusiasts, or the Odessa Society of Amateur Velocipedists. Collections available for public viewing at the museum of the Imperial Odessan Society of History and Antiquities told the story of the city's antique roots: its place in the ancient Greek system of trading *entrepôts* (trading posts) that once ringed the Black Sea.[4]

A stroll through the streets of the city would have led one to encounter some of the greatest writers and artists of the day, many of them towering figures in the history of east European Jewish, Yiddish, and Zionist culture. The Yiddish writer Sholem Aleichem—the codifier of *shtetl* culture whose stories would later inspire the musical *Fiddler on the Roof*—was living near the green expanse of Alexandrovskii Park. The historian Simon Dubnow, Russian Jewry's most celebrated chronicler, held forth at a well-known salon in his apartment on Bazarnaia Street. Leon Pinsker, whose pamphleteering would inspire Zionists for a generation, was on his deathbed in his flat on Rishelevskaia Street. Not far away a Christian family and a Jewish one were celebrating the arrival of two infants who would go on to become two of the twentieth century's defining Russian voices: Anna Gorenko (later Akhmatova) and Isaac Babel. For the more politically minded, organizations such as the Society for the Propagation of Enlightenment Among the Jews of Russia and the Society for the Support of Jewish Farmers and Artisans in Syria and Palestine—known informally as the "Odessa Committee"—offered differing visions of Jews' place in the Russian Empire, advocating either full assimilation or immigration to Ottoman-governed Palestine.

The cultural tapestry in the city was not always smooth. "[E]very year at Passover the Greeks beat up the Jews and robbed them," wrote the American Yiddish actor Jacob Adler, who grew up in the city.[5] Major anti-Jewish pogroms erupted in the 1870s and 1880s, often targeting the small shopkeepers and shipping merchants who had flourished in the city since the 1830s. But few people could have predicted the searing violence that descended on the city in 1905 and 1906. Over the course of a little more than a year, Jewish shops were ransacked. A carnival of looting and murder devastated the city center. Political assassinations skyrocketed. On one accounting, the death toll from targeted assassinations, bombings, shoot-outs, and mob attacks between February 1905 and May 1906 in the wider Odessa region included 13 provincial governors and mayors, 30 police captains and senior officers of the gendarmerie, 29 bankers and leading businessmen, 54 factory owners, 471 other police officers, and 257 local constables: in all some 1,273 deaths that the Russian imperial government attributed to "terrorist acts"—and not counting the hundreds of ordinary citizens killed or injured over the same period.[6]

Some of this violence would later be captured in Sergei Eisenstein's film *Battleship Potemkin* (1925), an artistically stunning but historically ludicrous account of the "uprising" in the city around the time of the 1905 Russian Revolution. Few people who actually witnessed the violence found much coherence in it, least of all a narrative of revolutionary idealism versus autocratic reaction. It was as if the city had suddenly learned how to devour itself. "Jewish pogroms are breaking out," wrote Liubov' Girs, the wife of a senior city official, in her diary. "[The Jews] have organized and armed themselves, and they are going so far as to shoot out of windows at the Russians. On Deribasovskaia Street all the Jewish stores have been smashed and the goods looted, and the riff-raff and their wives are strutting about in expensive clothes, boots, and fur coats. . . . The Jews on our street grabbed a dog and hung a label on his tail that said 'Nicholas II.'"[7]

The origins of the violence of 1905 had profoundly modern roots. The Russian state, increasingly wary of the revolutionary circles operating in the city's well-established political underground, fomented suspicion. Jewish workers and intellectuals, accustomed to previous waves of anti-Jewish violence and galvanized by the upsurge in looting in other cities, formed self-defense units armed with knives, clubs, and guns. The international context mattered as well. Odessa was the major shipping-out point for Russian soldiers and seamen dispatched to fight in the ongoing Russo-Japanese War. The influx of conscript soldiers into the city—and the impressment of former prisoners into a military desperate for manpower—created a mass of armed and often intoxicated young men eager to stave off boredom. While the upsurge in violence rested on older foundations—not least the widespread anti-Semitism of Russia's western borderlands and the distinctly discriminatory policies of the tsarist state—it was these more immediate factors that transformed the habitual rough-ups among Odessa's ethnic groups into large-scale violence.

But what is truly remarkable about the uptick in intercommunal violence in Odessa in the early twentieth century is how unimportant it actually turned out to be for the demographic structure of the city itself. Jewish out-migration increased immediately after 1905, but this pattern largely repeated historical patterns; the percentage of Jews in the city fell briefly after the pogroms of 1871 and 1881 but relatively quickly returned to, then surpassed, its previous level.[8] A similar thing happened after 1905. Despite the notorious pogroms throughout the western Russian Empire during World War I (1914–1917) and the Russian Civil War (1918–1920); successive military occupations of the city during those conflicts; and the cataclysms of collectivization, the Ukrainian famine, and Stalinism, the Jewish portion of the population continued to grow. The city was still a patchwork of ethnicities: Russians, Ukrainians, Jews, and Roma, along with smaller populations of Bulgarians, Moldovans, Greeks, and others. By 1926, the time of the last reliable Soviet census before World War II, of the 433,063 people living in the urban portions of the Odessa region, 38 percent were Russians, 36 percent were Jews, and 18 percent were Ukrainians, along with sizable populations of Germans, Poles, Armenians, Greeks, and Moldovans.[9]

The real end of Odessa's cosmopolitan culture came not from internal dissension among its many ethnic groups but rather via the determined pursuit of demographic purity by an occupying power: Romania. From 1941 to 1944 Odessa was controlled by a Romanian government allied with Nazi Germany. Romania had joined the German-led invasion of the Soviet Union in June 1941, and part of the reward for its services in that effort was Hitler's agreement to allow Bucharest to administer the territory immediately to the east of the Dnestr River—or Transnistria—including the largest city in the area, Odessa.

Romanian administrators were dispatched to the city soon after it came under full Axis control in October 1941. Shortly thereafter an attack by Soviet partisans on the Romanian military headquarters led to a huge wave of reprisals against partisans, Communists, and Jews, categories that the Romanians, like the Germans, saw as largely coterminous. The scale of the response was enormous. Hangings and shootings were carried out in the city center. Thousands of Jews were rounded up by Romanian security forces with the assistance of SS units and executed in the port, in military buildings on the outskirts of the city, and in sheds in the nearby settlement of Dalnik. The poles supporting overhead electric lines that serviced the city's trolley system were used as makeshift gallows.[10] Mass shootings and burnings were carried out in the weeks following the bombing of the military headquarters. "The chaos and the horrifying sights that followed cannot be described," a contemporary observer reported. "Wounded people burning alive, women with their hair aflame coming out through the roof or through openings in the burning storehouses in a crazed search for salvation."[11] Estimates based on witness reports, postwar trials, and limited survivor testimonies give a figure of at least 25,000 people killed in Odessa and Dalnik in the fall and early winter of 1941, that is, perhaps a third of all Jews who were living in the city when it came under Romanian control.[12] (The majority of Jews, along with other Soviet citizens, had been evacuated by Soviet authorities between June and October 1941.)

These were massacres carried out according to written orders passed down the Romanian chain of command. As such they were part of the "Holocaust by bullets," as one historian has called it: the mass murder of civilians in ditches, old buildings, and tank traps across Ukraine and other parts of the western Soviet Union.[13] The Romanians did not create extermination facilities, but they did construct an array of camps and ghettos in Transnistria to which the remainder of Odessa's Jews—and many other Jews and Roma (Gypsies) from Bessarabia and Transnistria itself—were eventually sent. Denunciations by average Odessans helped identify Jewish neighbors and ferret out those who attempted to hide their identity.[14] While Jews were more likely to survive the Holocaust in the areas controlled by Romanians than in those parts of the Soviet Union under German occupation, the remaking of Odessa's demographic landscape was gargantuan.

At the outbreak of the war there were around 200,000 Jews living in the city. By the time the Romanian forces arrived, there were perhaps 70,000 to 80,000. When the Soviet army returned in the spring of 1944, an informal census counted forty-eight Jews living there.[15] Tens of thousands returned after the war, arriving from the camps and relocation facilities in Central Asia, where many Soviet citizens had spent the war in relative safety. But the total number of Jews in Odessa never again rose above 12 percent. From the 1970s onward, as Jews were allowed to leave the Soviet Union for new lives in the United States, Israel, and elsewhere, the Jewish component of Odessa's population declined even further. Individual Jews remained, but the community as such was gone.

Istanbul from Imperial Metropolis to "Second City"

As people flooded out of the southern Russian seaports in 1905 and during World War I and the Russian Civil War, their first haven was often Istanbul. Successive waves of migrants—tsarist loyalists, failed nationalists fleeing the Bolsheviks, or failed Bolsheviks fleeing other Bolsheviks—found a congenial home south of the Black Sea. The city had long been a port of last resort for religious and other refugees seeking new lives abroad, most famously in the case of Sephardic Jews fleeing Catholic Spain in the fifteenth century. That long history repeated itself in the early twentieth century. To the long-standing communities of Greeks, Armenians, and European "colonies" of Italians, French, and Britons were added growing numbers of people escaping the century's rolling calamities. In 1920 alone, some 140,000 Russians, 70,000 Muslims, and more than 100,000 Greeks and

Armenians descended on the city fleeing violence in southern Russia, the Caucasus, and Anatolia.[16] For the first several decades of the century, in fact, the losers of Europe's successive wars, revolutions, and regime changes found a kind of temporary refuge in Istanbul.

As in Odessa, however, interactions among these various groups were not always peaceful, even if the large-scale rioting that affected Odessa in this period was unknown in Istanbul. The British commander of Allied occupation forces in Istanbul reported that he was busy arresting Bolshevik agents, attempting to deal with the parlous state of Russian refugees, evacuating British women and children in advance of an anticipated Turkish siege of the city, overseeing the removal of the sultan and his family to Malta, and taking sanitary measures against venereal disease "which is rampant in Constantinople."[17] The city, like the republic in which it was located after 1923, had as many enemies as it had guests. As one British diplomat noted succinctly on the eve of the declaration of the republic, a list of its opponents might include the following:

> All Old Turks and Sultanites.
> All the Generals who have been set aside by [Mustafa] Kemal.
> All the deputies of the old who have not been elected to the new Assembly.
> All the old C.U.P. [Committee of Union and Progress] stalwarts . . .
> All those with whom Mustafa [Kemal] has quarreled or of whom he is jealous or who are jealous of him . . .
> All those who prefer Constantinople to Angora [Ankara] as the capital.
> All Ulema, Imams, and Hojas . . .
> All civilians who get no pay, all demobilised soldiers who have no other occupation and can find none.[18]

After 1923, however, Istanbul settled into a kind of disimpassioned lull. Now a second city of a new republic rather than an imperial metropolis, its stakes were simply not what they once had been. The population was still mixed, but years of war and uncertainty had changed its structure profoundly. There had been perhaps 700,000 people in the city at the time of the last imperial census in 1906; just over twenty years later, when the new republican government organized its first official census, the figure was essentially the same, with the population probably dropping to around half a million by the end of that decade. Before World War I, Istanbul was a Muslim-majority city but just barely: 206,000 local Greeks, 84,000 local Armenians, and 130,000 expatriates (*ecnebi*) were concentrated in the hills and valleys flanking the Grande Rue de Pera.[19] After the war the city became steadily more Muslim with each passing decade, largely because of the steady flight of Christian and Jewish minorities.

The minority rights provisions of the Treaty of Lausanne (1923), while designed to protect religious groups within the republic, cast non-Muslims as potentially disloyal citizens. Likewise, the Law on the Maintenance of Order, promulgated in 1925, provided a legal justification not only for the suppression of open rebellion—most notably in the brutal defeat of Sheikh Said and his religious and protonationalist supporters among the Kurds—but also for limitations on press freedom, political organization, and cultural expression. Over the rest of the decade, one after another of the religiously defined minorities in Istanbul expressed their "voluntary" surrender of the collective rights laid out in the Lausanne accord. When local police in Istanbul suspected that the leadership of Orthodox Greeks, Gregorian and Protestant Armenians, or Ashkenazi and Sephardic Jews might not forward the required renunciation documents to the state, influential members of the minority communities were arrested. "Individuals are reported to be leaving the country as rapidly as they can amass the means," the US ambassador reported in November 1926.[20]

Many of these provisions, while directed against minority communities in Istanbul, were derivative of larger tendencies within the new Kemalist state: concern (often well-founded) about subversives, a commitment to building a strong one-party state, distrust of political or social dissent in virtually any form, and a belief in the additive power of seemingly contradictory impulses—revolution and stability, modernity and ethnic nationalism, populism and the overweening state.

But each of these elements of Kemalist governance had a particular meaning in the variegated social space of Istanbul. Despite the diminished status and population, the city was still a dynamic, even incorrigible, urban environment. Jazz bands performed at fashionable venues such as the Pera Palas Hotel and the Gardenbar. The Park and Tokatlian hotels hosted a steady stream of visitors from other parts of Europe and the Near East, who came to witness the transformation of the old Ottoman capital. Most repeated the common vision of Istanbul as a mixed and raucous city, just Oriental enough to be interesting but already Occidental enough to be visitable in comfort. From her train carriage leaving Haydarpaşa Station, Agatha Christie noted the "motley crowd of costumes, peasants thronging the platform, and the strange meals of cooked food that were handed up to the train. Food on skewers, wrapped in leaves, eggs painted various colours—all sorts of things."[21]

The desire to control the republic's second city was a constant feature of Turkish state policy from the 1920s onward, and during World War II the government stumbled into the policy that would end up having the greatest effect on the demographic complexion of Istanbul: the capital wealth tax, or *varlık vergisi*. After the outbreak of war between the Soviet Union and Germany in the summer of 1941, the need to maintain a large and ready military force, even as a neutral country, pushed the Turkish state to print more money; that approach in turn led to runaway inflation and the flight of wealth toward nonpaper havens such as gold and real estate. Seeking to squeeze resources from the citizens and corporations that controlled these appreciating assets, Ankara pushed through a major reform of the tax code in November 1942. Special commissions were appointed to levy new tax assessments; their deliberations were held in private, and their decisions were final. The new law came into effect a few weeks before Kurban Bayramı, the Muslim feast of sacrifice, and a dark joke circulated in Istanbul that this year the sacrifice seemed to be not a sheep but the city's Christians and Jews. "Many observers, including myself, concluded that the tax was intended to drive the non-Moslem element out of business," wrote Walter L. Wright Jr., the president of Robert College at the time, "and thus to 'solve' once and for all the problem of minority control of much of the country's commercial life."[22] Not since the early 1920s had the city seen a greater out-migration of Greeks and Armenians; faced with exorbitant tax bills, they were forced to liquidate their property or chose to move abroad rather than face incarceration in a debtor's prison.

The wartime experience of the *varlık vergisi* provided the basic context for narratives about Istanbul's minorities that would last well beyond the exigencies of the wartime economy. It cast Greeks, Armenians, and Jews as parasitical on the Turkish economy. It reinforced the view that these communities—of special concern to international actors from the Lausanne treaty onward—were of dubious loyalty to the Turkish state. It provided a template for punitive official action that could in turn be cast as promoting fairness and civic equality. And it justified what amounted to the seizure of private assets by neighbors and the municipal administration. After all, if a Greek or Armenian family decided to vacate their property and move abroad, how else were the assets to be treated than as abandoned property, available for the taking? Each of these policies was set in motion by the discrete actions of the Turkish state. When the remaining minority communities were attacked again after the war—most notoriously in the pogrom against Istanbul's Greeks on September 6–7, 1955—the targeting was possible precisely because minority communities had already been singled out as disloyal, dangerous, and illegitimate by a string of state policies. Popular mobilization was enhanced by a long-standing practice of the state's moving against its own minorities.

Of course, despite the coerced emigration of Greeks and other Christian communities, there was no experience in the city's history that came close to replicating the elimination of Odessa's Jews during World War II. But the two cities did have at least one feature in common: the key role of the state in changing what had been a workable, if not always peaceful, form of multiculturalism. Tax policy is obviously not the same thing as mass killing, just as antiminority riots are not the same thing as a state policy of forcefully eliminating an entire category of people. But the experience of both cities over the first half of the twentieth century is an important illustration of the way in which very different kinds of states can share a basic predisposition: a persistent worry that cosmopolitan cities, if not constrained and reformed, will inevitably spiral out of their control.

States and the Unbuilding of Cosmopolitanism

One of the most robust findings about social and political violence is its relationship to the policies and priorities of the state. While purveyors of violence might mask it as a natural outgrowth of ancient grievances, large-scale social violence—from riots to pogroms to genocide—rarely takes place without the encouragement and intervention of state institutions.[23] Does the same point hold with respect to the fate of cosmopolitan cities?

The respective experiences of Istanbul and Odessa seem to suggest that multicultural spaces have a substantial resilience on their own. They are rarely peaceful—few cities are, in fact—and tensions among religious, cultural, ethnic, and linguistic communities seem to be a constant feature of urban life. But there is a vast difference between the everyday, informal violence that attends urbanity and the systematic unmaking of cosmopolitan urban spaces. The latter only seems to be possible via the state. In Odessa a half century of repeated urban violence, mainly directed against the growing Jewish population in the city, did little to dampen the willingness of Jews to live there or to move there from the countryside or from other towns and cities. Each episode of anti-Jewish violence was followed by a short period of emigration and then by much longer periods of demographic growth. Istanbul, a city with its own long history of tensions among constituent religious communities, managed to remain a largely welcoming venue for multiple religious, ethnic, and linguistic groups, as well as to host successive waves of political refugees. It was not until states enacted systematic policies of transforming the urban environment—the occupation of Odessa by Romania in the 1940s and minority-restricting economic policies of the Turkish Republic in the same period—that the reality of cosmopolitanism was exchanged for concerns with purity.

Cosmopolitanism does not seem to need much encouragement. But it takes considerable work to unbuild it, which is where the formal institutions and ideologies of states often come in. Occupying powers create contexts in which actively denouncing one's neighbors is preferable to ignoring them. Soldiers and tax collectors create incentives for people to move. State-controlled educational systems make cultural purity the norm. The trick lies not in getting human communities to value cosmopolitanism. Left to their own devices, they seem to be more likely to learn to live with cultural difference than to expend valuable time, energy, and treasure seeking to eradicate it. Rather, the real difficulty lies in preventing states from caring too much about eradicating difference, that is, in blocking state institutions from seeing cosmopolitan values as inimical to state power, minority communities as secret threats or fifth columns for some foreign power, and the multifarious amalgam of language and custom in cities as somehow a natural impediment to progress and peace.

The experiences of Istanbul and Odessa seem to point toward both the power of cosmopolitanism as well as its natural limits. Over the centuries visitors to both cities have extolled its colorful streets; the mash-up of customs and costumes has been a cliché of travel writing about both locales from Herodotus onward. But the really durable kind of cosmopolitanism is not the variety in which one's barber is Greek, tailor Jewish, and bookseller Armenian—the "fantastic human ant-hill" version of a city, as Gustave Flaubert once described Ottoman Istanbul.[24] That variety has always been a thin bulwark against the determined interventions of the state. Instead, cosmopolitanism in its toughest form is not so much a virtue but a project: a continual effort to privilege the suffering of others, to affirm the practice of embracing one's own cultural discomfort, and to build a set of social networks and institutions that make the fate of other communities an inextricable part of one's own destiny. "Everything white in Constantinople is dirty white," Ernest Hemingway wrote during a visit to the city in October 1922.[25] And that, of course, is the point. Being messy is probably the natural state of cosmopolitan centers around the world. The tough thing is to preserve the mess against the cleaner ideologies and meaner intentions of the state.

NOTES

1. Kwame Anthony Appiah, *Cosmopolitanism: Ethics in a World of Strangers, Issues of Our Time* (New York: W. W. Norton, 2010).
2. Blair A. Ruble, *Second Metropolis: Pragmatic Pluralism in Gilded Age Chicago, Silver Age Moscow, and Meiji Osaka* (Cambridge, UK: Cambridge University Press, 2001).
3. James D. Fearon and David D. Laitin, "Explaining Interethnic Cooperation," *American Political Science Review* 90, no. 4 (1996): 715–735.
4. V. Kokhanskii, *Odessa za 100 Let* (Odessa: Tipografiia P. Frantsova, 1894).
5. Jacob P. Adler and Lulla Rosenfeld, *Jacob Adler: A Life on the Stage; a Memoir* (Winona, MN: Hal Leonard Corporation, 2001), 9.
6. Viktor Savchenko, *Anarkhisty-Terroristy v Odesse (1903–1913)* (Odessa: Optimum, 2006), 19.
7. Aleksei Girs and Liubov' Girs, Papers, October 19, 1905, Bakhmeteff Archive (Columbia University Rare Book and Manuscript Library).
8. Patricia Herlihy, *Odessa* (Cambridge, MA: Harvard University Press, 1986).
9. *Vsesoiuznaia Perepis' Naseleniia 1926 g.: Kratkie Svodki* (Moscow: TsS USSR, 1927), 115.
10. Alexander Dallin, *Odessa: 1941–1944. A Case of Study of Soviet Territory under Foreign Rule* (Santa Monica, CA: Rand Corporation, 1957), 74.
11. Quoted in *Report of the International Commission on the Holocaust in Romania* (2004), chap. 5, 54, http://www.yadvashem.org/events/11-november-2004.
12. See United States Holocaust Memorial Museum Archives, RG-25.004M, Reel 150; Litani, "The Destruction," 139; and Radu Ioanid, *The Holocaust in Romania: The Fate of Jews and Gypsies in Fascist Romania, 1940–1944* (Lanham, MD: Ivan R. Dee, 2000).
13. Patrick Desbois, *The Holocaust by Bullets: A Priest's Journey to Uncover the Truth Behind the Murder of 1.5 Million Jews* (London: Macmillan, 2008).
14. Charles King, *Odessa: Genius and Death in a City of Dreams* (New York: W. W. Norton, 2011), ch. 10.
15. Blinov to Polianskii, July 19, 1945, Yad Vashem Archives, Jerusalem, M-46/11.
16. British Forces in Turkey, Commander-in-Chief's Despatch, Period 1920–1923, National Archives of the United Kingdom (NAUK), CAB 44/38, f. 7.
17. Ibid., f. 8.
18. Henderson to Vansittart, October 31, 1923, National Archives of the United Kingdom (NAUK), FO 794/10, ff. 5–6.
19. Zafer Toprak, "La Population d'Istanbul dans les Premières Années de la Republique," *Travaux et Recherches en Turquie* 1 (1982): 63–70.
20. Bristol to Secretary of State, November 3, 1926, US National Archives and Records Administration (NARA), RG59, M353, reel 21.
21. Agatha Christie, *An Autobiography* (New York: Dodd, Mead, 1977), 354.

22. Walter L. Wright Jr., Memorandum on the Varlik Vergisi or Capital Wealth Tax, US National Archives and Records Administration (NARA), RG59, M1242, reel 31.

23. See, for example, Manus I. Midlarsky, *The Killing Trap: Genocide in the Twentieth Century* Cambridge, UK: Cambridge University Press, 2005); Christian Gerlach, *Extremely Violent Societies: Mass Violence in the Twentieth-Century World* (Cambridge, UK: Cambridge University Press, 2010); Timothy Snyder, *Bloodlands: Europe between Hitler and Stalin* (New York: Basic Books, 2012); Scott Straus, *The Order of Genocide: Race, Power, and War in Rwanda,* vol. 1 (Ithaca, NY: Cornell University Press, 2006); Ronald Grigor Suny, Fatma Müge Göçek, and Norman M. Naimark, eds., *A Question of Genocide: Armenians and Turks at the End of the Ottoman Empire* (Oxford: Oxford University Press, 2011); and Benjamin A. Valentino, *Final Solutions: Mass Killing and Genocide in the 20th Century* (Ithaca, NY: Cornell University Press, 2013).

24. Quoted in Kim Fortuny, *American Writers in Istanbul: Melville, Twain, Hemingway, Dos Passos, Bowles, Algren, Baldwin, and Settle* (Syracuse, NY: Syracuse University Press, 2009), 26.

25. Ernest Hemingway, "Constantinople, Dirty White, Not Glistening and Sinister," *Toronto Daily Star*, October 18, 1922, reprinted in Ernest Hemingway, *Dateline: Toronto; The Complete Toronto Star Dispatches, 1920–1924*, ed. William White (New York: Charles Scribner's Sons, 1985).

PART II

Paradise Lost

CONTESTED MEMORIES OF COSMOPOLIS

CHAPTER 5

Cosmopolitanist Nostalgia

GEOGRAPHIES, HISTORIES, AND MEMORIES OF THE RUM POLITES

İlay Romain Örs

Is Istanbul a cosmopolitan city, and if so, how so? Who is involved in such an identification, and what is their motive? To which period and where in Istanbul are they referring? Most importantly, what is meant by "cosmopolitanism"?

These questions form the departure point of this chapter. To address them, I begin by suggesting that Istanbul is a site for exploring the notion of an "essentially cosmopolitan" city, one in which practices of coexistence take place in an urban society that is conscious of cosmopolitanism as an idealized image of its own past. I first map how current and former residents reify their city as timelessly cosmopolitan, not only as a relic of its past but as a promise for its future. I then offer a critique of nostalgic discourses for their essentializing tendencies, which overlook the cultural and historical contexts within which cosmopolitanism prevails. This is done by way of an ethnographic intervention that contextualizes various cosmopolitanisms in Istanbul by providing spatial and temporal referents. My argument is that different modes of Istanbulite cosmopolitanism become visible through the eyes of different communities, who give meaning to their own cosmopolitan experiences within their time-space specific context. To illustrate, I bring attention to the case of Rum Polites, whose members have been both the leaders—and victims—of changing modes of urban cosmopolitanism throughout their long sojourn in the city.[1] The Rum Polites' narratives of Istanbul fix the otherwise nonreferential notion of cosmopolitanism by addressing questions of who, when, where, and how. This enables, in turn, critical reflection on the sites and modes of cosmopolitanism in Istanbul.

Cosmopolitanist Istanbul: A Relic to Be Revitalized?

Istanbul today is gripped by what could be called "cosmopolitanist nostalgia." This sentiment encompasses a wide array of past-oriented discourses preoccupied with describing Istanbul as a cosmopolitan city. Novels, articles, movies, television series, and exhibits seeking to demonstrate the cosmopolitan character of old Istanbul follow in swift succession. These paint a nostalgically constructed picture of the city from the gaze of locals and travelers, making the "multicultural" a dominant theme in post-1980 Turkish literature and public intellectual discourses.[2] Contributing to such narratives are local event organizers and policy makers who seek to establish Istanbul as a hub for tourism, conferences, and other international organizations on the premise that it has long been a cosmopolitan metropolis.[3]

The nostalgists of old Istanbul concur that this was a world city of amazing multicultural delights and tend to note regretfully its presumed loss. To paraphrase Robert Fine, who states that "we do not live in a cosmopolitan age, but we live in an age of cosmopolitanism," Istanbul's present may not be cosmopolitan, but due to abundant nostalgic narratives about its past and visions for the future, the city can be said to live in an age of cosmopolitanism.[4]

Following are the main themes of this cosmopolitanist nostalgia. For the last two millennia, Constantinople, then Istanbul, has been the largest and most important city in its geographical region as the capital of multicultural empires and a vibrant religious, political, economic, and cultural center. It has been home and refuge to a variety of peoples, who have coexisted in a rather peaceful fashion thanks to the cosmopolitan urban culture to which they belonged. Squeezed between its historical legacy and future calling, present-day Istanbul can hardly be characterized as properly cosmopolitan, which is highly regretted by the proponents of cosmopolitanist nostalgia. According to these discourses, cosmopolitanism in Istanbul today is a memory and a potential that has yet to be revitalized.

The much-valued presence of native non-Turkish and non-Muslim groups, known in Republican Turkey as minorities (e.g., Jews, Armenians, and Rum Polites), is an inherent dimension in cosmopolitanist nostalgic discourses. Contemporary author Leyla Erbil, for example, describes her experience of hearing Greek spoken in a patisserie-café as like hearing a "sweet background poem," which made Istanbul "a poetic city laced with the mixture of our voices with theirs."[5] Her words summarize a widely held stance, namely, the tendency of authors to portray the Rum Polites as the major figures in the cosmopolitan fabric of urban life. Often reduced to the sweet notes of a background symphony, minorities remain overrepresented yet understudied.

Narratives of this cosmopolitanist nonreferential nostalgia leave many questions about the very nature of cosmopolitanism unanswered. If, for example, Istanbul was quintessentially cosmopolitan, how did it give rise to its own dissolution, to the tragic destruction of the very cosmopolitan order it endorsed? How within such a cosmopolitanist landscape could a pogrom like that of September 6–7, 1955, take place, when a mob destroyed thousands of minority properties?[6] How could large amounts of wealth be seized from minorities by the force of law?[7] How could a campaign that promotes the sole use of the Turkish language in public prevail for years in the multilingual environment of cosmopolitan Istanbul?[8]

In cosmopolitanist nostalgia such questions remain largely uninvestigated, absent, or lost—like the cosmopolitans themselves. Cosmopolitanist nostalgia is apersonal because, in spite of the popularity of the nostalgic discourses—or perhaps because of them—there is little effort made to understand the subjectivities involved in the loss of pluralism. Minorities remain "both ubiquitous and unacknowledged, both remembered nostalgically and rejected ideologically."[9] The city is pictured, as Roland Barthes would have it, as "a place of our meeting with the other," yet the faces or stories of these others are rarely heard.[10] It is as if one morning people woke up to find that minorities' shops and patisseries were closed down. They had left all of a sudden, without telling anyone, and nobody knew where they had gone. The old Istanbul was a fairy tale, and the princess had disappeared.

This popular idea of "minorities as the disappearing colors" is met with ironical critique by non-Muslim intellectuals in Turkey today: Roni Margulies thanks the elites for their benevolence; Rıfat Bali criticizes narratives that talk about a sudden loss of Istanbul's cosmopolitan fabric just evaporated; and Mario Levi finds that the minorities are "not more than symbols" in a sentimental picture.[11]

Cosmopolitanist Interests: A Discourse of Nonalignment?

Who then are the nostalgists? Arguably, the primary proponents of cosmopolitanist nostalgia are members of the new urban elite since the 1990s. This group is composed of well-educated, secular, left-leaning, and Europeanist democrats, who can master several languages. This elite fosters a city identity or an Istanbulite consciousness that is based on the belief that old, cosmopolitan Istanbul was a much more civilized place. This turn to an urban cosmopolitan sensibility can be read, as noted, against the city's social-political landscape: massive migration from rural Anatolia, which has transformed the urban scene since the 1960s. In this same period, political Islam has gained greater social visibility and has dominated the municipal and central power centers.[12] The urban elite, feeling that their value systems and lifestyles are threatened, have turned to the past for assurance that a different future is possible.

For this group, the future is in a multicultural European community. By packaging Istanbul as a cosmopolitan center, secular urban cohorts mark their ability to embrace diversity at home, conforming to EU standards by displaying tolerance as a sign of European civility. Such attempts at political marketing experienced their heyday in the early 2000s, especially when Istanbul was being designated as 2010 European Capital of Culture. As Cengiz Aktar put it on that occasion: "Ever since its foundation, Cosmopolist Istanbul has been a city that bore different cultures, religions, and languages, which has always been able to synthesize them."[13]

Idealized cosmopolitanism is not, however, the monopoly of European-oriented liberals. As Nora Fisher-Onar points out, conservative and religious segments of urban society also partake in this endeavor, albeit with other visions about the future and the past. A nostalgic yearning for the Ottoman Empire in which a Turkish Muslim dynasty ruled over a multicultural population (at times referred to as "neo-Ottomanism") is evident in various realms of cultural and policy production. The popularity of television series depicting the golden era of the Ottoman past (such as *Süleyman the Magnificent*) attests to this point, alongside the increase in (re)invented traditions such as Conquest Festivals and Prophet Mohammed's Birthday celebrations.[14] This glorification of the Ottoman past, a trend that was absent in the first decades of the republic, comes with an elevated discourse of "tolerance" wherein the sultans generously allowed their different subjects to coexist. In the words of Sossie Kasbarian, this "nostalgia tends to gloss over the structural and everyday discrimination minorities experienced under the Ottoman regime, and it infantilizes and fossilizes the remaining communities as a historical relic."[15] In this mode of imperial cosmopolitanism the minorities are once again not more than ornate symbols of an idealized past; the severe conditions of non-Muslims in the empire, who endured arbitrary rule and often met with discrimination, are omitted from the rosy picture.

These differing yet similar cosmopolitan imaginaries are utilized both by NGOs and national and local authorities. The results of this cross-ideological convergence (liberal and conservative) are observable in the streets of Istanbul. Popular discourses have rendered fashionable those sites of multicultural coresidence that have long been deserted by their previous Rum, Armenian, or Jewish occupants and have been left to decay after being repopulated by poorer rural immigrants.[16] Upon their rediscovery by the urban elite, neighborhoods like Galata, Fener, Ortaköy, or Cihangir began to be restored with EU or UNESCO funding and reclaimed as representations of a lost but retrievable cosmopolitan urban past. Yet during this process little if any discussion took place regarding the disregarded legal and economic rights of the minorities in these districts. Without a critical approach to antiminority policies, attempts to reinstate the cosmopolitan fabric remain limited to cosmetic modifications: during the window-dressing of houses that used to be owned by minorities, questions of how these houses changed hands, when property rights were transferred overnight by the imposition of unconstitutional laws, remain unresolved. The construction of the cosmopolitan image of the city, based on a polished reimagination of historic cosmopolitanism, is advanced to capitalize on multiculturalism as a form of commercial and political marketing. Debates on preserving the physical

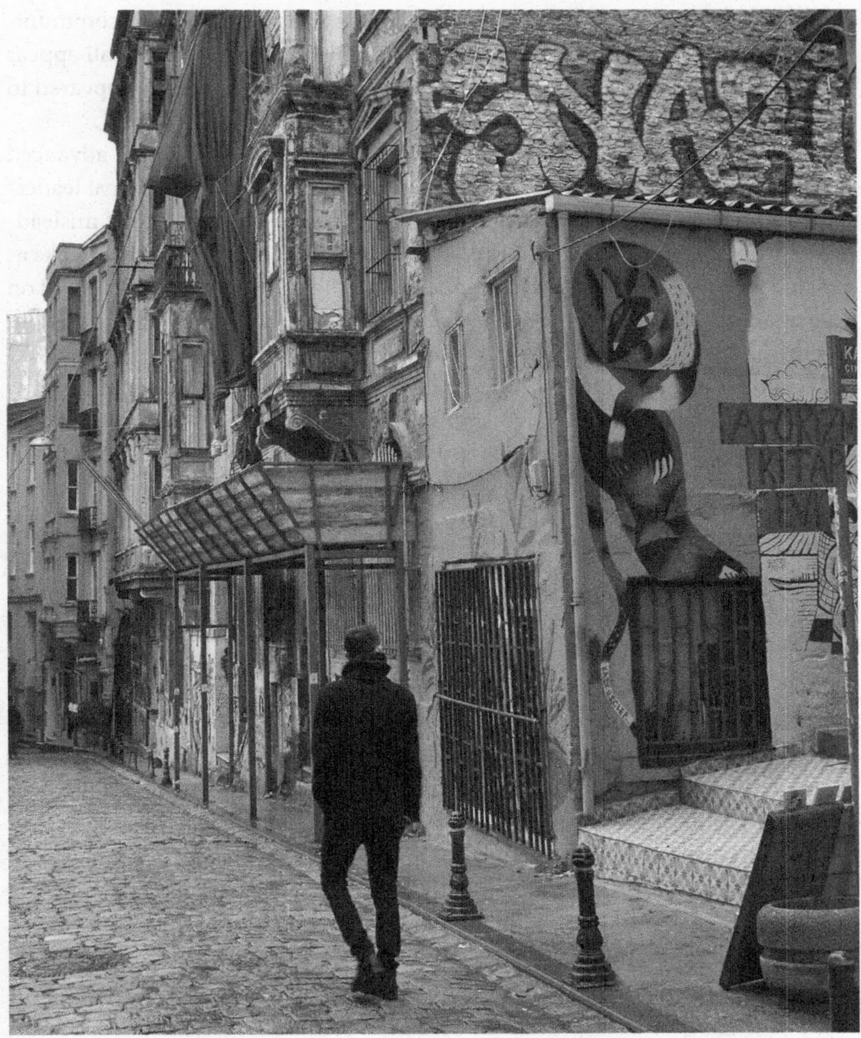

Figure 5.1. On a crumbling and reappropriated *Belle Époque* façade, a sign for the Aphorism Bookstore. Photo credit: Seray Pulluk.

surroundings or architectural landmarks in the city constitute visible manifestations of cosmopolitanist nostalgia and competing ideological narratives.

Recent developments in Turkish politics add yet another twist. As the reigning Justice and Development Party (AKP) encounters serious criticism in both its foreign policy and domestic politics, the party has decreased efforts—notable when it first came to power—to dress its practices in multiculturalist fashion. Failures in its foreign policy toward the Middle East, coupled with a near halt in the EU accession process, as well as inadequate efforts to improve minority policies (especially the failed outreach to the Kurdish and Armenian communities) amid rising xenophobic hostility and armed violence in society, all appear to reveal that the cosmopolitanist discourses that the party initially appeared to embrace were merely instrumental.

This claim that only self-serving versions of cosmopolitanism are advanced applies especially in the urban sphere, where the national and municipal leadership is under scrutiny for promoting projects based on a selective, if not misleading, representation of the past. The plan to rebuild Ottoman military barracks as a façade for a five-star hotel and shopping mall in Taksim Gezi Park was based on a certain imagination of Istanbul's imperial past and its commercial future, but this clashed with multiple rival views of pluralism among social actors demonstrating their right to the city.[17] The Gezi events became the pivotal point in the resistance of Istanbulites against ongoing rent-oriented development policies and antagonistic megaprojects of urban gentrification under cover of Istanbul's glorious past.[18] Yet the process of resistance is far from being successfully concluded, as a particularly vulgar program continues to be implemented under the rubric of *kentsel dönüşüm* (urban transformation), whereby no culturally, historically, or naturally significant site is spared from massive housing, transportation, or industrial projects. Public reactions to such destruction, as in the neighborhoods of Tarlabaşı, Sulukule, and Yedikule, has led to organizations of civil initiatives such as *Kuzey Ormanları Direnişi*, centered on promoting an appreciation and preservation of the cosmopolitan heritage and identity of Istanbul.[19]

While the public nostalgic discourses in Istanbul rarely specify what they romanticize, it is important, as Svetlana Boym maintains, to remember that there are two types of nostalgia: one that works as "restorative" by indicating a wish to return to the past, and one that is more "reflective" in that its proponents are more critically aware of their present circumstances.[20] Cosmopolitanist nostalgia in Istanbul arguably combines both of these aspects. As one of the oldest sites of continuous urban settlement, Istanbul has room to claim its importance as a site for exploring changing meanings of cosmopolitanism throughout the ages.[21] In that sense, as Keyder's, Zubaida's, and Baban's contributions to this volume affirm (see chapters 1–3), Istanbul's historical experience offers a window, for example, onto cultural diversity in great imperial and trading cities.[22] The histories and memories of native communities can help us develop a more nuanced understanding of the relationship between "cosmopolitanism" and "multiculturalism." Their stories focus our attention on these concepts not only as recent postnational projects but also as older cultural forms that preceded and resisted the nation-state, and which eroded in the postimperial unmixing of peoples.[23]

Yet, much cosmopolitanist nostalgia entails an essentialized and ambiguous ideal of cosmopolitanism with little specification of context, meaning, or agency, leaving the concept vulnerable to manipulation for political and material interests. Cosmopolitanist nostalgia—which has the potential to serve as both historical corrective and analytical tool—needs therefore be substantiated through an ethnographic intervention by cosmopolitans themselves; for example, by a historic community that once made up the longed-for and lost multicultural mix, the Rum Polites.

Cosmopolitanism Contextualized: An Ethnographic Intervention

The Constantinopolitan Greeks, the Rum Orthodox of Istanbul, or, using the term I prefer, the Rum Polites, are a mainly a Greek-speaking and Greek Christian Orthodox community by religion—a faith that links their heritage to the city's early rulers. Likewise, denoting the connection to Eastern Roman/Byzantine origins is *Rum*, which comes from *Romeos/Roman* and was used by the Ottoman administration for the religiously defined *millet-i Rum*. This identification of the Rum was inherited by the Turkish Republic to refer to a variety of the Christian Orthodox in the country, most of whom were expelled as part of the compulsory population exchange (*mübadele*) between Greece and Turkey in 1923. Among the few were exempt from the provisions of this convention, which was part of the Treaty of Lausanne. Among these were the *établis* Rum Polites, that is, members of the Greek Christian Orthodox community who had been allowed to settle within the city limits of Istanbul before 1918. Their number at that time is estimated to have been more than 100,000, in excess of 10 percent of the urban population. The rest of the century brought many other instances of displacement that affected the Rum Polites directly, such that their number shrank to a few thousands and they were brought to near invisibility in a city of about 20 million.

Today the Rum Polites are a transnational community living mostly between Greece—to which many have migrated—and Istanbul, their original homeland. Yet they are best defined as supranational, as their belonging to "the City" positions them beyond the two nation-states.[24] The Rum Polites' negative experience with nationalism nonetheless serves as a strong reminder of how cosmopolitan cities challenge the nation. Unable to comply with the standardized (Sunni/secular, Turkish-speaking) national ideal of the post-1923 Turkish Republic, the Rum Polites' experience in the twentieth century was of suffering from and witness to the extirpation of Istanbul's cosmopolitan order by agents of nationalism through a series of traumatic events.[25]

Upon their displacement, the Rum Polites found themselves scattered around the world, yet concentrated to a large extent in Athens, where they arguably perpetuate a "Diaspora of the City."[26] This is enabled through various means, but here I focus on how a diasporic memory of Istanbul is maintained through the written word. Being well known for their cultural productivity, the Rum Polites produce a body of literature relating to the past life of the Greek Orthodox in Istanbul that is kept vivid in personal and collective memory. With the nostalgic reminiscences it reveals, I present the Rum Polites literature as a source of nostalgia to be juxtaposed with other nostalgic discourses about Istanbul today. But I also offer it as a window onto the many contextualized modes of urban experience in different times and places that made up the "actually existing" cosmopolitanism of Istanbul. In the following I highlight three particular contexts of Istanbulite cosmopolitanism: those of Pera, Fener, and Tatavla.

Pera-style Cosmopolitanism

Pera is the Istanbul district that lies across the Golden Horn waterway, opposite the old city surrounded by Byzantine walls. Pera encompasses the quarters of Beyoğlu, Galata, Karaköy, Taksim, and beyond, but its center was the *Grand Rue de Pera, Stavrodromio/Isio dromo*, or today's İstiklal Avenue. This avenue serves as the foremost setting for cosmopolitanist nostalgia, not least in the Rum Polites literature. Pera had long been a center of maritime commerce, a function that impels toward cosmopolitanism as Keyder (see chapter 1 in this volume) and others have noted. Settlement in Pera dates to Byzantine times, when Genoans and Venetians established trade colonies opposite Constantinople. For the Rum, the earliest possible date of settlement in Pera is 1535, at the time of the opening of the French embassy, which invited some Rum Catholics to move across the Golden Horn. When other European countries began building their embassies in Pera around the eighteenth century, Rum families who had business relations with these countries followed. The year 1804 marked the construction of the first Greek Orthodox church, *Panagia*, in Pera, on the remains of an old Byzantine church. This accelerated the increase in Rum population, making the Rum the largest of the Pera resident communities. The height of Pera cosmopolitanism occurred after a trade treaty was signed with the British in 1838 and the subsequent periods of Reconstruction (*Tanzimat*) and Reformation (*Islahat*). During this age, economic advancement was coupled with political liberation—including citizenship status and the abrogation of the *millet* system—allowing them to participate actively in modern urban life.

Petros Markaris, a well-known Rum Polites author, writes that "a pedestrian walking around in Pera would find himself in an unequalled linguistic parade: Turkish, Greek, Armenian, Spanish from the Seferad, as well as Italian, French, and other Frank-Levantine languages."[27] Notably, Arabic, Persian, and Kurdish are not mentioned. There is thus a Western or Christian bias to Pera cosmopolitanism. As the journalist Petros Paleologos puts it, Pera was the extension of Turkey into Europe thanks to its "Christian, Rum and European" composition, reminiscent of the *Belle Époque* period of Paris.[28]

Researcher Soula Bozi similarly argues that Ottoman modernizers aimed to reshape Istanbul in the manner of other European capitals, such as Vienna, Paris, and Rome. Toward this end, Pera served as the window of Ottoman modernity.[29] Novelist Aglaia Konstantinou-Kloukina maintains that Pera was a cultural center that was "more European than Europe," undergoing constant modernization thanks to its patisseries, chocolatiers, florists, concert halls, theaters, pharmacies, and hotels, which mostly belonged to the Rum.[30] In this modernization narrative, the protagonists were the Rum Polites, whom Bozi also calls "metropolitans." An economic elite, the Rum Polites resided in private mansions for eight months, while spending the summer at houses in the Princes' Islands or along the shores of the Bosphorus to escape the city heat. Described as a "cosmic high-society," Pera cosmopolitans are the closest that Ottoman society came to having a bourgeoisie. And through their entertainments, they left their impression on the urban space in structures that reflected their abundant wealth and lifestyles.[31]

These representations are countless in Rum Polites literature. Pera-style cosmopolitanism is associated with a Europeanized version of modernity and a corresponding lifestyle and consumption culture enjoyed by a relatively well-educated bourgeois middle class. As Zubaida (see chapter 2 in this volume) notes, such sensibilities shaped a common public space and urban cultural life.

This memory of Pera-style cosmopolitanism raises questions. First, how mixed was the Pera population? There is clearly a middle-class bias to the memory, and some Rum scholars acknowledge that not every Rum living in Pera belonged to the urban elite. Poor migrants from islands such as Imbros (Bozcaada) and Chios were concentrated around the Pera neighborhoods of Tarlabaşı and Kasımpaşa during the nineteenth century. Yet such groups are not imagined among the cosmopolitans of Pera. The extent to which individuals and groups of diverse ethnic or religious backgrounds actually commingled likewise remains an open question.

As Baban (see chapter 3 in this volume) notes, cosmopolitanism is also a question of how far and deep relations went between people who shared the same public space and belonged more or less to the same social status groups. Could people of different religions marry one another, go to the same schools, form partnerships, share houses, or visit each other's homes? If intercultural closeness decreases in the transition from public to private, the institutional arrangements of multicultural communities in Pera suggest that public coexistence of separate communities did not necessarily translate into an integrated, multicultural urban society. Pera—a Greek word that means "other side"—was after all also home to other non-Muslim communities and foreigners, whose integration into the world of the Pera cosmopolitanism is an open question. Pera was organized, moreover, around separate places of worship, schools, cultural centers, publishing houses, newspapers, and even post offices for each resident cultural group. In short, Pera-style cosmopolitanism—and nostalgia for the era—is notable for its assertion of both vibrant plurality and subtexts of differentiation.

Fener-style Cosmopolitanism

Before posing for the popular sepia images of cosmopolitan Pera, the Rum of Istanbul had considered the center of prestige to be the district of Fener on the

Golden Horn. The status attached to Fener was elevated after the Ecumenical Patriarchate moved there in 1601 and reached its peak later in the seventeenth century during the time of the Fanariots.[32] These were wealthy merchant families originating from Aegean islands and Anatolian towns, who constituted a distinguished class thanks to their high position in both the Patriarchate and the Ottoman administration. The Fanariots held the exclusive title of governors (*voyvoda*) of Wallachia and Moldavia and Grand Dragomans, and often served also as the head of the Ottoman navy (*kaptan paşa*) and ministers of foreign affairs (*reis efendi*), among others. They were quite close to the sultans as their doctors, official translators, or trusted advisers. A member of one of the eminent Fanariot families wrote in his memoirs that they were "almost of equal level with the Grand Visier" and were allowed to grow a beard, wear high headgear, and enter the palace mounted on a horse.[33] Such titles could be passed on within the family, which is one of the reasons that Fanariots, who even had their own family crests, are regarded as the closest thing to an aristocracy within the Ottoman Empire. This distinct status of the Fanariots was shaken after the 1821 Greek revolt/revolution, with the hanging of the patriarch for not being able to control his community and the execution of many prominent Fanariots for having relations with the rebels.[34] Those who were able to escape death had to flee into exile, and this wealthy, religious, and sophisticated aristocracy, as described in the memoirs of Zarifis, a member of one of the most eminent Fanariot families, "almost disappeared from the face of the Earth."[35] Still, the Fanariot reign was not entirely over, as new families who replaced them continued to hold important posts, such as Ottoman ambassadors to London or Athens, until the late nineteenth century.

The Rum of Fener are represented as a noble, religious, traditional, and well-educated segment of the Istanbul population. Of great importance is the prestige of *Megali tou Genous Scholi* or the Fener Rum School, also known as the Red School, which was especially famous for its curriculum in history, philology, and philosophy. According to Haris Spataris, the magnificent building that housed the school appeared fascinating from all over the Golden Horn; the grandeur of the neighborhood was enhanced by the "dignified teachers," who were "scientists of the age," passing through the streets of Fener with their "dark-colored suits, woolen coats, briefcases, and high hats."[36] Founded in 1454 upon a royal decree (*ferman*) by Mehmet II the Conquerer (*Fatih*), *Megali tou Genous* (Fener Rum School) is said to have been linked to the Byzantine Ecumenical School, which had existed since the time of Constantine the Great, providing continuity with the Byzantine Empire.

One noteworthy aspect of Fener-style cosmopolitanism was the homogeneity of its population. In contrast to the multicultural society of Pera, almost the entire population of Fener was Rum Orthodox, to the extent that it "gave the impression of a living Byzantian corner inside the Turkish-held City."[37] In his memoirs, Rum author Nikos Apostolidis remembered when a Muslim from

Thrace wanted to move to Fener to be close to people who spoke his mother tongue. It took him a long time to find a house, which was then stigmatized as "the Turk's house." Another former Fener resident recounted that the only non-Rum business was the Jew Fiko's barber shop. The lack of a Jewish presence in this literature is noteworthy, given the Fener district's proximity to the Jewish-dominated neighborhood of Balat.[38] Spataris attests to this point by mentioning that the Fener Square was filled by Rum Polites; "there were no Istanbulite Turks, Jews, or Armenians."[39]

The Rum Polites' Fener-style cosmopolitanism, then, was very different from that of Pera. It invokes another elite group situating itself as superior to the rest of the population by virtue of its location at the center of the religious and political establishment, preserving and participating in the pluralist Ottoman system. The dissolution of Fener's elites or conservative cosmopolitanism parallels the demise of the very imperial status quo upon which it relied. While it was difficult for Fanariots to maintain their hybrid Ottoman-Rum identity with the onset of Greek nationalism in the first decades of the nineteenth century, the spread of nationalist separatism across the Balkans and Russia weakened the financial and demographic strength of the Ecumenical Christian Orthodox Patriarchate, with implications for the city of Istanbul. As a result, the grand era of Fener Rum cosmopolitanism ended by the mid-nineteenth century when Fanariot families moved abroad or elsewhere in Istanbul.

Tatavla-style Cosmopolitanism

Tatavla is a district where settlement started with the migration of laborers from the Aegean island of Chios/Sakız to work at the city's docks and harbors in the sixteenth century, many of whom were either slaves or prisoners of war from Crete, Mani, the Ionian islands, and the Peloponnese. Becoming a hub for the urban poor, Tatavla evolved to host the second biggest concentration of the Rum population after Pera. Before the 1740s, Tatavla was one of the poorest areas in the city.[40] A *ferman* from 1793 banned the non-Rum from residing in Tatavla. This gave the district an autonomous structure as a lively Greek cultural community (*politia*), institutionalized through its many churches, schools, sports clubs, theaters, places of entertainment, firemen (*tulumbacılar*), gangs and criminals (*külhanbeyi*), and renowned carnival (*Baklahorani*).

Tatavla became the second most affluent and populous center of the Rum Polites by the mid-nineteenth century. According to Thrasivoulos Papastratis, in its good times the population reached 20,000 souls. "Reading Kastanaki's *Pagida*, you may feel the spirit of Tatavla's golden age, when the heroic youth was fighting for the freedom of the City."[41] Greek was the only language heard in the neighborhood. The occasional Turkish salesmen who roamed the streets had to advertise their products in Greek, as Nikos Valasiadis wrote in his memoirs, because the housewives insisted on not shifting to Turkish when buying their groceries in Tatavla. "They were good and kind, but they had to speak Greek if they wanted to sell anything here."[42]

Tatavlan cosmopolitanism was very different from the Pera and Fener variants. There was neither much cultural mix nor any extravagant European, bourgeois lifestyle as in Pera. Nor was there religious, economic, or political prestige comparable to Fener's. Tatavla cosmopolitanism was a function of its relationship to the city overall; by having a purely Rum Orthodox neighborhood, Istanbul was coded as a multicultural space.

The concentration of Rum Polites in one district made Tatavla an easy target for Turkification policies as the nation-building project took hold in Istanbul. Street names were replaced in 1927 with exceedingly Turkish names (Bozkurt, Ergenekon). Tatavla itself was renamed Kurtuluş (Salvation) following a major fire in 1929, which destroyed the Rum Polites fabric of Tatavla, both symbolically and physically.

Comparing Rum Polites Cosmopolitanisms

I have examined the memories of the Rum Polites in order to access the different meanings of cosmopolitanism in the context of Istanbul, uncovering at least three modes of cosmopolitanist nostalgia. The best known, Pera-style cosmopolitanism, marks the closing decades of the nineteenth and the first half of the twentieth centuries, invoking a sense of the multicultural coexistence. It recalls religiously and ethnically diverse groups that belonged to the upper middle classes and maintained a Western, modern, bourgeois lifestyle that was visible in the common public space. Tatavlan cosmopolitanism, by way of contrast, entailed the spatial separation of an autonomously organized and homogenous cultural community made up of lower income groups. Tatavla nevertheless could be viewed as a building component of the wider cosmopolitan composition of Istanbul. Fener-style cosmopolitanism was a conservative cosmopolitanism linked to preserving an imperial and patriarchal order that was essentially multicultural. I have connected the dissolution of these cosmopolitanisms with the onset of nationalism, a story that is missing in many popular nostalgic idealizations of cosmopolitan Istanbul.

Perhaps the most apparent feature of these expressions of Rum Istanbulite cosmopolitanism is their strong sense of locality. For the Rum Polites cosmopolitanism was about being from an intrinsically cosmopolitan part of the city which, paradoxically, was rooted in the uniqueness of the place itself. Istanbul, as the City (*i Polis*), was able to alter the meaning of cosmopolitan etymologically by shifting the weight back and forth from "cosmos" to "polis." The Rum Polites thus took their cosmopolitanism from their Istanbul roots, not from their world travels.

Reading the Rum Polites literature, one is gripped by a sense of nostalgia emanating from an emic sense of Istanbulite cosmopolitanism. This imbues cosmopolitanist platitudes with substance and concrete references. Rum Polites' rooted cosmopolitans, in turn, can serve to compare other localized and historicized understandings of the concept: an ethnographic opening onto etic discussions regarding cultural and political theories of cosmopolitanism.

In conclusion, current and former Istanbulites perpetuate cosmopolitanist discourses in various ways and for different reasons. Yet almost all participate in creating an essential, timeless, nonreferential cosmopolitan image of Istanbul. As illustrated in this ethnographic and discursive analysis, the meanings of cosmopolitanism are rooted in specific temporal and spatial contexts. While the Rum Polites evoke their memories for reasons such as retaining their belonging to a cosmopolitan Istanbul that they have lost, current residents nostalgize the lost cosmopolitanism out of yearning for a multicultural European future. Cosmopolitanist discourses attempt to bring Turkey closer to the West, while also implying that the EU, because it is built on multicultural premises, must acknowledge the extraordinary cosmopolitan heritage of Istanbul and thus embrace the Turks as Europeans. Others see alternative visions for Turkey in a revival of the Ottoman legacy, wherein Turkish Muslims reigned over a cosmopolitan population. Cosmopolitanist discourses help raise awareness of these histories and shed light on forgotten modes of sharing the city. However, while they tend to blame nationalism in general for the dissolution of the multicultural fabric, they rarely acknowledge the persistence of state policies, legal codes, and social practices that discriminate against minorities. Cosmopolitan nostalgia thus provides its adherents with a refuge from pressing issues and challenges—such as addressing the rights of Turkey's much-diminished Rum Polites community.

ACKNOWLEDGMENTS

This chapter draws on my dissertation research on the Rum Polites in Athens, which is forthcoming in revised and expanded form from Palgrave Macmillan.[43] Earlier versions of this chapter have been presented at a Cambridge University workshop on Black Sea cities, as well as at a seminar on old and new Istanbulites in the Istanbul Ottoman Bank Archives. My gratitude goes to the conveners of these occasions and other colleagues for their feedback on the first draft. I am also thankful to the editors of this volume, particularly Nora Fisher-Onar, for the diligent work that made this publication possible.

NOTES

1. The Rum Polites (also known as *İstanbullu Rumlar* or *Konstantinoupolites*), are Greek-speaking Christian Orthodox natives of Istanbul. During Ottoman times, they composed a majority of the urban elite until the end of the empire. Their numbers exceeded 200,000 by the beginning of the twentieth century, forming around one-fourth of the city's population. The community has decreased to a few thousand in the face of tragic events and processes that have forced their displacement from Istanbul. Alexis Alexandris, *The Greek Minority of Istanbul and Greek-Turkish Relations 1918–1974* (Athens: Centre for Asia Minor Studies, 1992); İlay Romain Örs, "Identity and the City: the Rum of Istanbul and Athens," in *Economy and Society on Both Sides of the Aegean*, ed. Lorans Baruh and Vangelis Kechriotis (Atina: Alpha Bank, 2010) 175–198; and Samim Akgönül, *The Minority Concept in the Turkish*

Context: Practices and Perceptions in Turkey, Greece, and France, Muslim Minorities (Leiden: Brill, 2013) and *Türkiye Rumları: Ulus Devlet Çağından Küreselleşme Çağına Bir Azınlığın Yok Oluş Süreci* (Istanbul: İletişim, 2012).

2. Catharina Dufft, *Turkish Literature and Cultural Memory: "Multiculturalism" as a Literary Theme after 1980* (Wiesbaden, Germany: Harrassowitz, 2009); see also Amy Mills, "The Ottoman Legacy: Urban Geographies, National Imaginaries, and Global Discourses of Tolerance," *Comparative Studies of South Asia, Africa and the Middle East* 31, no. 1 (2011): 183–195, and "Reading Narratives in City Landscapes: Cultural Identity in Istanbul," *Geographical Review* 95 (2006): 441–462

3. Deniz Göktürk, Levent Soysal, and İpek Türeli, eds. *Orienting Istanbul: Cultural Capital of Europe?* (London: Routledge, 2010).

4. Robert Fine, *Cosmopolitanism* (London: Routledge, 2008), 19.

5. Leyla Erbil, "Trianon Pastanesi," in *İstanbul'da Zaman*, ed. Tomris Uyar and Sırma Köksal (Istanbul: Büke, 2000), 14.

6. The overnight pogrom known as *Septemvriana* in Greek occurred on September 6–7, 1955. Mobs attacked Rum-owned private and public buildings in Istanbul, İzmir, Imros, and Tenedos.

7. Wealth tax is a wartime fiscal measure that was enforced in 1942–1944. The amount to be paid was proportional to the taxpayer's ethnoreligious category and was sanctioned with harsh, arbitrary, and inhuman conditions, including expulsion to a labor camp in Eastern Turkey.

8. Citizen, Speak Turkish! was a government-backed popular campaign in the 1930s that prohibited the use of non-Turkish languages in public, including in personal conversations among native speakers of other languages.

9. Amy Mills, James A. Reilly, and Christine Philliou, "The Ottoman Empire from Present to Past: Memory and Ideology in Turkey and the Arab World," *Comparative Studies of South Asia, Africa and the Middle East* 31, no. 1 (2011): 135.

10. Roland Barthes, *Camera Lucida: Reflections on Photography* (New York: Hill and Wang, 1981), 96.

11. Ali Kırca, *Azınlıklar: Kaybolan Renkler* (İstanbul: Sabah, 2000); Roni Marguiles, *Bugün Pazar, Yahudiler Azar* (Istanbul: Kanat Kitap, 2006); Rıfat N. Bali, *Tarz-ı Hayat'tan Life Style'a: Yeni Seçkinler, Yeni Mekanlar, Yeni Yaşamlar* (Istanbul: İletişim, 2002); and Mario Levi, *İstanbul bir Masaldı* (Istanbul: Remzi, 1999).

12. Ayşe Öncü, "Istanbulites and Others: The Cultural Cosmology of 'Middleness' in the Era of Neo-Liberalism," in *Istanbul: Between the Global and the Local*, ed. Çağlar Keyder (New York: St. Martin's Press, 1999), 95–119.

13. Cengiz Aktar, "Cosmopolist: European Capital of Culture Istanbul," *Istanbul* 41 (2002): 182–190.

14. Nora Fisher-Onar, "Echoes of a Universalism Lost: Rival Representations of the Ottomans in Today's Turkey," *Middle East Studies* 45, no. 2 (2009): 229–241.

15. Sossie Kasbarian, "The Istanbul Armenians: Negotiating Co-existence," in *Post-Ottoman Coexistence: Sharing Space in the Shadow of Conflict*, ed. Rebecca Bryant (Oxford: Berghahn Press, 2016), 210.

16. Zerrin Özlem Biner, "Retrieving the Dignity of a Cosmopolitan City: Contested Perspectives on Rights, Culture and Ethnicity in Mardin," *New Perspectives on Turkey* 37 (2007): 31–58.

17. İlay Romain Örs, "Genie in the Bottle: Gezi Park, Taksim Square, and the Realignment of Democracy and Space," *Philosophy and Social Criticism* 40 (2014): 489–498.

18. Çağlar Keyder, *İstanbul: Küresel İle Yerel Arasında* (Istanbul: Metis, 2000); and Ayşe Öncü, "The Politics of Istanbul's Ottoman Heritage in the Era of Globalism: Refractions through the Prism of a Theme Park," in *Cities of the South: Citizenship and Exclusion in the 21st Century*, ed. Barbara Mermier, Franck Drieskens, and Heiko Wimmen (Beirut: Saqi Books, 2007), 233–264.

19. Tarlabaşı is a neighborhood in Pera that has been subjected to major projects of urban development and gentrification. Sulukule is an area located inside the Byzantine city walls that for many centuries housed the Romani/Gypsy populations. Despite major international campaigns, the area was subjected to urban gentrification projects. Located by the Byzantine city walls, Yedikule is the site of one of the oldest continuing practices of urban agriculture and is currently resisting demolition through gentrification. *Kuzey* Ormanları *Direnişi* is a civil environmentalist initiative that was founded initially to protect the forest area in northern Istanbul, which is being destroyed for megaprojects such as the third Bosphorus bridge and third airport (www.kuzeyormanlari.org).

20. Svetlana Boym, "Nostalgia and Its Discontents," *The Hedgehog Review* 9, no. 2 (2007): 7–18; and Svetlana Boym, *The Future of Nostalgia* (New York: Basic Books, 2001).

21. Carolyn Cartier, "Cosmopolitics and the Maritime World City," *Geographical Review* 89, no. 2 (1999): 278–289; Nancy Foner, "Transnationalism, Old and New: New York Immigrants," in *Urban Life: Readings in the Anthropology of the City*, ed. George Gmelch and Walter P. Zenner (Prospect Heights: Waveland Press, 2002), 341–356; and Aristide Zolberg, "Contemporary Transnational Migrations in Historical Perspectives: Patterns and Dilemmas," in *U.S. Immigration and Refugee Policy*, ed. Mary M. Kritz (Lexington: Heath, 1983), 15–51.

22. Craig Calhoun, "The Class Consciousness of Frequent Travelers: Toward a Critique of Actually Existing Cosmopolitanism," *South Atlantic Quarterly* 101, no. 4 (2002): 869–897; see also Kimberly Hutchings and Roland Dannreuther, eds. *Cosmopolitan Citizenship* (New York: St. Martin's Press, 1999); Sami Zubaida, "Middle Eastern Experiences of Cosmopolitanism," in *Conceiving Cosmopolitanism: Theory, Context, and Practice*, ed. Steve Vertovec and Robin Cohen (New York: Oxford University Press, 2003), 32–42; Karen Barkey, *Empire of Difference: The Ottomans in Comparative Perspective* (Cambridge, UK: Cambridge University Press, 2008); and Keyder, *Istanbul*.

23. Rogers Brubaker, "Aftermaths of Empire and the Unmixing of Peoples: Historical and Comparative Perspectives," *Ethnic and Racial Studies* 18 (1995): 189–218.

24. İlay Romain Örs, "Beyond the Greek and Turkish Dichotomy: The Rum Polites of Istanbul and Athens," *South European Society and Politics* 11, no. 1 (2006): 79–94.

25. Ayşe Kadıoğlu, "The Paradox of Turkish Nationalism and the Construction of Official Identity," *Middle Eastern Studies* 32, no. 2 (1996): 177–193.

26. İlay Romain Örs. *Diaspora of the City: Stories of Cosmopolitanism from Istanbul and Athens* (New York: Palgrave Macmillan, 2018).

27. Petros Markaris, "Εισαγωγή." Introduction to *Και στα Ταταύλα Χιωνή*, by Nikos Valasiadis (Athens: Ekdoseis Gavrilidis, 2002), 11.

28. Petros Paleologos, "To Peran," *To Vima*, May 8, 1971.

29. Soula Bozi, *Ο Ελληνισμός της Κωνσταντινούπολης: Κοινότητα Σταυροδρομίου-Πέραν* (Athens: Ellinika Grammata, 2002).

30. Aglaia Konstantinidou-Kloukina, *Οπου Λοιπόν . . . μια Φορά και έναν Καιρό στην Πόλη. 1949–1958* (Athens: Ikaros, 2003).

31. Bozi, *Ο Ελληνισμός της Κωνσταντινούπολης*, 57.

32. Christine Philliou, *Biography of an Empire: Governing Ottomans in an Age of Revolution* (Berkeley: University of California Press, 2010).

33. Georgios Zarifis, *Oi Anamniseis Mou: Enas Kosmos pou Efige* (Athens: Troxalia, 2002), 37.

34. A member of a prominent Fanariot family, Alexandros Ypsilantis, founded Filiki Etairia with a number of his friends in Odessa in 1814; the group then organized a revolt in March 1821. Although the conspiracy was denounced by the Patriarchate and the Fanariots under threat of excommunication, the soon-defeated rebellion was met with severe punishment by the Ottomans. Sporadic revolts in the Peloponnese evolved into a revolution accepted as the beginning of Greek independence on March 25, 1821.

35. Zarifis, *Oi Anamniseis Mou*, 47.

36. Haris Spataris, *Biz İstanbullular Böyleyiz! Fener'den Anılar* (Istanbul: Kitap, 2004), 104.

37. Zarifis, *Oi Anamniseis Mou*, 26.
38. Nikos G. Apostolidis, *Αναμνήσεις απο την Κωνσταντινούπολη* (Athens: Trochalia, 1996), 284.
39. Spataris, *Biz İstanbullular Böyleyiz!*, 81.
40. Georgios Kamarados-Vizantios, *Ta Ellinika Tatavla* (Athens: Kamarados-Vizantios, 1980).
41. Thrasivoulos O. Papastratis, *Eptalofou Bosporidos Odoioporia: Ellines, Armenoi, Tourkoi, Evraoi* (Athens: Irodotos, 1998), 75.
42. Nikos Valasiadis, *Kai sta Tatavla Chioni* (Athens: Ekdoseis Gavrilidis, 2002), 34.
43. Örs, *Diaspora of the City*.

CHAPTER 6

Cosmopolitanism as Situated Knowledge

READING ISTANBUL WITH DAVID HARVEY

Amy Mills

Since the turn of the millennium, rapid globalization has generated debates about how to live with diversity. These are often framed within the concept of cosmopolitanism: Is a "cosmopolitan ethic" that values universal rights to hospitality and belonging increasingly possible, or increasingly under threat? The question is an inherently geographic one. It compels us to examine the extent to which our social and political relationships are conditioned by experiences in locality. The question is also suggestive of the interrelatedness of places through transnational political and economic formations.

David Harvey examines this relationship between living in diversity and place in his 2000 essay in *Public Culture*, "Cosmopolitanism and the Banality of Geographical Evils," and in a later book of essays titled *Cosmopolitanism and the Geographies of Freedom*.[1] Harvey argues that recent developments such as the expansion of the European Union, the global spread of neoliberalism, and massive cross-border flows "open a space for active revival of cosmopolitanism as a way of approaching global . . . questions."[2] However, Harvey cautions that geographic realities limit what he criticizes as universalizing cosmopolitan theory. The geographic particularities of specific places—together with the ways in which they are connected to other places—condition the politics of realizing cosmopolitanism. To carry Harvey's argument fully forward—namely, to examine the lived cosmopolitanism of "Other" places—we must turn to geographically situated knowledge.[3] What does cosmopolitanism mean on the ground to those who experience or create hospitality or exclusion in diverse places?

Drawing on three empirical case studies from Istanbul, this chapter shows that even though the notion of cosmopolitanism is central to Istanbulites' imagination of their city, the city's ethos—both past and present—might more accurately be described as "throwntogetherness," a concept that captures the lived dynamics of multi- or intercultural interaction.[4] Throwntogetherness illuminates the complexity, ambivalence, and geographic contingency of social interactions, without assuming *a priori* modes of relation. As I demonstrate, Istanbulite understandings of cosmopolitanism, however much they figure in stories the cities' denizens tell, are laden with multiple values and embodied in people and places that are shaped by a throwntogetherness that is highly ambivalent in its engagement with the "Other."

Cosmopolitanism and the Geographies of Freedom

Questions about cosmopolitanism in the English-speaking academic world over the past twenty years share a concern for human rights and mutual recognition in an era of intensifying globalization, nationalism, transnationalism, and multiculturalism.[5] A common starting point of this conversation has been Immanuel Kant's conceptualization of cosmopolitanism as a way of being a "citizen of the world" and of the cosmopolitan ethic as a human right to hospitality and the tolerance of difference within and beyond state borders.[6] Kant's cosmopolitanism is also the root of the notions of cosmopolitanism that I examine in this chapter. At the center of the Kantian cosmopolitan ideal is a view of the world as a shared geographic space that remains divided by the territorial boundaries of states.[7] The nature of this shared and yet divided geography creates tensions between feelings of belonging and regard for others within and across sovereign communities.

Seyla Benhabib frames this tension as friction between universal human rights and humanity on one hand and the boundaries of state citizenship and nationalism on the other.[8] How, for example, can international human rights laws be enforced across all contexts when they may conflict with the laws of particular states or create tensions within specific cultural and political situations?[9] Seeking answers to this question, theorists apply cosmopolitanism, and its Kantian lineage, to diverse empirical situations. Scholars examine the degree to which particular sites and peoples exemplify or undermine cosmopolitanism, and they refine cosmopolitanist theory by attending to its diverse lived, empirical, and historical realities. We see this in formulations such as "vernacular cosmopolitanism,"[10] "visceral cosmopolitanism,"[11] and "actually existing cosmopolitanism."[12]

Harvey enters the conversation by accentuating how power and agency shape cosmopolitan encounters in local places. He argues that scholars should explicitly consider what he calls the "space-times"—the specific, emplaced histories/geographies—of cosmopolitanisms. He criticizes cosmopolitan theories for being Eurocentric, for reinforcing the production of inequality, and especially for being "formulated without reference to the realities of geography, ecology, and anthropology."[13] Questions about cosmopolitanism should be grounded, he argues, not only in the local and temporal particularity of place, but also in the ways that particularity is produced through global interconnections with other places. For Harvey, this spatial theory disrupts universalistic, Kantian understandings of cosmopolitanism, which imagine a seamless cosmopolitan space outside of history or local particularity.[14] His spatial theory also subverts anthropological approaches to "rooted" cosmopolitanism, which do not grapple with the ways in which local economic and political disparities are produced through the global relationships that link the histories and futures of distant places.[15]

Yet because Harvey is not working from an empirical study, he does not historicize cosmopolitanism by examining the construction of the "cosmopolitan" itself as a meaningful category in any specific geographic context. Nor does he examine the ways in which cosmopolitanism, as an idea, operates in the cultural politics of diverse lived geographies.

Doreen Massey's work offers a way to deepen Harvey's critique of cosmopolitanist theory. Her conceptualization of space is similar to Harvey's in that it involves a simultaneous consideration of the relational location of place and its interconnection with other places. However, Massey is also interested in emplaced histories and the ways residents mobilize the pasts of places to direct their futures.[16] Massey's theoretical intervention builds on Harvey's conceptualization of space-time to think explicitly about social relations in an interdependent context.[17] She further develops these ideas to consider the ways that emplaced social interactions are conditioned by meaning and imagination. Massey introduces the concept of throwntogetherness to elucidate the essential role of the material, emplaced circumstances that condition how social relations take place. The concept also invokes the imagined or remembered nature of previous interactions.[18] Throwntogetherness refers to the ways social relations depend on the actual space—an urban street, a bus, a park bench, a café—in which people encounter one another. Those encounters are influenced by the social and personal ideas that people bring to the space: the ideas about others that condition how we relate to strangers in particular contexts, how close we sit next to someone on a bus, and whether we talk to the person next to us on the park bench. These ideas about others inhere in personal and social memories and cultural histories: *local* memories and histories.

Importantly, for Massey, spatial situations are always open. They are not predetermined by assumptions regarding political-economic structures or the relative power of participants in an encounter. Nor are they troubled by Eurocentric boxes that attempt to locate people, conceptually, in predictable and static subject positions. Massey's conceptualization invites scholars to think about spaces and encounters as flexible, dynamic, and unpredictable, making it possible for us to imagine that mutual recognition and coexistence are possible even within a fragmented city full of conflict, and even in moments of almost unbearably rapid and dramatic urban change. Throwntogetherness thus shifts attention away from whom or what is cosmopolitan to focus on the fluid and complex nature of social exchanges, which may be both hospitable and hostile. It is these emplaced spatial encounters that propel social change and create history.[19]

What then do Istanbulites understand *cosmopolitanism*—a term so often invoked by both denizens and outsiders to describe the city—to mean? How have Istanbulite understandings of cosmopolitanism propelled the city's power-laden cultural politics in various moments in history? I consider these questions by briefly examining three Istanbulite cosmopolitanisms and the work they do to produce distinct forms of urban culture. Because I derive these categories from an empirically grounded inductive analysis, they are not meant to be applied to other geographic contexts.

In my first example, "cosmopolitans" are the actual non-Muslim minorities and Levantines of Istanbul whose European languages and political and economic connections and privileges facilitated a Western-oriented Ottomanism in the late nineteenth and early twentieth centuries. This way of using the word cosmopolitanism, I explain, reflects how Turks themselves used the word *kozmopolit* in this era, and it was laden with negative connotations.

In my second example, cosmopolitanism is a concept of late twentieth-century Istanbul that refers to a socially constructed cultural memory of the city's past. In this case, local Istanbulites of diverse identities and origins use the word *kozmopolit*, but it refers to a nostalgic memory of better times in the past, when Turks and minorities mixed, knew each others' languages, and shared the proper modern manners of neighborliness in daily life. The words *cosmopolitanism* and *cosmopolitans* here signify a seamless, idealized past of tolerant multiculturalism, unburdened with negative connotations. However, my reading of this Istanbulite understanding of cosmopolitanism is a critical one. I argue that this nostalgic cosmopolitanism obscures the tensions of past and ongoing relations between majority and minority populations in the city. As such, it attempts to assuage Turkish anxiety or guilt about the role of the state and of Turkish citizens in past and present nationalist violence.[20]

In my third example, I consider lived actions of hospitality, belonging, or exclusion among diverse people. I do so with the theoretical tool of throwntogetherness, which privileges the role of space in social interaction. That is, I examine the ways that sharing physical space and the mutuality that necessarily arises from actually interacting with others create complex dynamics of belonging and exclusion. This approach helps me to interpret ethnographic observations of neighboring among various women—Turkish, Greek, Jewish, and Armenian, of various social classes and places of origin—who share neighborhood space and whose memories of the national past in the city both converge and diverge. I argue that these spatial interactions among Istanbulites, who in earlier times may have been called *kozmopolit*, are in fact best interpreted through the notion of throwntogetherness, which better captures the role of memory, trauma, and imagination in visions of living together—or not—in diversity.

Three Kozmopolit Imaginaries

In my first example, one vision of Istanbulite cosmopolitanism was that of a value or an ideal linked to nineteenth-century Western modernity that traveled to Istanbul and described as "cosmopolitan" the local non-Muslim elites with European ties and modern lifestyles. As Baban and Örs (see chapters 3 and 5 in this volume) observe, these people could negotiate national and linguistic differences and move between "worlds," facilitating the political and economic changes that counted for modernity in Turkey of that period. They did so, however, from positions of political and economic privilege that provoked resentment and anxiety among local Turkish Muslims. Cosmopolitans were admired for their modern ways of life but also were resented and feared because they represented European political and economic intervention that posed a crisis for the Ottoman Empire. Reading this Istanbulite cosmopolitanism, we must consider the historic, geographic relations—the linkages between places—that created a "West" and a local/other imaginary in these Ottoman contexts.

Ottoman-European economic and political integration had intensified rapidly in the nineteenth century, although it began much earlier. Ottoman cities of the period were places of encounter among Turkish, Arab, Jewish, Christian, and other Ottoman citizens with diverse resident foreigners, including Europeans. European citizens were exempt from local laws, while Ottoman Jews and Christians were frequently given political privileges, consular rights, or European citizenship through the agreements that facilitated Ottoman-European trade.[21] Karen Barkey argues that in increasingly globally integrated Ottoman cities, this integration began to create "bounded identities" from what had been "mobile markers of difference": religion and ethnicity became grounds for intercommunal conflict because trade networks and political connections affected Muslims and non-Muslims in different ways.[22] Non-Muslims facilitated Ottoman-European economic integration because they knew European languages, constituted the trading classes, understood the practice of finance, and had protected status.[23] These were the people known locally as "cosmopolitans," because the word traveled through the geographic relationships that connected them to Europe, where cosmopolitanism had already gathered meaning to describe multilinguistic, pluralistic modernity. These cosmopolitans grew wealthier through the political and economic privileges they held as those who facilitated Ottoman-European interaction. As such, they created spaces of Ottoman-European culture.

In this culture-making capacity, the Istanbulite cosmopolitans were positioned to create conflict as well as mutuality. Muslims' perception of their own relative impoverishment or lack of political power, in comparison to the cosmopolitans, led to intercommunal conflict. In 1850 in Aleppo, for example, Muslims rioted against wealthy (but not against poor) Christians.[24] The dynamics of nineteenth-century globalization similarly brought sectarianism to Lebanon.[25] Social relationships in so-called cosmopolitan space-times were conditioned by the power dynamics of *fin de siècle* globalization, the ties of money, power, political privilege, and commodities that brought people into encounters in the first place. The growing European dominance in the global political economy produced cosmopolitans, in Istanbul, as a social category laden with negative connotations.

This local, geographically integrated, urban political economy created particular cultures, ways of making meaning of who or what was related to the West. Notably, "Ottoman non-Muslims as a whole had the unusual experience of modernization as a process of noticeable gain with little added pain."[26] This meant that modernity in late Ottoman and post-Ottoman places was laden with a Janus-faced quality for Muslims who did not enjoy the privileges that gave access to modern ways of life, even as they found the commodities, symbols, and practices of modernity increasingly desirable. The term "alla Franca," which carried negative associations in the early nineteenth century, referring to a "particular type of Westernized individual," became layered with new, positive connotations of cultural superiority and modern progress by the end of the nineteenth century.[27]

Local cultures of cosmopolitanism were thus inseparably bound up with the power relations that structured the late nineteenth- and early twentieth-century global economy. For example, a French visitor to a music café in Smyrna in 1896 described the crowd, the music, and the performers as "cosmopolitan." Precisely what kinds of people were present remained unidentified, except that they were contrasted against (noncosmopolitan) Turkish, Jewish, traditional, and lower-class people. Cosmopolitanism in this case reproduced a sense of European cultural and economic superiority located in the predominantly European entertainment districts of the wharf area, not the social clubs and taverns of the multiethnic districts farther from the port.[28] Cosmopolitanism reflected European, elitist, and orientalist imaginations about Mediterranean cities.[29] This European-inflected cosmopolitanism could not accommodate historic, Muslim understandings of social difference or universal belonging that were grounded in memories of a recent history, in which Muslims were privileged.[30]

In such contexts, people may have multiple and seemingly contradictory allegiances to both patriotism and cosmopolitanism, identifying with many places at once and on multiple scales of belonging.[31] Indeed, as Malte Fuhrmann argues with regard to late nineteenth-century Smyrna, "The dividing line between social practices inspired by nationalism and those inspired by cosmopolitanism does not reveal two neatly separated camps. Instead, the actions of individuals often followed both of these seemingly contradictory modes of social intercourse."[32] Fuhrmann suggests that articulations of identity that create both flexible ties of belonging and exclusionary boundaries are spatially dependent. Contemporary Istanbulite Jews in private spaces, for example, may strategically reveal their Jewish identity to other Jews through the use of Ladino (Judeo-Spanish originally brought to the Ottoman Empire by Sephardic Jews) or through jokes or games that depend on insider knowledge. Yet such moves conceal this aspect of their identities in the public sphere.[33] Globally interconnected, local spaces of mixed social encounters are fraught with antipathy as well as openness.

From Harvey's geographic perspective, the space of the city itself is crucial to these encounters. Indeed, Ottomans and Europeans were compelled to interact and negotiate with one another around common issues of importance, such as the expansion and shared management of the urban fabric.[34] Neither religion nor citizenship status predetermined the nature of urban social relations. Intercommunal dynamics were influenced by class, status, ethnicity, and religion and were sometimes characterized by solidarity and sometimes by conflict.[35] The relative power of different actors in the making of the city differed, however, according to how they were positioned in a given space-time—in a city's locality and, simultaneously, in its throwntogether globality as a hub of social contact, commerce, and politics.

Early twentieth-century Istanbul, like late nineteenth-century Smyrna, was a place of globalized encounter in which lived cultural boundaries of belonging and exclusion were produced at the nexus of the city's historic particularity and its globalism. Istanbul was the capital of the Ottoman Empire; before and after the turn of the century, it had become fragmented as local nationalisms, imperial overreach, and European political and economic penetration weakened imperial hold over its territories. Western powers were partitioning the Ottoman Levant into European mandate territories and were proposing to similarly partition the Anatolian peninsula.

The Ottoman imperial capital was briefly occupied by Allied forces between 1919 and 1923, as the Turkish revolutionary leader Mustafa Kemal defended Turkish territory in what would be called the War of Independence, an effort that included fighting forces from Greece on the Aegean coast. By the time the new Republic of Turkey was declared in 1923 and Ankara became the capital, Istanbul's old Turkish political and economic elite had become marginalized by the state leaders of the new republic. Istanbul, as many have noted, experienced a period of economic, political, and demographic decline. National belonging in Turkey was increasingly framed in secular Sunni Muslim and ethnically Turkish terms. In this context, Greeks, Armenians, and Jews were increasingly seen as traitors because of their relationships to the powers that were or could be fragmenting the state's territory.[36]

Those most affected by Istanbul's relative decline in the early years of the republic were the city's non-Muslims, who became ethnic minorities. At the turn of the century they had been dominant in Istanbul's population and economy. In the early decades of the twentieth century, however, the city's wealth was increasingly available to Turks as non-Muslims began to lose their historically dominant role in the city's economy. This was the result of state-led policies meant to dispossess non-Muslims of their wealth and nationalize it by transferring it to Muslim Turks. Instruments included taxation, forced deportations, the confiscation of property, and the closure of predominantly non-Muslim dominant professions to Greeks. Such pressures caused extensive minority emigration from Istanbul; simultaneously, wealthy provincial Turks and rural migrant poor were expanding the city's population. These economic pressures resulted in an increasingly stark contrast in the city between the fortunes and circumstances of the elite and the growing, impoverished poor, manifested in the differing quality and availability of modern infrastructure and the increasing segregation of urban districts by class. Many of the remaining non-Muslim minorities were among these elites. They were joined by the Turkish Muslim nouveau riche. For these reasons, Istanbulite cosmopolitanism, as an idea, was imbued with the tension that surrounded economic inequality and the sense that the city's cosmopolitan things, lifestyles, and places were not accessible to the majority of Turks.

As Zubaida (see chapter 2 in this volume) has shown, Beyoğlu was the site of Istanbul's most modern, European-style entertainment and social spaces as well as the city's foreign consulates and shops selling European goods catering to the cosmopolitan elite. Beyoğlu's cosmopolitanism embodied both the secular modernity and Western identity desired by Turkish nationalists. At the same time, it represented national political betrayal, cultural decadence, and social immorality.[37]

Women's bodies and behaviors, in particular, became sites of anxiety. While the image of the modern, European-dressed woman became a nationalist ideal, women were also idealized as mothers, the symbolic maternal bearers of the new nation.[38] Various cultural representations of women in Beyoğlu illustrate the modernity/immorality paradox of cosmopolitanism from a Turkish perspective. Turkish etiquette manuals, for example, provided instructions to women on how to behave in places like Beyoğlu to protect their moral standing.[39] Quintessentially modern and ethnically mixed new social spaces like *pastane* (European-style cafés that sell desserts) demanded new cultural rules for interaction. The manuals accordingly advised that women should not go to a *pastane* alone but only in groups, and that a man should not offer a single woman in a *pastane* a dessert.[40] The signs and symbols of cultural modernity were also the constant subject of satire. An essay published in 1922 presents the various social meanings or values of the *manto*, the modern woman's overcoat. The painful labor of a poor girl sewing a *manto* is contrasted with the activities of the *manto*'s wearer, a modern woman secretly leaving the home of a foreigner in Beyoğlu.[41]

Turkish satirical depictions of elite immorality were deeply inflected by ethnicist depictions of non-Muslims, including representations of fat and wealthy or sexually open Christian women and of usurious Jewish merchants and their cunning wives. In a short essay from 1930, for example, the author depicts an urban encounter in Galata, near Beyoğlu. A group of people stand on the street in front of Unyon Han (a *han* is a large building housing multiple shops and businesses). Galata had a large Jewish population at the time, and the Ladino name of the *han* suggests a Jewish owner. The essay describes fat-faced rich people wrapped in fur coats, healthy young people, and merchants standing around a poor person who has lost his eyes and is lying freezing on the ground. Someone in the crowd asks him, "Neyin var?" ("What [illness or problem] do you have?"). And the man says, in a play on words, "nothing, I have nothing, nothing wrapped around me, nothing on my head, nothing in my belly."[42] Satirical depictions of urban life in this era linked modern, European-like districts (like Galata) and ethnic minorities with notions of moral depravity. The ambivalence of the notion of cosmopolitanism in this period was produced then in great part by popular cultural media. By the end of the twentieth century cultural media in Istanbul had greatly shifted in their representations of non-Muslim ethnic minorities, to a second reading of cosmopolitanism. This entailed a nostalgic discourse of harmonious multiculturalism that hid or erased the negative values so dominant nearly a century before. Istanbulite understandings of cosmopolitanism were bounded by a cultural memory of past tolerant pluralism among Greeks, Jews, and Armenians and the Turks who lived among them. By the turn of the twenty-first century, Istanbul was a nationally "Turkish" city, in that very few of its historic non-Muslim minorities remained, although the population had increased dramatically with migrants, including rural people who identified as ethnically Turkish as well as thousands of displaced Kurds. Prospects for European Union accession in the 1990s placed ethnicity and human rights on the public agenda, and the ascending power of Islamically oriented political parties challenged the political and economic dominance of the city's secular, Turkish elite. The cultural and economic polarization of the city also had increased as a result of post-1980s globalization and widening income disparities.[43]

For all of these reasons, Istanbul had become a culturally alienating and politically fraught city for many of its residents. This postmodern urbanism generated a Turkish cultural nostalgia for better times, for an imagined historical moment when everyone knew everyone else, and daily life took place on a smaller scale.[44] This imagined historical moment became embodied in the word cosmopolitanism, which was used to describe people and places that embodied an imagined cultural memory of the city's historic tolerant pluralism.

As I describe in my ethnography of the formerly Greek, Jewish, and Armenian Istanbul neighborhood of Kuzguncuk, this nostalgia, authored by the city's cultural elite, is presently imbued with the idea that the city's multicultural past had been one of tolerance, harmony, and cosmopolitan belonging.[45] Istanbul's historic non-Muslim districts began to be gentrified by a secular Turkish elite, moved by ongoing representations of Istanbul's harmonious past and its correspondingly beautiful landscapes in various cultural media. These narratives of tolerance, and the gentrification of the city's historic urban fabric, signify a Western-oriented, Turkish elite cultural identification with global democratic values and political pluralism. The neighborhood's landscape of churches and mosques serves as persuasive evidence of this reading of the neighborhood's history.

This renewed and romantic cosmopolitan narrative, however, is a Turkish one. By glossing over the historical processes by which the city lost its non-Muslim minorities, the cosmopolitanist narrative works to deny the lived histories of state and social violence. The reasons that Greeks, Jews, and Armenians almost completely disappeared from the city, while their properties became available for development, are obscured. Although this Istanbulite cosmopolitanism appears, on the surface, to hold the inclusionary values of Kantian cosmopolitanism, in actuality it redraws ethnic and economic boundaries and thus forecloses possibilities for contemporary pluralistic belonging.

In my third and final example of Istanbulite cosmopolitanism, I return to my ethnography to discuss the practices of neighboring among female neighbors.[46] Neighboring is a traditional practice among women that involves ongoing reciprocal visiting and hosting of fellow female neighbors. As a social practice that creates bonds of belonging or boundaries of exclusion in shared neighborhood space, neighboring is a fruitful source for examining lived, mutual recognition among diverse people. Neighboring, in this sense, involves practicing hospitality, the rights to hospitality, and a shared sense of belonging to the neighborhood. While scholars seeking evidence of cosmopolitanism might see neighboring as cosmopolitan in its ideal Kantian sense, residents themselves do not think about these activities in terms of cosmopolitanism and would not use that word to describe neighboring. A better scholarly language would include the Turkish word for neighboring (*komşuluk*) while perhaps invoking an explicitly theoretical concept such as throwntogetherness to analyze the complexity of social relations involved.

Traditional neighboring has disappeared in much of contemporary Istanbul, where most people live in large apartment buildings and may not know their neighbors, and where many women work outside their homes during the day. In Kuzguncuk, however, neighboring continues to involve diverse members of the neighborhood (although not everyone approves of or participates in this practice). Kuzgunuck's population varies greatly by region of origin, ethnicity, beliefs, and practices regarding secularism or piety, and in terms of class and occupation. People who migrated from rural areas in the Black Sea region over several decades live near generally poorer and more pious rural migrants. This mix is complicated by the presence of an urban, educated cultural elite who include some foreigners and wealthier secular Turks who purchase and restore Ottoman-era wooden houses. Various students, single people, and others rent apartments or live in cooperative arrangements and are there to enjoy the relatively liberal social and political atmosphere and the peaceful landscape of this neighborhood. Kuzguncuk also has a smaller resident group of Jews, Greeks, and Armenians who remain from these historically dominant populations, most of whom are intermarried with Muslims.

Neighboring is practiced most regularly by lower-middle class women who are long-term residents of Kuzguncuk. They share news and support and enforce propriety. Wealthier women also neighbor among one another, but less frequently. Some of them explained that they found traditional neighboring to be far too time consuming as well as transgressive of their higher expectations for privacy and freedom from neighbors' opinions and observations. Neighboring creates belonging in Kuzguncuk through emplaced attachments to one another and to this microscale environment of local immediacy. This "emplaced cosmopolitanism" is, like Sheldon Pollock's "vernacularism," an "action rather than an idea, . . . something people do rather than something they declare, as practice rather than proposition."[47] However, my study of neighboring illuminated the extraordinary complexity of the terms of social identification and social interaction that condition relationships among neighbors. Such terms articulate whether, where, or when there may be a shared belonging that transcends ethnicity, class, origin, or other boundaries.

There is evidence that positive interethnic relationships have always existed and yet have also always been deeply threatened in Kuzguncuk. In interviews with Greeks and Jews, they recall examples of interethnic marriages as far back as the 1920s. Greeks and Turks also told me stories of lovers whose families refused them permission to marry because they were not from the same ethnoreligious group. In contrast, I know of an example of an intermarried couple today who have been happily married for over thirty years. However, the wife has been told she cannot be buried in the graveyard of her people because she married outside her religion. An elderly Jewish man told me that his daughter was "dead to him" because she married a non-Jew, and a Greek woman warned me "never to take a Turk." An intermarried secular Turkish Muslim woman told me about her positive relationship with her husband's Christian family, but told me that she would never eat "Jewish food." Jews and Turks alike remembered their mothers neighboring with Armenian mothers on the same street, while they also remembered sometimes fighting with other Armenian children who lived in the upper part of the neighborhood.

Gender and class complicate ethnicity as a facet of identity that bonds or excludes people. An intermarried Jewish woman, for example, lives in a relatively lower income part of Kuzguncuk next to Turkish families of Black Sea origin. She visits every day with the women next door. They make each other food and tea, and her Turkish neighbors help her with errands, including paying her utility bills at the post office. They will visit her if she is ill, and they will comfort her if she grieves. Their shared economic circumstances, ages, and gender give them a lot in common. But when she and I sat together and she told me about her memories of the 1943 property tax (levied disproportionately against non-Muslims) and of the 1955 riots (against Greek properties), she closed her front door behind us and told me I could never trust a Turk. In that moment, her experiences with and memories of Turkish state nationalism and of violence against people like herself created a boundary that separated her from her neighbors and bonded us together simply because we are both not ethnically Turkish, in spite of the fact that I am a foreigner, am much younger, and had known her for only a matter of months.

Cosmopolitanist theory cannot accommodate the complexity of the social relationships I observed in Istanbul. As these examples illustrate, spaces of hospitality rely on careful negotiation and are intensely dependent upon very small interactions in shared spaces over time. These spaces are very fragile and are easily destroyed at heightened moments of state nationalism or global crisis, such as before and after the attempted coup in July 2016.

Throwntogetherness

The three understandings of cosmopolitanism discussed above are produced at the intersection of the city's local histories with the global circulation of ideas, money, and power. Reading these Istanbulite cosmopolitanisms with Harvey's proposal to consider the space-times of cosmopolitanism aligns with his agenda to disrupt both the universalizing and localizing approaches to cosmopolitanism. However, these Istanbulite cosmopolitanisms undermine Harvey's assumptions regarding cosmopolitanism's emancipatory potential. Harvey sees this potential in our contemporary global moment, in which old forms of state power and national belonging are undermined by the massive movements of people and things across boundaries and the increasing power of transnational political bodies and social movements. In the case of Istanbul, however, these connections can redraw social boundaries that fragment the urban social and material fabric.

So what can we make of the potential Harvey envisaged for lived practices of democracy, mutual recognition, and advancing human rights in Istanbul? Resistance movements that promote these ideals have long existed in Istanbul in various forms, and they include movements based on Marxist, socialist, anarchist, feminist, environmentalist, or other generally leftist ideals. Resistance movements are increasingly visible in the city's public spaces and in international media, and as the 2013 Gezi protests demonstrated, they can momentarily become broadly inclusive of diverse agendas. The terms of belonging to particular resistance movements can also make them exclusive, however, because they prioritize various narrow agendas over others. The feminist movement, for example, has not always been tolerant of broader LBGT rights and has not included the agendas of transgendered women, for example, who are excluded from the mainstream identity politics of the movement. Women's rights organizations provide a platform for a shared agenda of political activism even while various organizations and organization members also prioritize different and sometimes competing interpretations of women's rights.[48] Spaces of blending, hybridity, and mutual recognition have existed and continue to exist in the city, but the social relations that create these spaces involve complex processes of negotiation.[49]

Cosmopolitanism, in the ideal form that Harvey and others want to realize, is not possible as a social and political formation that can transcend the cultural identity politics that fragment the city but also create important ties of belonging. Mutual recognition and recrimination are contingent, highly dependent on particular spaces and circumstances, and more common than we might assume in the realm of ordinary life. Importantly, mutual recognition is also not necessarily consistent among spaces, groups, or even individuals and is not definable by a single conceptual term or ideal. There is no single way to theorize the possibilities for, or to identify, actually existing examples of cosmopolitanism.

Istanbul's cosmopolitanisms are produced through the city's historic and contemporary relationships to its own complex histories and to global economic, political, and cultural power. However, questions *about* Turkish cosmopolitanism, in scholarly discourses in Turkish studies and in popular political commentaries, continue to reify orientalist or Turkish nationalist imaginations of the world. For neo-Ottomanist commentators in Turkey, the Ottoman past was indeed cosmopolitan, an assertion produced in a contemporary Turkish context in which the ruling Justice and Development Party positions itself against the recent, secular political Turkish history.[50] For liberal leftist secular Turks, remembering the city's cosmopolitan past articulates a cultural and political reaction to the presumed political intolerance of an Islamist present. Bringing an explicit consideration of space-time to understanding specific contexts means surrendering the ideal of cosmopolitanism, because space-time is itself the process of historic and spatial encounter and is thus always in the making.

Does contemporary globalism provide new opportunities for cosmopolitanism because of the erosion of the state or cross-border flows? Today, the increasing complexity of Turkey's globalization (including "massive cross-border capital flows, migratory movements, and cultural exchanges") has *not* come with a commensurate challenge to the powers of the state and has *not* necessarily "opened a space for an active revival of cosmopolitanism."[51] That said, new forms of social and political plurality and association occur every day in Istanbul. Beyond cosmopolitanist theory, the less value-loaded idea of throwntogetherness makes it possible to study and participate in spaces and moments of diverse kinds of mutual recognition amid a complex and changing urban context.

NOTES

1. David Harvey, "Cosmopolitanism and the Banality of Geographical Evils," *Public Culture* 12, no. 2 (2000): 529–564; and David Harvey, *Cosmopolitanism and the Geographies of Freedom* (New York: Columbia University Press, 2009).

2. Harvey, *Cosmopolitanism and the Geographies of Freedom*, 78.

3. Donna Haraway, "Situated Knowledges: The Science Question in Feminism and the Privilege of Partial Perspective," *Feminist Studies* 14 (1998): 575–599.

4. Doreen Massey, *For Space* (Thousand Oaks, CA: Sage, 2005).

5. Steven Vertovec and Robin Cohen, eds., *Conceiving Cosmopolitanism: Theory, Context, and Practice* (New York: Oxford University Press, 2003); Dipesh Chakrabarty, Sheldon Pollock, Homi K. Bhabha, and Carol A. Breckenridge, eds., *Cosmopolitanism* (Durham, NC: Duke University Press, 2002); Seyla Benhabib, *Another Cosmopolitanism*, The Berkeley Tanner Lectures (Oxford: Oxford University Press, 2006); and Pheng Cheah and Bruce Robbins, eds., *Cosmopolitics: Thinking and Feeling Beyond the Nation*, vol. 14 (Minneapolis: University of Minnesota Press, 1998).

6. Vertovec and Cohen, *Conceiving Cosmopolitanism*, 10; David Harvey, *Cosmopolitanism and the Geographies of Freedom* (New York: Columbia University Press, 2009); and Seyla Benhabib, *The Rights of Others: Aliens, Residents and Citizens* (New York: Cambridge University Press, 2004).

7. Harvey, *Cosmopolitanism*.

8. Benhabib, *The Rights of Others*.

9. Harvey, *Cosmopolitanism*. See also Benhabib, *The Rights of Others*.

10. Sheldon Pollock, "Cosmopolitanism and the Vernacular in History," in *Cosmopolitanism*, ed. Dipesh Chakrabarty, Sheldon Pollock, Homi K. Bhabha, and Carol A. Breckenridge (Durham, NC: Duke University Press, 2002), 15–53; and Mamadou Diouf, "The Senegalese Murid Trade Diaspora and the Making of a Vernacular Cosmopolitanism," trans. Steven Rendall, in *Cosmopolitanism*, ed. Dipesh Chakrabarty, Sheldon Pollock, Homi K. Bhabha, and Carol A. Breckenridge (Durham, NC: Duke University Press, 2002), 111–137.

11. Mica Nava, *Visceral Cosmopolitanism: Gender, Culture and the Normalisation of Difference* (New York: Berg, 2007).

12. Scott Malcomson, "The Varieties of Cosmopolitan Experience," in *Cosmopolitics: Thinking and Feeling Beyond the Nation*, ed. Pheng Cheah and Bruce Robbins (Minneapolis: University of Minnesota Press, 1998), 233–245.

13. Harvey, *Cosmopolitanism*, 99.

14. See chapter 3 in this volume.

15. Harvey, *Cosmopolitanism*.

16. Doreen Massey, "Places and Their Pasts," *History Workshop Journal* 39 (1995): 182–192.

17. Doreen Massey, "Power-geometry and a Progressive Sense of Place," in *Mapping the Futures: Local Cultures, Global Change*, ed. Jon Bird, Barry Curtis, Tim Putman, and Lisa Tickner (New York: Routledge, 1993), 59–69.

18. Massey, *For Space*.

19. Ibid.

20. Amy Mills, *Streets of Memory: Landscape, Tolerance, and National Identity in Istanbul* (Athens: University of Georgia Press, 2010); and Fatma Müge Göçek, *Denial of Violence: Ottoman Past, Turkish Present, and Collective Violence Against Armenians: 1789–2009* (New York: Oxford University Press, 2015).

21. Ian Coller, "East of Enlightenment: Regulating Cosmopolitanism Between Istanbul and Paris in the Eighteenth Century," *Journal of World History* 21 (2010): 450.

22. Karen Barkey, *Empire of Difference: The Ottomans in Comparative Perspective* (Cambridge, UK: Cambridge University Press, 2008), 277–279.

23. Ibid.

24. Bruce Masters, *The Arabs of the Ottoman Empire, 1516–1918: A Social and Cultural History* (New York: Cambridge University Press, 2013), 190.

25. Ussama Makdisi, *The Culture of Sectarianism: Community, History, and Violence in Nineteenth Century Lebanon* (Berkeley: University of California Press, 2000).

26. Frederick F. Anscombe, *State, Faith, and Nation in Ottoman and Post-Ottoman Lands* (New York: Cambridge University Press, 2014), 108.

27. Şükrü Hanioğlu, *A Brief History of the Late Ottoman Empire* (Princeton, NJ: Princeton University Press, 2008), 100.

28. Maureen Jackson, "'Cosmopolitan Smyrna': Illuminating or Obscuring Cultural Histories?," *The Geographical Review* 102 (2012): 337–349.

29. Coller, "East of Enlightenment"; Jackson, "'Cosmopolitan Smyrna'"; Paolo Giaccaria, "Cosmopolitanism: The Mediterranean Archives," *The Geographical Review* 102 (2012): 293–315; Will Hanley, "Grieving Cosmopolitanism in Middle East Studies," *History Compass* 6 (2008): 1346–1367; and Hala Halim, *Alexandrian Cosmopolitanism: An Archive* (New York: Fordham University Press, 2013).

30. See Sami Zubaida, "Middle Eastern Experiences of Cosmopolitanism," in *Conceiving Cosmopolitanism: Theory, Context, and Practice*, ed. Steve Vertovec and Robin Cohen (New York: Oxford University Press, 2003), 32–42; and chapter 2 in this volume.

31. Katharine Mitchell, "Geographies of Identity: The Intimate Cosmopolitan," *Progress in Human Geography* 31 (2007): 714; and Julia Phillips Cohen, *Becoming Ottomans: Sephardi Jews and Imperial Citizenship in the Modern Era* (New York: Oxford University Press, 2014), 131.

32. Malte Fuhrmann, "Cosmopolitan Imperialists and the Ottoman Port Cities: Conflicting Logics in the Urban Social Fabric," *Cahiers de la Méditerranée* 67 (1995): 149–163, para. 46.

33. Marcy Brink-Danan, *Jewish Life in Twenty-First-Century Turkey: The Other Side of Tolerance* (Bloomington: Indiana University Press, 2011).

34. Sibel Zandi-Sayek, *Ottoman İzmir: The Rise of a Cosmopolitan Port (1840–1880)* (Minneapolis: Minnesota University Press, 2012).

35. Michelle Campos, *Ottoman Brothers: Muslims, Christians, and Jews in Early Twentieth-century Palestine* (Stanford, CA: Stanford University Press, 2011), 11.

36. Göçek, *Denial of Violence.*

37. Carole Woodall, "'Awakening a Horrible Monster': Negotiating the Jazz Public in 1920s Istanbul," *Comparative Studies of South Asia, Africa and the Middle East* 30 (2010): 514–582.

38. Yasemin Gencer, "We are Family: The Child and Modern Nationhood in Early Turkish Republican Cartoons (1923–28)," *Comparative Studies of South Africa, Asia, and the Middle East* 32 (2012): 294–309.

39. Nevin Meriç, *Adab-ı Muaşeret: Osmanlı'da Gündelik Hayatın Değişimi (1894–1927)* (Istanbul: Kapı Yayınları, 2007).

40. Ibid., 86–87.

41. Kirpi, "Mantolar Neye Mal Oluyor?," *Aydede* 1 (1922): 2.

42. Yusuf Ziya, "Hiç Bir Şeyi Yoktu!," *Akbaba* 751 (1930): 1.

43. Çağlar Keyder, ed., *Istanbul: Between the Local and the Global* (New York: Rowman and Littlefield, 1999).

44. M. Christine Boyer, *The City of Collective Memory: Its Historical Imagery and Architectural Entertainments* (Cambridge, MA: MIT Press, 1996).

45. Mills, *Streets of Memory.*

46. Ibid., ch. 5.

47. Pollock, "Cosmopolitanism and the Vernacular in History," 17.

48. Nora Fisher-Onar and Hande Paker, "Towards Cosmopolitan Citizenship? Women's Rights in Divided Turkey," *Theory and Society* 41, no. 4 (2012): 375–394.

49. Ibid.

50. Amy Mills, "The Ottoman Legacy: Urban Geographies, National Imaginaries, and Global Discourses of Tolerance," *Comparative Studies of South Asia, Africa and the Middle East* 31, no. 1 (2011): 183–195.

51. Harvey, *Cosmopolitanism*, 78.

CHAPTER 7

Hagia Sophia's Tears and Smiles

THE AMBIVALENT LIFE OF A GLOBAL MONUMENT

Anna Bigelow

On November 14, 2013, at the opening of a textile museum in part of the Hagia Sophia museum complex in Istanbul, Turkey's deputy prime minister, Bülent Arınç, announced: "Ayasofya is telling us something. I wonder what Ayasofya wants to tell us?"[1] Ayasofya is Turkish for Hagia Sophia, the grand structure that served as a cathedral and monument under the Byzantine Empire and became a mosque under the Ottomans and a museum after the establishment of the Turkish Republic. Regaling those gathered with his view of the great building's innermost desires, Arınç argued that after Hagia Sophia became a mosque in 1453, its essential Islamic identity could not be changed: once a mosque, always a mosque. Arınç further claimed that the Hagia Sophia wished to join two other church-mosque-museums (also named Hagia Sophia) in the Turkish cities of Trabzon and İznik, which had partially reverted to mosque status earlier in 2013 after decades as museums. Arınç's public channeling of the building's thoughts was built on the argument that the church and museum periods were aberrations from its essential mosque nature.

Such claims are but the most recent in a centuries-old debate. For a millennium and a half, Hagia Sophia has represented the imperial aspirations of its possessors, those who aspire to possession, and their competing claims to determine the identity of the critically important polis now known as Istanbul and its inhabitants. The city's strategic location at the convergence of Asia and Europe, the bridge between the Aegean and Black Seas, at the mouth of the Bosphorus explains why so many settlements that have been placed here, from Lygos to Constantinople to Istanbul, have been central to the imperial powers that controlled the promontory. The ideal topography and location as a crossing point among empires, cultures, languages, and continents also means that this site has always been a global city, virtually from its origins in the fifth millennia B.C.E. As one of the most famous architectural wonders and a UNESCO world heritage site, the Hagia Sophia has long been recognized as the quintessential symbol of the metropolis into which the city has grown. And so it is not surprising that heated debates accompanied its transformation from church into mosque and mosque into museum, as well as its increasingly contested status as a museum today.

This chapter examines the ways that Hagia Sophia is universally recognized as a monument by Christians, Muslims, and secularists, but is perennially contested. Not one of these groups has been able to fully dominate its identity. The chapter shows that their contesting claims become salient at times of transition in state and society during which each group—proponents of church, mosque, and museum—mobilizes aesthetic languages of power that have resonated across centuries. For each constituency Hagia Sophia is the object of intense efforts to control the interpretive possibilities of the building discursively and physically, and through it to determine national identity. Examining these contests, the chapter argues that the very forces that make Hagia Sophia cosmopolitan, namely the multiplicity of meanings embodied in its single powerful space, also make it a site of mutually exclusive universalisms on the part of religious and secular actors.

The Long History of a Global Attraction

Hagia Sophia has a long history as a holy place. The Orthodox basilica was built in 537 C.E. on the grounds of an earlier church, before which there had been a pagan temple on the site. It became a Catholic cathedral briefly during the Fourth Crusade (1204–1261). It was then returned to Orthodoxy for almost two centuries, until the 1453 Ottoman conquest of Constantinople, when the church became a mosque and the city became Istanbul. The latest phase in Hagia Sophia's life began in 1935, when it became a museum, as ordered by the founder of the Turkish Republic, Mustafa Kemal Atatürk, following its excavation and restoration by the Byzantine Institute of America. Today, it is the crown jewel of Istanbul's Golden Horn, with the famous Sultanahmet mosque (Blue mosque) and the Topkapı Palace among the area's other attractions. According to UNESCO, "The Outstanding Universal Value of Istanbul resides in its unique integration of architectural masterpieces that reflect the meeting of Europe and Asia over many centuries, and in its incomparable skyline formed by the creative genius of Byzantine and Ottoman architects."[2] The Golden Horn's skyline is dominated by the Hagia Sophia, which is the most popular site in all of Turkey for both tourists and citizens, today drawing over three million people a year.[3]

While its global appeal (and the vast revenue generated, at 30 YTL (~US$10) per visit by non-Turkish citizens as of this writing) would seem to solidify Hagia

Sophia's status as a museum, this position is by no means unchallenged. Some Muslims call for it to be opened for *namaz* (ritual prayer), just as many Orthodox and other Christians hope to see the building restored as a church. Such debates mark the latest layer in the long history of Hagia Sophia's relationship with state authority and the increasingly ambivalent history of Turkey's relationship with state secularism. They also highlight the tensions between the site's cosmopolitan character and the competition it engenders among rival and exclusionary visions of collective identity.

Hagia Sophia, in short, is at once a universally recognized "wonder" and a central component of competing visions of the universal. In the early twenty-first century it plays this role by serving as a stage upon which secular nationalists, but also supporters of the (neo)liberal heritage sites regime, vie with Islamists and others who argue for its use in competing constructions of national identity and religiosity. For Kemalists and other secular nationalist movements, Turkey's secularism is the *sine qua non* of the republic. Turkish laicism became state policy with the birth of the republic through the charismatic leadership of Mustafa Kemal Atatürk and other protagonists of the Turkish nationalist movement. They envisioned a public sphere devoid of observable religious practices, symbols, and ideas. To the extent that religion would persist, it would be strictly controlled by the state. The museumification of the Hagia Sophia was one of many symbolic acts taken in the early republican period that helped to articulate the vision for the new nation-state.

However, Islamist political parties—especially the Justice and Development Party (AKP), in power since 2002—have eclipsed the secular establishment in recent years. In tandem with this transformation, debates in Turkey about the role of religion in national identity frequently focus on visible signs of religiosity in public spaces with regard, for example, to women's headscarves, the role of Sufi orders, and the status of historic sacred sites. Religious sites have been an especial battleground between secularists and Islamists, particularly evident in the conversions of the Trabzon and İznik Hagia Sophia museums into active mosques and in efforts to do the same with the much more famous Istanbul Hagia Sophia.

These controversies are reshaping Hagia Sophia and its status as a museum. In 1991, during the tenure of the right-leaning ANAP (Motherland Party), an Islamic prayer space was opened in the passageway leading from the road closest to the Topkapı Palace.[4] This space remains open for prayer today, having undergone major renovations in recent years. There are increasing public calls to open the entire building for Muslim worship. Each change—and the public perceptions and debates surrounding it—helps to illuminate the ambivalence of the building. On the one hand it is a monument to secularized cosmopolitanism—a universal heritage shared by multiple but disenchanted religions. On the other it embodies the aspirations of groups who claim the sacred authenticity or primacy of only one religious identity. Such debates at this nexus of universal resonance

Figure 7.1. Exterior, Hagia Sophia. Photo credit: Anna Bigelow.

and particularistic claims entail creative reinterpretations of historical events that illuminate deeply held fears and hopes for the Turkish state among the groups in question.

New Materialism and the Phenomenology of Space

At least two literatures can help us to unpack this paradox, addressing the question of what, as Arınç enigmatically suggested, Hagia Sophia might be telling us. First, in the field of religious studies, new materialists argue that the building is a form of "vibrant matter" having force and agency beyond that imputed to it by human interlocutors.[5] This suggests that certain themes associated with the building will persist over time and space. The idea that buildings as material objects have agency independent of the humans who construct and construe them is gaining ground in recent materialist theory. As Diana Coole and Samantha Frost argue, we must "give material factors their due in shaping society and circumscribing human prospects."[6] Buildings, especially those deemed "monuments," outlive their makers and remakers, existing symbolically and discursively far beyond their immediate locations. They contain and distill memories, as well as the diverse entanglements and interconnections often associated with cosmopolitanism.[7] Multiply occupied, the "Other" is always present in a place like Hagia Sophia, even if no longer allowed entrance or publicly disavowed. The often forgotten or suppressed "Other," after all, built, embellished, prayed, or desired the building much like the present owners.

These variant conceptions are fixed in place through popular narratives and practices, becoming "sites of memory." As art historian Gülru Necipoğlu notes:

> Hagia Sophia was therefore a true *lieu de memoire* in which a wide variety of memories (Christian-Byzantine and Islamic-Ottoman) crystallized, passing down from one generation to the other and continually being reinterpreted according to changing contexts. While it had a remarkable capacity to condense memory, Hagia Sophia was not an open signifier to which any signifier could arbitrarily be attached by changing audiences. Its meanings revolving around the twin themes of universal empire and religion remained surprisingly constant before and after the conquest of Constantinople.[8]

In this passage, Necipoğlu addresses the shift from church to mosque. In the republican museum period, however, the same themes of universal empire and religion continue to resonate with constituencies who long for Hagia Sophia's "restoration" as a mosque or a church. Triumphal neo-imperialist narratives are evident in both Orthodox and Islamist sources. For even in a postimperial age, imperial imaginaries persist, the resurgence of "neo-Ottoman" nostalgia in Turkey being a case in point.[9]

Religion too has proved resilient, with many Islamists speaking of turning Hagia Sophia from a museum into a mosque as a key part of a "second conquest." A dramatic case in point is the argument put forth in the so-called Islamic State or ISIS's glossy Turkish-language magazine *Konstantiniyye'nin Fethi* (*The Conquest of Constantinople*). One claim made therein is that Istanbul essentially has become Constantinople again at the hands of tyrants, despots, and infidels. The city therefore demands reconquest. This argument is part of ISIS eschatology, which draws on some hadith that suggest the (re)conquest of Constantinople will occur shortly before the return of Jesus and the end times. Although ISIS advocates a more violent path to bring about the apocalypse, such hadith are well-known outside of extremist circles as well. For many Muslims throughout the world, the Hagia Sophia was and is one of the most powerful symbols of a period of glory during the Ottoman era and is linked in narratives to the Prophet Muhammad. One legend claims that the great church's dome collapsed when Muhammad was born, another that it could not be repaired until his saliva was added to the cement.

But monuments like Hagia Sophia are not mute witnesses to efforts to speak on their behalf. As a second literature on the phenomenology of space tells us, they can facilitate or thwart certain usages, both conceptually and literally. This may be the particular power of space. Phenomenologists of space from Martin Heidegger and Henri Lefebvre to Edward Casey argue in various ways that spaces are capable of containing multiple meanings and sustaining those contradictions in ways that allow interlocutors to experience and represent the space in a variety of ways simultaneously.[10] In other words, two individuals could stand in nearly the same spot at the same time but interpret a building in entirely different ways. On this point, theories of space intersect with the tension in cosmopolitan thinking between how to reconcile "thin" recognition of the universal with "thick" universalisms.[11]

In the case of Hagia Sophia, this may mean one person sees an aesthetically pleasing, multilayered structure to be celebrated for its spiritual and historic significance to multiple religious communities. Another sees a church in chains buried under a veneer of Islamic decoration and secular occupation. Some may look beyond or behind those features that detract from their ideal vision, while others embrace the multiplicity. That said, the physical features of a building determine to some degree the possible interactions between visitors and structure. Thus while there are continuous efforts to transform a monument's identity, transformations are often incomplete and contested.

Between Cosmopolitanism and Contending Universalisms

"All societies invest a great deal," as David Morgan suggests, "in teaching their members to feel similarly."[12] Shaping the collective response to the Hagia Sophia has been the object of its custodians since it was built in the aftermath of riots that threatened the Byzantine emperor Justinian's legitimacy. Monumental spaces do not merely structure the experiences of individuals, but are also constituted by the social systems that produce, inherit, reconfigure, and control the site. As Lefebvre explains, there is a power feedback loop between monuments and the political regimes by which they are created and claimed: "Each monumental space becomes the metaphorical and quasi-metaphysical underpinning of a society, this by virtue of a play of substitutions, in which the religious and political realms symbolically (and ceremonially) exchange attributes—the attributes of power; in this way the authority of the sacred and the sacred aspect of authority are transferred back and forth, mutually reinforcing one another in the process."[13] In the case of Hagia Sophia, mutually constitutive but contested expressions of emplaced power have been intensified by the role of multiple religious and political regimes centered in the iconic city: Christianity and Byzantium, Islam and the Ottoman Empire, secularism and the Turkish Republic. Although each layer may seem to negate (or attempt to negate) the previous stage, they are also mutually reinforcing. In this way the Hagia Sophia became the template for Ottoman mosques even before the conquest. The aesthetic principles of the site—domed roof, mosaic embellishment, elite and public spaces—were expressive of imperial authority and were mastered, mimicked, and embellished. Though mutually recognizable as marks of power in both Christianity and Islam, these features also leave the building open to essentialist claims by those seeking to control its interpretation. For example, for some Islamist interlocutors, Hagia Sophia's Byzantine (Christian) mosaics may be evidence of the superiority of Islamic tolerance due to Ottoman preservation of the mosaics, but that also makes them targets for removal, as they challenge the efficacy of the transformation into a mosque.

From Church to Mosque

Through the centuries, to control the Hagia Sophia's identity has meant controlling the identity of society more broadly. From its origins onward, the monumental site both validated and manifested power, for it could only have been built, maintained, or improved by an imperial state with substantial economic and technological resources. At each time of transition from one empire to another the Hagia Sophia must have been reinvented discursively and materially. As Berin Gür argues: "Each [political regime] has produced its own spatial and social lexicon, architectural index of signs and symbols; in other words, each constitutes a social thought having an existence in space through architecture. Then, each political and in turn social domination has marked its existence on the urban space in the Sultanahmet district [where Hagia Sophia is located] by erecting its own architecture and by converting the existing ones in accordance with the norms of the new domination."[14] And so it was that Mehmet II, conqueror of Constantinople in 1453, did not destroy or ignore the Hagia Sophia but claimed it—the first of a series of Ottoman rulers to place his imprimatur upon the building. His material imprint attests to the intertwining of universal resonance and particularistic claims that make Hagia Sophia so ambivalently cosmopolitan. He ordered that in the Byzantine structure be built a *mihrab* (niche to mark the direction of prayer), a *minbar* (staircase used as a pulpit) for delivery of Friday sermons, and a platform for recitation of the Qur'an. Mosaics directly within the line of sight for those at prayer were covered with plaster, but those in the upper galleries and elsewhere that did not confront the congregation were left uncovered until the seventeenth century.[15]

Conceptually too, Mehmet II sought to reconfigure the place of Hagia Sophia in relation to Islam by commissioning a history of the building, *Diegesis peri tes Hagias Sofias* (*Narrative concerning Hagia Sophia*). The text appropriated Byzantine history by including stories connecting the building to Islam before the Ottomans' arrival in 1453. Among these accounts was the widely circulated story mentioned above that the dome had collapsed at the moment of the Prophet Muhammad's birth, and that only the Prophet's saliva could secure the cement that would keep the great dome in place. "In this way Justinian's monumental church [was] reconstituted in the Ottoman text as a symbol of universal rule that reflected a perfect concordance between divine will and imperial power."[16]

That these narratives remained powerful is attested to by later descriptions of the Islamic significance of the structure. For example, the Sufi writer and thinker Sâmiha Ayverdi (1905–1993) wrote: "There is nothing more natural than myths surrounding a temple that carries the weight of centuries. And in one of these myths, despite the fact that Ayasofya is an Orthodox Church, the tradition that it would one day become a mosque circulated."[17] Ayverdi also appropriated the story of the Byzantines needing the Prophet Muhammad to solidify the dome. The narrative not only invoked the recurring themes of imperial power and divine will, but also claimed the Islamic essence of the building as predating the arrival of the Ottomans.

But if monuments are in many ways distillations of the societies and regimes that produce them, the dominant set of claims also often masks oppositional interpretations. At each time of transition there have been communities who refused to acknowledge the validity of the recent transformation and who directed their energies toward making the building fit their alternative expectations and interests. For example, just prior to the Ottoman conquest of 1453, some Orthodox Christians boycotted the space due to their objections to efforts at rapprochement in that period between the Roman and Orthodox Churches.[18] Distressed by the possibility of the Eastern and Western churches reconciling, some Orthodox faithful may have been better able to digest the Ottoman conquest.

With the swift conversion of the church into a mosque, newcomers likewise did not universally accept the altered status of the Hagia Sophia. Some Muslims objected to efforts to preserve the building at all. Restraining them required imperial intervention through an official declaration (*ferman*) that proclaimed "those who opposed the sultan's orders as tyranny, arguing that Hagia Sophia need not be preserved since it had been built by non-Muslims, deserved to be executed as infidels"; the measure further demonstrated that "despite largely successful official efforts to Islamize the building, its Christian memory had not been completely erased" even in the eyes of Muslim interlocutors.[19] The need for the *ferman* indicates ongoing resistance among some Muslims to using the structure for prayer, since to them it was manifestly Christian in its orientation, decoration, and aesthetics.

Orthodox Nostalgia and Neo-Imperial Ambition

Greek poetry and folk songs invoke the miracle of the Hagia Sophia and the tragedy of its appropriation. In a lament (*feryat*) reminiscent of contemporary Islamists who advocate reopening the building as a mosque, poetry that may date back to Hagia Sophia's conversion in 1453 expresses both a longing for and an expectation of the eventual return of the church. In a recent article, Marios Philippides excavates the roots of a still popular folk song describing the moments just before the Ottoman conquest. The lyrics depict an angel announcing that God has willed the fall of the city but also consoling the weeping Mary that eventually the loss will be redeemed. "Be still Madonna and weep no more: / With the passage of years and time, it will be yours again," the song concludes.[20] As Philippides argues, the "last line with its promise of eventual salvation and liberation, endeared this poem to the Greeks. The poem succeeds in creating an atmosphere of impending doom and of a sorrowful end to the millennial empire. . . . [and]

an oracle that offers a ray of hope to a nation about to be enslaved."[21] Whether all of or merely elements of this song can be traced to the time of the conquest, it certainly persists as a common theme in the emancipatory literature produced by contemporary advocates for a return of the church.

For the Orthodox community, the Hagia Sophia is the historic seat of the patriarchate. Though pressing these claims is politically impossible for the small Orthodox minority in Turkey (less than 1 percent of the population), they watch any activity related to the Hagia Sophia closely. Many Orthodox Christians outside of Turkey are more vocal in their desire to "liberate" the structure from the secular Muslim "prison" of the museum.[22] For example, Greek American author Theodore G. Karakostas states in a self-published work that the essence of Hagia Sophia can never be anything but a church. Karakostas sees a "heaven-inspired edifice" that can never be truly superseded: "Whether used as a Latin church by the crusaders or as a mosque by the Ottomans, the theological and political foundations upon which this heaven-inspired edifice was built can never be replaced or subjugated. It is a Greek church—a fact that all Greeks are well aware of—and Greeks are the real guardians of Hagia Sophia even though our nation has been exiled and we are deprived of access to our great church."[23]

If the conquest of 1453 and the transformation into a mosque were violations according to many Orthodox Christians, so was its conversion into a secular space. According to the New Byzantines website (www.newbyzantines.net), a site dedicated to celebrating and restoring Byzantine culture:

> Where once potentates and patriarchs, prelates and priests, saints and sinners moved in solemn procession, tourists now loiter and stare. The images looking down from the walls are no longer the windows to heaven but silent witnesses to the profanities of the Muslims and the vulgarities of the tourist trade. Gone are the chanting priests; gone too are the smells and bells of the East. No longer do the cherubim descend to accompany and to praise the Holy Mysteries. The Great Church is little more than a mound of architecturally ordered stones devoid of the life of liturgy.[24]

In this rendering, the New Byzantines equate Islam and tourism as corrupting forces even as they invoke the Orthodox sensorium—a powerful memory tool—of "smells and bells" as that which gave life to Hagia Sophia.

While some such claims are rooted in Orthodox redemptive history, there is also a more generalized antipathy among many Orthodox for the mosque/museum phases of Hagia Sophia's existence. Arınç's statements in November 2013, for example, provoked a reaction from the Greek government. Interestingly, the response mixed secular and religious criticism, claiming Hagia Sophia as both a Christian and a world heritage site. According to the Greek foreign ministry: "The repeated statements from Turkish officials regarding the conversion of Byzantine Christian churches into mosques are an insult to the religious sensibilities of millions of Christians and are actions that are anachronistic and incomprehensible from a state that declares it wants to participate as a full member in the European Union, a fundamental principle of which is respect for religious freedom."[25] By thus invoking religious freedom rather than theology, the argument is embedded simultaneously in liberal secular universalism and Orthodox universalist critiques of Islamist aspirations.

The Ambivalent Museum and the Global City

Such hybrid rationales have been in evidence since at least the early twentieth century, when the museum's founders—at the behest of the new Turkish republican regime—restored the monument in order to garner the goodwill of Christians in the region and the West. In a letter requesting funds for additional excavations and restorations, the Byzantine Society of America stated that the goal of the museum was to "promote goodwill for America in Turkey and in all Christian communities of that region, by insuring the completion of the work which Kemal Atatürk and successive governments have asked Thomas Whittemore to carry on; principally in Haghia Sophia."[26]

The project of restoring Hagia Sophia and making it available to the public fit perfectly into the modernization project Atatürk envisioned for the country. "The discourse brought forth by the civilization project was utopist and reformist yet centralized. It constituted its own actors, the ideal citizen of the Turkish Republic (reformist and modernist). The discourse was constructed around notions of civilization, modernization, and nationalism."[27] This ideal citizen wore Western clothes, spoke and read modern Turkish in the Latin script, kept religion in private, and visited sites of cultural and historical significance as a spectacle or an artifact. The ideal marked a change from the intended effect of visiting Hagia Sophia in Byzantine or Ottoman times, when the scale, aesthetics, and acoustics would have reminded the visitor of the divine and the imperial. Now the pilgrims are tourists, observing from a cultivated distance the artifice of the museum. For secularists, Hagia Sophia is emblematic of a composite history that can be archived and controlled.

But if the conversion into a museum appeared to cut Hagia Sophia off from its imperial and religious heritage, Christian and Islamic alike, it has hardly been a definitive transformation. To be sure, some scholars of Hagia Sophia assert that becoming a museum ossified, even killed, its living spirit. Art historian Robert Nelson, for example, argues in an essay on the touristic dimension of the monument that "the reconstitution of the building as a museum and a monument constituted a further break from either its Byzantine or its Ottoman past and marked its demise as a living, social organism."[28] But the Hagia Sophia is clearly alive and speaking to Arınç as well as those who dream of the second conquest or the restoration of Constantinople. And while in the wake of Arınç's November 2013 statement, then prime minister and current president Recep Tayyip Erdoğan refuted any immediate plans to convert Hagia Sophia—saying that the

Figure 7.2. Interior, Hagia Sophia. Photo credit: Anna Bigelow.

neighboring Sultan Ahmet mosque (also known as the Blue Mosque) must first be filled with the faithful to rationalize a change—he has made other comments indicating support for the plan.[29] In August 2015 Culture and Tourism Minister Yalçın Topçu also called for prayer to be allowed in the Hagia Sophia.[30]

The Islamist revival in Turkey has been accompanied by increasingly public challenges to the institutions and symbols of the secular state. Among these symbols, the Hagia Sophia is perhaps most prominent. This is particularly the case among legalistic-minded Islamists, who argue first that the transformation from mosque to museum is existentially impossible (once a mosque, always a mosque) and second that the museumification itself was illegal. For example, a bill introduced in 2013 by an ultranationalist with Islamist roots argued on the latter grounds that the original cabinet decree declaring the Hagia Sophia a museum was released in 1934, but not published in the *Official Gazette* or any other similar official publication. Since the Constitution of 1924 and the current Constitution stipulate that all bills, proposals, or decrees need to be published in the *Official Gazette* after presidential approval in order to be accepted as law, the Hagia Sophia's museum status is illegal.[31] The bill was accompanied by a petition and bolstered by online campaigns gathering tens of thousands of signatures.[32] In recent years, moreover, on the May 30 anniversary of the conquest of Constantinople, ever larger crowds have come to pray outside the Hagia Sophia, hoping for the building's restoration as a mosque.[33] Activists outside of Istanbul, where support for the AKP and other Islamist or ultranationalist parties is strongest, lead many such efforts.

The project of restoring Muslim prayer in Hagia Sophia was advanced to some extent in 1991 when a small series of rooms serving as an entryway to the Sultan's prayer platform (*hünkar mahfili*) were opened for daily prayer (*namaz*).[34] Since 2008 a good deal of restoration work has been done inside the space, with new carpets, a new *minbar*, and a new office for the imam taking shape. Located on the corner of the Hagia Sophia closest to the Topkapı Palace (the hub of Ottoman governance), this space was the passageway that allowed the sultan private entrance to the raised imperial prayer space. Nowadays the midday and afternoon prayers bring together several dozen people from the surrounding area—as well as cab drivers and some tourists—to pray. Friday congregational prayers and *hutbe* (sermons) are full to overflowing with approximately 200 men filling every corner of this asymmetrical, multichambered, and somewhat awkward area. Many Turkish Muslims openly state that since they were the victors in the battle that transformed Constantinople into Istanbul, there should have been no problem in maintaining the structure as a mosque even after the Ottoman Empire fell. Indeed, several Muslim visitors at the Ayasofya to whom I spoke claimed that if the Christians were to retake the region, it would be fully within their rights to make it into a church.

By June 2014 most of the restorations, paid for by private funds, were completed, with the interior made to resemble the space during the time of Abdülmecit I (r. 1839–1861). There is a section of the *kisve* (the cloth that drapes the Ka'ba in Mecca) framed on the wall of the imam's chamber. The ceiling in the last room before the passage opens into the platform on which the sultans would pray has been restored in the style of Abdülmecit I's time. According to the imam, the sultans would wait in this room until the call to prayer was complete and the people had gathered for prayer. As the sultans could not leave their capital city to perform the hajj, the ceiling was painted with images of Mecca and Medina. Nowadays the small central room of the three-chambered passageway is used for women's prayer (except during Friday congregational prayers).

Though this current usage of this space is an innovation, its proponents frame it as a restoration of past practice. Furthermore, it is—at least to some—rationalized as true to the foundational principles of the republic and the true intention of Atatürk himself. One person in attendance at this designated area of the building even claimed that Atatürk opposed cessation of prayers in the Hagia Sophia, but he was sick at the time and the "people in power were completely against Islam and so after his death it [prayer] was stopped."[35] Although the building was closed for prayers in 1934 and Atatürk died in 1938, the argument underscores the complicated way in which Atatürk figures in Islamist discourses in Turkey. For while Atatürk's policies toward religion and religious institutions (e.g., outlawing Sufi orders and the Perso-Arabic script) indicate antipathy toward public religiosity, some Islamists, as Esra Özyürek has argued, still claim Atatürk as their own. Özyürek illustrates this through the images and rhetoric deployed in media linked to Islamist interests. For example, in an editorial marking Republic Day in 1998 the ultrareligious newspaper *Akit* displayed a picture from 1923 of Atatürk praying next to a religious official and accompanied it with text glorifying the military victories that led to the establishment of the republic.[36]

It is true that it was not until April 10, 1928, that the Turkish Republic became officially secular, but this representation of the past clearly serves a more pressing present interest. The appropriation of Atatürk as the founder of a religious nation gives legitimacy to the contemporary quest to bring Islam more into the public sphere. Just as there is a constituency that regards the restoration of a New Byzantium as a desirable and achievable goal, there is another group longing for a New Ottoman Empire, or even a New Caliphate. Proponents of this narrative invoke past glories to critique the present, arguing that Turkey's financial, political, and social problems could all be resolved by Islamic governance. In this regard, Alev Çınar notes, Islamism has taken on the formations of power developed by the secular state.[37] In its vision of the future, Istanbul is conquered again through the reformation of Islam and the overthrow of the secular state. Istanbul is a particularly powerful site for this project: a problematic cosmopolis that is vulnerable, degenerate, and corrupt. In the Islamist sources Çınar examines, "images of Istanbul, depict [. . .] the city as suffering at the hands of corruption, alienation, and degeneration"; according to these Islamist publications and performances, Istanbul has been made open to "penetration and destruction, a place that is defenseless in the face of the modernizing and Westernizing influences of the secular state."[38] For these constituencies, Istanbul's cosmopolitan quality as one of the great contemporary and historic places of cultural, ethnic, and religious mixing is a cause for alarm, not celebration.

Just as such groups seek to capture and "purify" the quintessentially cosmopolitan site of Hagia Sophia, they also claim its environs, like the historic district of Sultanahmet, the main tourist area in Istanbul. As Yusuf Halaçoğlu, who drafted the parliamentary resolution seeking the museum's reinstatement as a mosque, put it: "Hagia Sophia has been standing with the echoes of prayers for 481 years. It is the symbol of the conquest of Istanbul."[39] The argument corroborates a long line of Islamist claims, cited by Çınar, that the Prophet Muhammad had foreseen "that Istanbul would be conquered not once but many times," if "Fatih Sultan Mehmet saved Istanbul by conquering it, [but] who is going to save the people who are sleeping now? This will happen with the second conquest."[40]

The language of conquest marks Hagia Sophia as a symbolic space, ownership of which signals the preeminence of the regime. The proponents of the mosque, as noted, make their case in a variety of forms. One case is based on democratic procedural grounds, noting irregularities in the notice of a parliamentary act. Another case for mosque conversion emanates from theological and ontological claims about mosque status as an eternal designation. Reproducing moreover the imperial and religious rationales for making Hagia Sophia a mosque, such discourses claim that its conversion would herald the actual ascension of the new Turkey to a position of power regionally and globally, without a need to accommodate other imaginaries.

Conclusion

On July 1, 2016, toward the end of the fasting month of Ramadan, the call to prayer was given inside the main body of the Hagia Sophia for the first time in eighty-five years. Two and a half years after Bülent Arınç mourned, "We are looking at a sad Ayasofya now, but hopefully we will see it smiling again soon," it appears that he may not mourn much longer.[41] As this chapter has shown, Arınç was neither the first nor the last to suggest Hagia Sophia should be an active place of worship. Similar invocations—and narratives of resistance—have marked previous transitions in the building's ownership. Today it remains an open question whether Hagia Sophia will be opened for prayer permanently or if the recent rituals were a one-time event. If a lesson is to be drawn from the historical record, however, any change in the building's signification requires an enormous amount of energy to achieve even partial consensus among constituents, much less adversaries, of a particular project. As a layered monument, replete with symbols central to multiple imaginaries of Istanbul-Constantinople, the Hagia Sophia is both quintessentially cosmopolitan and emblematic of the limitations of cosmopolitanism. The disenchanted secular vision of the building as a museum and world heritage site will never be reconciled with the particularistic universalisms of the Islamists or neo-Byzantines. And at each juncture when a change or potential change to the status of the building appears possible due to a power shift in the polity, recurring tropes of empire and divine will be mobilized toward an elusive consensus about what makes Hagia Sophia smile.

NOTES

1. "Deputy PM Signals Conversion to Mosque," *Sunday's Zaman*, November 15, 2013, http://www.todayszaman.com/national_deputy-pm-signals-conversion-of-hagia-sophia-to-mosque_331606.html.

2. "Historic Areas of Istanbul," World Heritage Convention, UNESCO, http://whc.unesco.org/en/list/356.

3. Data cited in Edhem Eldem, "Istanbul as a Cosmopolitan City: Myths and Realities," in *A Companion to Diaspora and Transnationalism*, ed. Ato Quayson and Girish Daswani (Oxford: Blackwell Publishing, 2013), 226 and 228 n11.

4. Tahsin Gökmen, "Ayasofya'da ilk namaz," *Türkiye*, February 12, 1991, 1 and 11.

5. Jane Bennett, *Vibrant Matter: Towards a Political Ecology of Things* (Durham, NC: Duke University Press, 2010).

6. Diana Coole and Samantha Frost, eds., *New Materialisms: Ontology, Agency, and Politics* (Durham, NC: Duke University Press, 2010), 3.

7. Ulrich Beck, "We Do Not Live in an Age of Cosmopolitanism, but an Age of Cosmopolitanisation: The Global 'Other' Is in Our Midst," *Irish Journal of Sociology* 19, no. 1 (2011): 18–19.

8. Gülru Necipoğlu, "The Life of an Imperial Monument: Hagia Sophia after Byzantium," in *Hagia Sophia from the Age of Justinian to the Present*, ed. Robert Mark and Ahmet Çakmak (New York: Cambridge University Press, 1992), 225.

9. See Nora Fisher-Onar, "Echoes of a Universalism Lost: Rival Representations of the Ottomans in Today's Turkey," *Middle East Studies* 45, no. 2 (2009): 229–241.

10. See Edward S. Casey, "How to Get from Space to Place in a Fairly Short Stretch of Time: Phenomenological Prolegomena," in *Senses of Place*, ed. Steven Feld and Keith Basso (Santa Fe, NM: School of American Research Press, 1996), 13–52.

11. For a discussion of "thin" and "thick" values in cosmopolitan theory, see Nora Fisher-Onar and Hande Paker, "Towards Cosmopolitan Citizenship? Women's Rights in Divided Turkey," *Theory and Society* 41, no. 4 (2012): 375–394.

12. David Morgan, "Materiality, Social Analysis, and the Study of Religions," in *Religion and Material Culture: The Matter of Belief*, ed. David Morgan (London; Routledge, 2010), 58.

13. Henri Lefebvre, *The Production of Space* (New York: Wiley-Blackwell, 1991), 225.

14. Berin F. Gür, "Spatialisation of Power/Knowledge/Discourse: Transformation of Urban Space through Discursive Representations in Sultanahmet, Istanbul," *Space and Culture* 5, no. 3, (2002): 243.

15. Gülru Necipoğlu, "The Life of an Imperial Monument: Hagia Sophia after Byzantium," in *Hagia Sophia from the Age of Justinian to the Present*, ed. Robert Mark and Ahmet Çakmak (New York: Cambridge University Press, 1992), 212.

16. Ibid., 200.

17. Samiha Ayverdi, *Ah Tuna vah Tuna (Oh Danube, Oh Danube)*, trans. Yekta Zülfikar (Istanbul: Kubbealtı Neshriyati, [1990] 1996), 227–228.

18. Marios Philippides, "Tears of the Great Church: The Lamentation of Santa Sophia," *Greek, Roman, and Byzantine Studies* 52 (2012): 724.

19. Necipoğlu, "The Life of an Imperial Monument," 208.

20. Philippides, "Tears of the Great Church," 735.

21. Ibid., 717.

22. An example of such efforts is the website of Chris Spirou, at http://www.freeagiasophia.org/. The Free Agia Sophia Council of America's declared mission is "to restore the great church of Agia Sophia located in Istanbul (Constantinople), Turkey, as a functioning church of the Orthodox Christian faith, and to re-establish Agia Sophia as the Holy House of Prayer for all Christians of the world and the Basilica (Seat) of Orthodoxy that it was before the conquest of Constantinople by the Ottoman Turks in 1453 AD." The site has been taken down since I referenced it, but others not unlike it appear all the time. Most English-language sites seem to emerge from the United States.

23. Theodore G. Karakostas, *In the Shadow of Hagia Sophia* (n.p.: Author, 2013), 5.

24. "Hagia Sophia: The Mother Church," http://www.newbyzantines.net/byzcathculture/hagiasophia_mc.html.

25. Statement by the Greek Ministry for Foreign Affairs, November 18, 2013, http://www.mfa.gr/en/current-affairs/statements-speeches/foreign-ministry-spokespersons-response-to-statements-from-turkish-officials-regarding-the-conversion-of-hagia-sophia-into-mosque.html.

26. Thomas Whittemore, letter of application for funds to continue restoration work of Hagia Sophia, March 30, 1950, Dumbarton Oaks archive.

27. Gür, "Spatialisation of Power/Knowledge/Discourse," 248.

28. Robert S. Nelson, "Tourists, Terrorists, and Metaphysical Theater at Hagia Sophia," in *Monuments and Memory, Made and Unmade*, ed. Robert S. Nelson and Margaret Olin (Chicago: University of Chicago Press, 2003), 74.

29. "PM Erdoğan Planning Prayers with Islamic Leaders at Hagia Sophia," *Hürriyet Daily News*, April 29, 2014, http://www.hurriyetdailynews.com/pm-erdogan-planning-prayers-with-islamic-leaders-in-hagia-sophia.aspx?PageID=238&NID=65717&NewsCatID=338.

30. "Yalçın Topçu Ayasfoyanın Acılması icin Garakete Geçti," *Yeni Akit*, August 31, 2015, http://www.yeniakit.com.tr/haber/yalcin-topcu-ayasofyanin-acilmasi-icin-harekete-gecti-90203.html.

31. "Turkey's Nationalist Party Seeks Prayers in Hagia Sophia," *Hürriyet Daily News*, November 9, 2013, http://www.hurriyetdailynews.com/turkeys-nationalist-party-seeks-prayers-in-the-hagia-sophia.aspx?PageID=238&NID=57632&NewsCatID=338.

32. "Özgür Ayasofya için İmza Kampanyası," *Risale Haber*, May 22, 2014, http://www.risalehaber.com/ozgur-ayasofya-icin-imza-kampanyasi-210600h.htm.

33. "Thousands Perform Morning Prayer Near Hagia Sophia, Call for Its Reopening as a Mosque," *Today's Zaman*, May 31, 2015, http://www.todayszaman.com/anasayfa_thousands-perform-morning-prayer-near-hagia-sophia-call-for-its-reopening-as-mosque_382166.html.

34. It was also opened briefly in 1980 during a period of coalition government between Islamist and nationalist parties, but it closed again after the military coup in that year.

35. Interview by author with visitor to Hagia Sophia's mosque section, June 19, 2009.

36. Esra Özyürek, *Nostalgia for the Modern: State Secularism and Everyday Politics in Turkey* (Durham, NC: Duke University Press, 2006), 158.

37. Alev Çınar, *Modernity, Islam, and Secularism in Turkey: Bodies, Places, and Time*, vol. 14 (Minneapolis: University of Minnesota Press, 2005), 30.

38. Ibid., 165.

39. "Plans for Hagia Sophia Stir Debate," *SETimes.com*, http://www.setimes.com/cocoon/setimes/xhtml/en_GB/features/setimes/features/2013/11/27/feature-03.

40. Çınar, *Modernity, Islam, and Secularism*, 165.

41. Agence France Press, "Greece and Turkey Feud over Hagia Sophia," *Daily Star*, Beirut, November 20, 2013, http://www.dailystar.com.lb/News/Middle-East/2013/Nov-20/238455-turkey-and-greece-feud-over-hagia-sophia.ashx.

PART III

Actually Existing Conviviality

SHARING SPACE IN A GLOBALIZING CITY

CHAPTER 8

Living Together in Ambivalence in a Migrant Neighborhood of Istanbul

Kristen Sarah Biehl

Today, as for centuries, Istanbul's historical peninsula stands at the heart of immense and highly diverse flows of peoples. A short trip through several of the tram stations cutting across the center of the peninsula offers a window onto this diversity. Arriving at the Beyazıt-Grand Bazaar tram station, one leaves behind most of the thousands of tourists from all corners of the world flocking to the historical palaces, mosques, and bazaars of the Eminönü and Sultanahmet districts. On a weekday and around rush hours, many of the men getting off here and turning right onto the hills of Gedikpaşa are likely to be working in the hundreds of small garment and apparel workshops hidden within the many buildings in the area. The ateliers are audible on the streets through the cacophony of sewing machines and hammers molding shoes. One station further on, at Laleli-Üniversite, Turkish and foreign students will cross to the right of Ordu Avenue, rushing off to class at Istanbul's oldest university, dating back to the fifteenth century. Eager traders from Eurasia, the Middle East, and Africa will cross to the left, venturing into the wholesale retail district of Laleli, where the breadth and colors of product displays and advertisements exhaust the eyes both horizontally and vertically. Go one station further to the Aksaray station, which adjoins the densely trafficked Atatürk Boulevard, and one will see many commuters and travelers hopping on or off the tram, as this is the location of one of the two main transport arteries of a megacity of some 15 million people. The second such hub, Yenikapı Marmaray station, opened in 2013, is the first underground transport system to connect the European and Asian continents, contentiously built over the remains of the Byzantine Theodosius harbor.

Nested within this commotion and facing the Marmara Sea, where dozens of freighter ships wait docked for their turn to pass through the Bosphorus strait and on to the Black Sea, lies the neighborhood of Kumkapı.[1] The district has come to serve a somewhat different function than its neighboring localities, which cater primarily to tourists, traders, and workers. Today Kumkapı has emerged as a central residential hub for a great diversity of international migrants who have come to Istanbul with the intention of staying and/or working, seeking asylum, or transiting to a third country.[2] In this process, housing practices in Kumkapı have been evolving to accommodate the distinct demography and needs of these migrant populations, most notably in the form of room rentals and shared housing. As a result, it has become a place where residents, both longer settled ones and newcomers, must confront differences regularly within close public quarters and the privacy of home. Based on ethnographic research on housing practices and experiences, this chapter analyzes how Kumkapı residents experience this process of living together with differences.

Contexts such as Kumkapı are not an exception in a contemporary world where migration and urbanization are leading to new, intensified forms of diversity.[3] In the past decade this pattern has spurred growing academic interest in exploring how people adopt and respond to, or as more popularly expressed, "live with," differences in contexts in which diverse groups reside in close proximity. A number of terms bearing family resemblances have been coined to describe these experiences. Gilroy, for one, expands on the notion of conviviality to describe "the processes of cohabitation and interaction that have made multiculture an ordinary feature of social life in Britain's urban areas and in postcolonial cities elsewhere."[4] In a similar vein, Wise and Valeyutham, as well as Neal et al., speak of an everyday multiculturalism/multiculture approach to identify the ways that people routinely manage interactions and relations in multicultural environments.[5] A separate but related strand of literature is that of scholars working with the concept of cosmopolitanism. The notion can be used to describe ordinary people's everyday openness and practical competence in bridging boundaries with those who are different from them, especially in localized work/trade/commercial relations. Analysis is often framed in terms such as "ordinary,"[6] "strategic,"[7] "tactical,"[8] and "corner-shop"[9] cosmopolitanism.

A shared aspect of most of this literature is that while it examines ways of constructively living together despite differences, there is also recognition that diverse social realities are defined by ambivalence. Positive encounters and daily courtesies among groups do not necessarily imply an appreciation of differences or even a neutral or careless stance. This is especially apparent if attitudes are shaped by pragmatism, such as the need to maintain commercial interests, avoid conflict, or just get on with day-to-day life.[10] Everyday local encounters and relationships can be characterized at the same time by boundary crossing, friendly reception, and solidarities, as well as by boundary maintenance, intimidation, and violence.[11]

My ethnographic research in Kumkapı affirms the presence of this ambivalence in the ways that differences are accommodated today. Similar to Karner and Parker's findings in their study of relations between residents and entrepreneurs in a deprived inner-city area of Birmingham, Great Britain, I describe how Kumkapı is a space defined by a series of "co-existing and intersecting ambivalences [that] defy clear-cut taxonomies of localities, communities (or even individuals) as either cohesive/integrated or not."[12]

However, in contrast to the various literatures cited above that focus on commercial and public spaces, I reflect on ambivalence within the private spaces of housing, which is rarely recognized as a space in which conviviality and cosmopolitanism take shape. I begin by introducing this study's methodology, then trace the different factors leading to Kumkapı's gradual emergence as a residential neighborhood for migrants of diverse backgrounds. Two ethnographic sections exploring housing practices follow. In the first, I show the ways in which Kumkapı welcomes migrants' differences and needs that are not as admissible elsewhere in the city. The second section reveals how boundary making and exclusion nevertheless also run deep in Kumkapı, as reflected in examples of highly discriminatory housing practices related to gender and race. In the concluding section I draw these two aspects together and discuss implications for understanding how ambivalence informs convivial living and cosmopolitan openness.

Methodology

This chapter is an outcome of a larger doctoral research project for which I carried out ethnographic fieldwork in Kumkapı over a period of fifteen months (from August 2012 to October 2013). As part of this research, I applied a combination of methods, including socio-spatial mapping of the locality (i.e., differences in physical structure and use), as well as extensive informal discussions and semistructured interviews with more than eighty people of varying national, ethnic, religious, and gender backgrounds living and working in the locality. I spoke with them about their migration motives and histories, housing experiences, and everyday lives in Istanbul. Also, for a period of six months, from March to August 2013, I rented a small room in an apartment building offering room rentals in shared flats to migrants. This housing complex became the primary site of my participant observations in Kumkapı, and some of its residents became my closest informants. During fieldwork I kept daily field notes on activities and observations. All interviews were recorded and transcribed. Field notes and transcripts were then coded for aspects related to sense of place, local economic practices, discourses of social differentiation, housing use practices, and neighborly relations. The data I have used in this chapter are based primarily on these transcripts.

Setting the Stage: From a Minority Quarter to a Migrant Hub

For several centuries Kumkapı remained a residential, religious, and educational center of the Greek and Armenian citizens of the Ottoman state, then the Turkish Republic. The many churches and minority schools located in the area make this evident, though only a few remain active. After the 1950s the demographic profile of Kumkapı began changing due to forces that similarly affected other minority quarters of Istanbul.[13] In the face of discriminatory state policies and growing nationalistic public hostility, this is the period during which large segments of the religious minority populations of Kumkapı emigrated abroad. The exodus was matched by major rural immigration to Istanbul due to a decline in agriculture and the rise of urban industrialization. Hence as minority populations steadily emigrated, their neighborhoods throughout Istanbul began transforming into points of arrival and settlement for internal migrants. In Kumkapı's neighboring districts the spread of commercial businesses also had a key impact in instigating this change: after the mid-1960s, Gedikpaşa rapidly emerged as a central node of small-scale shoe manufacturers and traders,[14] while automotive-related galleries, spare-part, and repair shops opened up across Laleli.[15] In the face of such changes, settled residents of these old districts were drawn to the newly developing middle-class areas, while for incoming internal migrants, commercialization in the area was attractive, implying availability and proximity of jobs.[16] To this day, both housing availability and accessibility of economic opportunities have remained important pull factors for the continuous flows of internal migrants arriving in Kumkapı. Yet the profile of these migrants has changed in terms of regional origin, ethnic composition, migration motive, and local reception, in parallel with changes in larger patterns of internal migrations to Istanbul.

In recent decades Kumkapı also has become a significant destination for international migrants and a center for transnational activities, especially in commerce. The radical transformation in the neighboring Laleli district from the late 1970s onward in the face of new economic opportunities, catering initially to Arab tourists and traders,[17] then to "suitcase traders" from Russia,[18] is very likely to have been the initial trigger for the arrival of foreigners in the surrounding area, whether as tourists, traders, customers, or migrants. Today Laleli remains a significant marketplace for cross-border trading, while the customer profile has greatly diversified from the previous predominance of Russians to include many countries in the Caucuses and Central Asia, and increasingly more in the Middle East and Africa. Moreover, an ever-escalating number of foreigners are integrated into the Laleli economy and its manufacturing counterpart in Gedikpaşa, not just as traders, but in a plethora of job opportunities such as menial worker, sales assistant, or transnational broker.

While these transformations have been taking place in the surrounding area, Kumkapı has emerged as the residential counterpart. In the past decade in particular, given the increasing arrival of migrant populations in Kumkapı, housing has become highly commercialized and adapted to the conditions and needs of such people. With increasing demand, an ever-growing number of both landlords and tenants have engaged in the practice of letting and subletting rooms in their own households, and even in sheds, in basements, or on rooftops. Some buildings are fully refurbished for these purposes, with flats converted into studio rooms with shared kitchen/bathroom facilities. The density of this housing type is very high, as several people often share single rooms. The turnover of people is also extremely rapid, as most do not arrive with the intention of settling.

In parallel with the housing market, Kumkapı's service economy has been transforming. Because of the density of the resident population and high turnover rate, the number of supermarkets, real estate offices, and secondhand furniture shops is much higher than what would be expected in an average residential neighborhood of this scale elsewhere in Istanbul. Many foreign migrants have started establishing their own businesses as well, including dozens of country- and region-specific cargo shipping companies established to serve suitcase traders, as well as ethnic restaurants and hairdressers. A notable aspect is that most business practices in Kumkapı are characterized by informality, in two senses: they are often only partially licensed if at all, and they provide informal employment opportunities for migrants.

As an outcome of these decades-long overlapping processes of migration and urban change, Kumkapı stands out as one of the most diverse residential neighborhoods of present-day Istanbul in terms of both population composition and settlement patterns. The "locals"—meaning those who are territorially rooted in and are citizens of the Turkish state—include a small number of ethnic Greek, Armenian, and Assyrian Christian minorities, ethnic Turks who came to the area during the 1960s and 1970s at the peak of rural-to-urban migrations, ethnic Kurds, and to a lesser extent ethnic Arabs, as migrant arrivals during the 1990s. Foreign nationals have also been arriving in Kumkapı in increasing numbers since the 1990s and have greatly intensified this already-existing local diversity. They come from a wide range of countries: from Moldova to Uzbekistan in Eurasia, Somalia to Nigeria in Africa, and Syria to Sri Lanka in the Middle East and Asia. In addition to their ethnic, national, and religious backgrounds, both the native and foreign populations of Kumkapı are differentiated along lines such as migration motive and channel, gender, age, family composition, legal status and entitlement, and labor opportunities, among other characteristics. Finally, it is notable that a great majority of the foreign nationals can be described as being irregular migrants with respect to entry, residence, and/or work status under Turkish laws. In the following sections I focus primarily on the experiences of Kumkapı's migrant foreigners.

Inclusive and Flexible Accommodation

As noted previously, in recent decades Kumkapı has been drawing increasingly more diverse groups of international migrants, having gained a reputation as a place that is welcoming to foreigners. This allows the formation of subcommunities and solidarity networks vital to survival in the city. The stories of several denizens are illustrative. Hasan came from Guinea to Istanbul in 2006 as a seventeen-year-old. He arrived in the central Taksim district, where he was left by his smuggler and told to approach the office of the United Nations High Commissioner for Refugees (UNHCR) to file a refugee application. Due to his age, he was immediately placed in a state-run shelter for unaccompanied minor asylum seekers in Istanbul, located in the Kadıköy district on the Asian side of the city. When he was about to turn eighteen, however, the shelter staff told him that he would have to find his own housing and advised him to visit Kumkapı. There, he was told, he would find "people of his own kind," implying other foreigners, and African nationals/persons of color in particular.

Yıldız and her husband Kamil, who moved from Turkmenistan to Istanbul six years before this study, came to Kumkapı on similar grounds. Initially, they stayed with relatives living in the Zeytinburnu district of Istanbul, but following some visits with other acquaintances living in Kumkapı they noticed from walking on the streets that, in contrast, being a stranger was the norm there: "Zeytinburnu is like a village, everyone knows each other and looks at you because you are a foreigner. Here we are comfortable, everyone is foreign so no one looks at you." As indicated by this comment, the extent of diversity in Kumkapı provides migrants with a sense of anonymity and normalcy compared to other parts of the city, where they are otherwise reminded of their outsider position. These are desirable experiences given the irregular legal status of most migrants in the neighborhood. In another discussion with Yıldız, who has remained in Turkey undocumented for over three years, I asked whether she had any concerns about encountering authorities in Kumkapı, and she replied, "No, because anyhow everyone here is *kaçak* [illegal]."

What draws migrants to Kumkapı is also the fact that here they can more easily access housing, which has evolved in a way that responds to the differences and needs of migrants. The migrant populations in Kumkapı bring with them varying demographic traits. Most often they are solo travelers like Hasan; they are rarely couples or extended families. There are also significant variations in the gender and age composition of different national groups, as well as marked racial distinctions. Due to established cultural beliefs in Turkey about protecting family honor and popular prejudices that have emerged against migrant others, especially if one is single and a foreigner, one's chances of being offered housing in other districts of Istanbul are lower. In Kumkapı, however, such barriers are less significant, though not entirely irrelevant, as discussed further in the following section. An exemplary marker of this is the rental advertisements in

Kumkapı that specify property being made available to these groups, as in *bekar için oda* (room for bachelor), *bayana oda* (room for woman), and *yabancıya oda* (room for foreigner).

Besides incorporating such demographic differences, Kumkapı also has emerged as a place that accommodates differences in housing usage. As suggested by the rental advertisements cited, this is evident in the increasingly more popular practice of room rentals, wherein homeowners either rent out one or more rooms in their households while still living there or rent out all the rooms to different individuals. Shared housing among migrants with a similar national/ethnic background is also popular, particularly after longer periods of stay in Kumkapı, when people have enlarged their social networks. Most migrants residing in Kumkapı see their stay as only temporary and functional, like Yıldız and Kamil, who came to Istanbul with the intention to save enough money to build a new house and make investments in Turkmenistan, where their child also awaits them. Similarly, Hasan was waiting for finalization of his asylum application, which if approved could lead to his resettlement in a third country.

Given these motives, room rentals and shared housing offer opportunities that are vital to migrants' survival in Istanbul. First, rent is charged per room rather than for an entire flat, which both makes rent more affordable and allows for savings. At the time we met in the spring of 2013, Yıldız and Kamil were making close to 2,000 Turkish liras (TL) a month in salary through domestic and textile work and paid 350 TL for rent. Living in a shared household allowed them to accumulate substantial savings, and they had already succeeded in building their house in Turkmenistan. Second, there is more flexibility regarding tenancy arrangements, as long as rent is being paid. For Hasan and his four other Guinean housemates, having more freedom in determining who comes, stays, and goes was a feature they greatly valued. This was partly about decreasing their share of the rent, though there was also a strong solidarity aspect in that they could accommodate friends and acquaintances in need of a temporary place to stay. Another aspect of the flexibility of shared housing in Kumkapı is the freedom to vacate on very short notice. Demand for rooms in Kumkapı is so high that landlords and lead tenants have little concern about finding replacements; hence rental contracts are rarely signed. In my own flat, the rooms vacated were usually reoccupied within one day.

I was a neighbor to Yıldız and Kamil in the five-room flat we all shared. They were the longest-term tenants, having moved in some two years before when the building was refurbished to accommodate more room shares. I observed the couple as being quite friendly and proactive in neighborly relations, especially with those coming from the same geographic region. They would regularly socialize at dinner or afterward with other neighbors in the flat coming from Uzbekistan and Azerbaijan. They were also friendly to other neighbors. Yıldız sometimes visited and chatted with the Sri Lankan woman living on a room built on the rooftop. She also would greet the Ugandan woman living upstairs, though language barriers did not permit further conversation. Yıldız joked that Kamil was the *muhtar* of the apartment building, the Turkish term for an elected neighborhood official, as the landlord would ask Kamil to keep an eye on people in the building when he was away.

For Yıldız, "cleanliness" was the main criterion on which she distinguished between and approved of people. A new Uzbek couple had moved in while I was away temporarily. When I returned Yıldız commented: "She is a very clean woman, she uses *ACE* everywhere" (ACE is a brand of bleach). Similarly, when talking about a Senegalese woman who had lived in my room before and had to move out after a violent dispute with a Turkish man living across the hall, Yıldız commented: "She was actually really clean. She wouldn't use a mop but would sit on the floor to clean the floors with a cloth."

Another criterion for Yıldız's approval was not bringing in too many strangers, especially boyfriends or girlfriends. A single Uzbek woman moved into my flat toward the end of my tenancy. A couple of weeks later she started having a male companion stay overnight, who was a Kurdish man she had met locally. The news quickly reached the landlord, who demanded either that she stop this practice or move out. As reflected in the example of this flat, private spaces of housing are equally significant sites of encounter and negotiation of differences. In this case, convivial living was made possible through a shared understanding about respecting cleanliness and privacy/honor of individuals and families.

Drawing and Ordering Boundaries

In the previous section I explained how Kumkapı can be seen as a place that is welcoming toward differences, citing the example of migrants' flexible access to housing. However, differences are not entirely overlooked. There is a strong gendered dimension to being a *yabancı* (foreigner) in Kumkapı. In Turkey, migrant women, especially those from the former Soviet Union, have for a long time been overrepresented in the entertainment and sex work sectors.[19] The districts of Laleli, as well as neighboring Yenikapı and Aksaray, were the historic centers of this trade and largely remain so. Even for the foreign women who do not engage in prostitution per se, intimate engagements with Turkish/ Kurdish men are popular, and romantic and economic motives are often enmeshed.[20] This has a strong impact on the experiences of migrant women living in Kumkapı, who are perceived by locals as promiscuous.

This is an aspect that gives added meaning to the emphasis on having *bayan* (women) occupy rental rooms. Today in Kumkapı the preference for women as tenants is embedded in, or does not preclude, the desire to pursue them for romantic and sexual relations. In turn, there are women who willingly enter into such relations. For some this is strategic, a way to have their rent paid, while for others it involves genuine romantic interest. For still others both motives apply. As a result, Kumkapı has gained a reputation as a space where such relations can take place in an otherwise conservative society. When I asked a close informant, a Kurdish man from the city of Batman in southeastern Turkey who runs a phone shop, whether this was actually a common local practice, he replied, "it's all over the place." As an example, he mentioned a man he knows who lives in a three-bedroom flat across the street, keeping one room to himself and renting out the other two. "No one lasts longer than two months" he joked, "because either he hits on them or walks around naked." Another informant, a Kurdish man from Diyarbakir, who rents two rooms in his flat, frequently boasted to me about his success in getting to sleep with his female tenants and once used a derogatory term to describe "all these 'Russians' who one day," he contended, "will look at you, while the next day they have someone else behind the door."[21]

Due to such perceptions, sexual harassment is a daily occurrence with which migrant women dwelling in Kumkapı must cope. I was visiting the home of Mehtap, an Uzbek woman in her thirties living with her young son from her first marriage. Soon after my arrival our conversation was interrupted by a phone call from her landlord, who lived with his family in another neighborhood but kept a room upstairs from her. He said he wanted to talk to her and asked her to come up. She was wearing a long, sleeveless dress and wore a T-shirt on top to cover her chest; she headed upstairs, looking annoyed. When she came back shortly afterward, she explained: "He wants us to vacate the house. He says 'you didn't fulfill my request.' I lived in Russia for one year and the Russians are also dirty people but never have I seen a place like Turkey. I mean they look at you in such a way like you are a whore." Only a week later Mehtap moved out, as she was eager to get away from his persistent harassment. The case of Mehtap reveals how unequal relations between landlords and tenants also become a site of managing and negotiating differences.

Race is another significant register of differentiation in present-day Kumkapı. Hasan explains: "It was very hard for us to find housing when we first came. We spent over a month to find this place, we went to different real estate agents but when they see you are black they say no, or they ask for payment in dollars. What you find has really bad conditions or is too expensive." Natives and foreigners alike in Kumkapı who distinguish themselves as "white" use the Turkish expression *zenci*, which in Turkish slang denotes a person of black color, when speaking about migrants from the African continent, or darker skinned migrants from Pakistan, Bangladesh, and Sri Lanka. Among this "white" population, there is a common tendency to associate being *zenci* with filth. Underlying this is partly a more universal racism, in which filth is attributed to mere skin color, but it is also associated with differences in certain cultural attributes, such as food consumption and language communication practices. When I moved into my flat, one of the first persons I met was the Turkish man who lived in a corner room alone. He was a friend of the landlord and in charge of renting rooms in the flat. He complained extensively about the Senegalese woman who had previously lived in my room: "The bathroom walls became all black when they were living there." A presumed primitiveness of life in the African continent also feeds these perceptions of filth. The same Turkish man noted: "My blood never warmed up to Africans, spitting on the stairs and stuff. They are really dirty. They live there in tin homes, do their toilet outside and throw dirt on it, here of course it seems like heaven to them." As recounted in the previous section, my other neighbor Yıldız did not share this opinion at all, saying the woman was very clean. She believed that the real matter of dispute was different: "I heard that he hit on her and tried touching her, but she refused." While these two opposing narratives suggest different causes behind the departure of the Senegalese woman from the flat, what is interesting, as in Mehtap's comment above, is the way that themes of "filth" and "cleanliness," referring to both physical and moral qualities, are commonly used in drawing boundaries.

The dialogue below also invokes highly discriminatory discourses. I overheard this exchange during an interview with a real estate agent at his office when a Senegalese man walked in.

> SENEGALESE MAN (SM): *Selamun aleyküm* (Turkish/Muslim greeting). Did you find a house?
>
> REAL-ESTATE AGENT (RA): No. I haven't.
>
> SM: You told me the other day to come back tomorrow.
>
> RA: I said come by once in a while. Really, I don't have anything now but I am saying something will come up. You know, not every house can work for *you.*[22] Either it has to be a basement, or an individual house. All buildings say we don't want them. Families are afraid of you.
>
> SM: Why are they afraid?
>
> RA: Because you are barbarians, you talk too loud. You cook and it smells very bad. Is this right?

The discussion continued for a little longer, and I will return to it in the conclusion of this chapter. After the Senegalese man left, I asked the real estate agent why Africans are always the ones given basement flats. He replied:

> RA: When you say basement perhaps there is an aspect you are missing. Now if a person lives in a basement, he walks straight away downstairs. His voice will not go upstairs and he will not run into people. Because it is usually upper floors where families live.

Besides the racial and cultural stereotypes, what is also notable in this dialogue is the way that socially produced differences permeate the urban fabric through the physical ordering of space, which in apartment blocs is reflected in a sort of vertical hierarchy in tenancy.

CONCLUSION

Conviviality and cosmopolitanism are terms that are most often associated with the commercial and public spaces of global cities, where diverse people are more inclined to interact with one another,[23] as opposed to "communalism in the home."[24] In this chapter I have shown that the private sphere of housing is equally affected by migration and the diversification to which it gives rise as are public spaces, since residents must live with and negotiate differences with their flatmates, neighbors, and landlords. The case of Kumkapı illustrates how everyday convivial relations in houses and buildings are maintained through developing shared understandings, such as physical cleanliness and respect for privacy. At the same time though, deep-seated prejudices toward the "other" are widespread, as illustrated with regard to gendered and racial difference. Such biases are often informed by and directly impact housing practices.

It is possible to argue that in today's Kumkapı differences are accommodated mainly for pragmatic purposes. For most residents and business owners, there is a shared interest in maintaining diversity in the locality. As one of the neighborhood authorities said to me: "Here it has become like a trade center; for the local population the foreigners are profit. That is why they ignore them. The foreigners are also content. From here they find work, money. . . . While having no house or income back in their country, in three or four years here they become rich and can invest there." Pragmatism is also reflected in the prevailing patterns of social relations across groups, which is one of minimizing encounters to daily courtesies. When I asked Hasan who his neighbors were in the building, he said: "We don't know each other. Everyone minds his or her own business. If we meet in the stairways we greet each other, that is really it."

Does pragmatic openness then imply that Kumkapı residents are in fact intolerant or don't have any empathy toward differences? In "Cosmopolitans and Locals in World Culture," Ulf Hannerz presented one of the first anthropological engagements with cosmopolitanism, a definition that echoes through much contemporary ethnographic work. In Hannerz's account, tourists, migrants, and refugees are lumped together as "fake cosmopolitans" for whom "often the involvement with another culture is not a fringe benefit but a necessary cost, to be kept as low as possible."[25] In turn, he described a "genuine cosmopolitanism" as "a willingness to engage with the Other. It is an intellectual and aesthetic stance of openness toward divergent cultural experiences."[26] Hannerz's categorization has since been countered by many scholars, who have exposed the ways that ordinary people living and working in multicultural/multiethnic settings display everyday pragmatic openness and practical competence in bridging boundaries with people who are different from them.[27] "Openness" as an attribute of the cosmopolitan disposition has also come under scrutiny. As Noble states, "'openness to otherness' doesn't tell us much; such openness can only begin an encounter, it is not the encounter itself."[28] Similarly, Glick-Schiller et al. argue that "openness" should not necessarily imply a welcoming or celebration of cultural and other differences, but rather a focus on "experiential commonalities despite difference."[29]

In Kumkapı, as I have aimed to show, the experiential commonality is that living together amid such diversity is an ambivalent process. This was a feeling that most residents I met in Kumkapı harbored. For migrant inhabitants, regardless of background, Kumkapı was a place where they said they could find comfort, security, and solidarity with people of similar backgrounds. In the case of housing, it is also a liberating space enabling accommodation of differences and needs not as readily addressed in the wider city. On the other hand, Kumkapı is also a place where migrants said they encountered threatening and demeaning forms of exclusion. As illustrated, such stances seep into both everyday discourses about different migrant groups in the locality and the physical ordering of space. Kumkapı, as such, is far from being a place where multicultural living is celebrated. Boundary making is strong, whether due to ethnicity, as in the case of the local Kurdish and Armenian population, or to the "illegal" status of foreign migrants. It can, moreover, take violent forms, given deprivation, the competition for resources, and marginalization from the larger society.

In the previous section I narrated a dialogue between a real estate agent and a Senegalese man who was looking for a rental room, which ended with a derogatory statement citing food preferences as a reason that local families don't want Africans in their buildings. That dialogue continued:

SM: Everyone has different tastes: Chinese food is different; Senegalese food is different.

RA: Well yes, yours is good for you, tastier for you. Ours tastes better for us.

SM: We have many problems like this. We are given rental homes and we pay for it. Then friends come for a visit and we aren't allowed to talk. I am here four years and there is a difference. Three years I was in one house and had no such problems. There are good people here and there are bad.

As this exchange shows, the real estate agent's demeaning stereotypes were tempered, at the end of the exchange, with an acknowledgment of relativity. And while I would have expected the Senegalese man to walk out in response to such statements, he stayed in the room for some time, sensing perhaps (or having heard from others) that this realtor was nevertheless helpful in finding housing for black persons. In Kumkapı, even as exclusionary discourses loom large there is room for discussion, and individual attributes may be recognized over stereotypes. I argue that it is these daily encounters and their ambivalent openness that also makes convivial living possible, as it is through this process that individuals continuously engage and question the ethics, capacities, and resources for tackling difference in everyday life.

NOTES

1. Kumkapı, like the names of neighboring Laleli and Gedikpaşa, is a historical district name that is known and used more commonly in place of the official neighborhood names. These districts roughly encompass the following administrative neighborhood units: Kumkapı (Katip Kasım, lower part of Nişanca, and Muhsine Hatun), Gedikpaşa (Mimar Hayrettin), and Laleli (Mesih Paşa, Mimar Kemalettin, upper part of Nişanca, and Saraç İshak).

2. Kristen Biehl, "Spatializing Diversities, Diversifying Space: Housing Experiences in a Migrant Hub of Istanbul," *Ethnic and Racial Studies* 38, no. 4 (2015): 596–607.

3. Steven Vertovec, *Diversities Old and New: Migration and Socio-Spatial Patterns in New York, Singapore and Johannesburg* (Basingstoke, UK: Palgrave Macmillan, 2015); and Mette Berg and Nando Sigona, "Ethnography, Diversity and Urban Space," *Identities* 20, no. 4: 347–360.

4. Paul Gilroy, *After Empire: Melancholia or Convivial Culture?* (London: Routledge, 2004), xi. See also Nowicka, Magdalena and Steven Vertovec. "Comparing Convivialities: Dreams and Realities of Living-with-Difference." *European Journal of Cultural Studies* 17, no. 4 (2014): 341–356.

5. Amanda Wise and Salvaraj Valeyutham, eds., *Everyday Multiculturalism* (Basingstoke, UK: Palgrave Macmillan, 2009); and Sarah Neal, Katty Bennet, Allan Cochrane, and Giles Mohan. "Living Multiculture: Understanding the New Spatial and Social Relations of Ethnicity and Multiculture in England," *Environment and Planning C* 31 (2013): 308–323.

6. Michele Lamont and Sada Aksartova, "Ordinary Cosmopolitanisms: Strategies for Bridging Racial Boundaries among Working Class Men," *Theory, Culture and Society* 19, no. 4 (2002): 1–25.

7. Craig Jeffrey and Colin McFarlane, "Performing Cosmopolitanism," *Environment and Planning D: Society and Space* 26 (2008): 420–427.

8. Loren Landau and Iriann Fremantle, "Tactical Cosmopolitanism and Idioms of Belonging: Insertion and Self-Exclusion in Johannesburg," *Journal of Ethnic and Migration Studies* 36, no. 3 (2010): 375–390.

9. Susanne Wessendorf, *Commonplace Diversity: Social Relations in a Super-diverse Context* (Basingstoke, UK: Palgrave Macmillan, 2015).

10. Jennifer Lee, *Civility in the City: Blacks, Jews, and Koreans in Urban America* (Cambridge, MA, and London: Harvard University Press, 2002); Wessendorf, *Commonplace Diversity*; and Gill Valentine, "Living with Difference: Reflections on Geographies of Encounter," *Progress in Human Geography* 32 (2008): 323–337.

11. Christian Karner and David Parker, "Conviviality and Conflict: Pluralism, Resilience and Hope in Inner-City Birmingham," *Journal of Ethnic and Migration Studies* 37, no. 3 (2011): 355–372; Loren Landau, "Conviviality, Rights and Conflict in Africa's Urban Estuaries," *Politics and Society* 42, no. 3 (2014): 359–380; and Darshan Vigneswaran, "Protection and Conviviality: Community Policing in Johannesburg," *European Journal of Cultural Studies* 17 (2014): 471–486.

12. Karner and Parker, "Conviviality and Conflict," 366.

13. Amy Mills, *Streets of Memory: Landscape, Tolerance, and National Identity in Istanbul* (Athens: University of Georgia Press, 2010).

14. Berna G. Müftüoğlu, *Fason Ekonomisi: Gedikpaşa'da Ayakkabı Üretimi* (Istanbul: Bağlam Yayıncılık, 2005).

15. Çağlar Keyder, "A Tale of Two Neighborhoods," in *Istanbul: Between the Global and the Local*, ed. Çağlar Keyder (Lanham, MD: Rowman & Littlefield, 1999), 173–187.

16. Çağlar Keyder, "Globalization and Social Exclusion in Istanbul," *International Journal of Urban and Regional Research*, 29, no. 1 (2005): 124–134.

17. Keyder, "A Tale of Two Neighborhoods."

18. Deniz Yükseker, "Trust and Gender in a Transnational Market: The Public Culture of Laleli, Istanbul," *Public Culture* 16, no. 1 (2004): 47–65.

19. Leyla Gülcur and Pınar İlkkaracan, "The 'Natasha' Experience: Migrant Sex Workers from the Former Soviet Union in Turkey," in *Deconstructing Sexuality in the Middle East: Challenges and Discourses*, ed. Pınar İlkkaracan (London: Ashgate, 2002), 199–215.

20. Yükseker, "Trust and Gender"; and Alexia Bloch, "Intimate Circuits: Modernity, Migration and Marriage among Post-Soviet Women in Turkey," *Global Networks* 11, no. 4 (2011): 502–521.

21. During my fieldwork I did not meet any Russian nationals living in Kumkapı. However, locally the term "Russian" is actually used in reference to nationals of former Soviet Union

countries residing in Kumkapı, with Georgia, Armenia, Uzbekistan, and Turkmenistan being the largest groups.

22. While beginning the talk in the formal singular (*sen*), here the agent changed to the use of the plural for you (*siz*), making reference to ascribed group identity as Africans and persons of color.

23. Vertovec, *Diversities Old and New*.

24. Geertz 141, cited in Pnina Werbner, "The Dialectics of Urban Cosmopolitanism: Between Tolerance and Intolerance in Cities of Strangers." *Identities* 22, no. 5 (2015): 577.

25. Ulf Hannerz, "Cosmopolitans and Locals in a World Culture," *Theory, Culture & Society* 7, no. 2 (1990): 239.

26. Ibid., 239–240.

27. Craig Jeffrey and Colin McFarlane, "Performing Cosmopolitanism," *Environment and Planning D: Society and Space* 26 (2008): 420–427; Michele Lamont and Sada Aksartova, "Ordinary Cosmopolitanisms: Strategies for Bridging Racial Boundaries among Working Class Men," *Theory, Culture and Society* 19, no. 4 (2002): 1–25; Uma Kothari, "Global Peddlers and Local Networks: Migrant Cosmopolitanisms," *Environment and Planning A* 26 (2008): 500–516; and Wessendorf, *Commonplace Diversity*.

28. Greg Noble, "Everyday Cosmopolitanism and the Labour of Intercultural Community," in *Everyday Multiculturalism*, ed. Amanda Wise and Salvaraj Valeyutham (Basingstoke: UK: Palgrave Macmillan, 2009), 50–51.

29. Nina Glick-Schiller, Tsypylma Darieva, and Sandra Gruner-Domic, "Defining Cosmopolitan Sociability in a Transnational Age. An Introduction," *Ethnic and Racial Studies* 34, no. 3 (2011): 403.

CHAPTER 9

Contesting the "Third Bridge" in Istanbul

LOCAL ENVIRONMENTALISM, COSMOPOLITAN ATTACHMENTS?

Hande Paker

"We are environmentalists," claimed Recep Tayyip Erdoğan, Turkey's then prime minister and current president. He was speaking at the launch ceremony for the construction of a third bridge over the Bosphorus strait in Istanbul in May 2013. "This bridge will have features that protect the environment," he declared.[1] The protesters at the city's Gezi Park, having gathered that same month to protect what Erdoğan had dismissed as "just a couple of trees" from demolition for urban structures, disagreed vehemently. The incompatibility of the Turkish leader's and the protestors' readings of environmentalism was underscored by Erdoğan's taunt: "Do whatever you want in Gezi Park, we have made up our mind" (about the park's fate). This stance conveyed Erdoğan's confidence that, like the park, the construction of a third bridge was a service of the Justice and Development Party (AKP) government—which he defined as a "civilizational project"—to the ancient yet global city of Istanbul.

Erdoğan's short speech contained all the elements of contestation surrounding the project to construct a third bridge over the Bosphorus strait linking the European and Asian sides of Istanbul. The debate, I suggest, centered around three dimensions: environmentalism, the idea of Istanbul as common value and global heritage, and democratic participation. This chapter examines how these concerns, read as loosely defined cosmopolitan commitments, were perceived, constructed, contested, and crosscut by particularistic positions emanating from local sensibilities. By situating analysis in concrete networks of action, I unpack the dynamic process via which cosmopolitan commitments and particularistic attachments shape one other. Attention to how these processes come together in the global city,

I argue, can help to address a major criticism of cosmopolitan democracy, namely that it offers a weak basis for political action. But while mobilization against the "third bridge" enabled collective action across diverse positions, participants also at times prioritized their particular interests over the cosmopolitan coalition.

The relationship between democracy and environmentalism has cropped up not only in debates over the third bridge but in practically all recent environmental struggles in Turkey. These struggles have multiplied due to the aggressive policies of neoliberal growth perpetuated by the AKP government.[2] If the Gezi Park events were an expression of concerns about the environment, the city, and the nature of democratic participation, such concerns were articulated long before the protests. This was evidenced by repeat mobilizations against the construction of the third bridge. People came together around this common cause, yet not as smoothly as some recent work on cosmopolitanism and citizenship might suggest.

Ecological risks are among the most important global risks that challenge territoriality, generate transnational concerns relevant to the whole of humanity, and necessitate common bases of action. This chapter explores whether environmental concerns for Istanbul can indeed create common platforms of action. Can mobilization for the environment and the city form the basis of cosmopolitan commitments that strengthen democratic processes? Cosmopolitan democratic theorists argue that "democratic iterations" can turn encounters with Others into a transnational political process in which various actors participate.[3] The chapter examines how this process unfolds in practice.

Sassen has underlined the importance of specific places and institutional arrangements in situating cross-border dynamics, especially the global city.[4] The (global) city emerges as a significant location of contentions shaped by integration into the neoliberal global economy and mobilizations against its adverse impacts. In the case of the mobilization against the third bridge across the Bosphorus, the loosely constructed common referents—environmental conservation, Istanbul as common value and global heritage, and democratic participation—were crosscut by alternative references or competing affiliations. This is why, at times, the social or political location of an individual as a denizen of the neighborhood that would be adversely affected by the construction of the bridge, a supporter of the government, or a supporter of the opposition political party could determine participation (or not) in a platform. Yet common antibridge platforms and mediating actors emerged that negotiated solidarities by accommodating diverse commitments in the campaigns that they organized: the Arnavutköy Neighborhood Initiative, the Life Instead of the Third Bridge Platform (LTBP), and the Green Party of Turkey.

Cosmopolitanism and the Environment

The idea of cosmopolitanism as navigated through recognition of the Other has been embraced by some as an opportunity to democratize a new social geography characterized by globalizing dynamics and nonterritorial constraints. For others, it has remained an elitist idea without a solid social basis on which political action can be built.[5] These criticisms have spurred scholars who are proponents of cosmopolitanism to make explicit the processes that underlie cosmopolitanism as lived experience. Such experiences include postnational politics, nation-state transformations, the rise of a participatory global civil society, changing forms of citizenship, and the intensification of global risks that transcend national borders. Urban contexts such as global cities are key sites at which these processes unfold.

The growing literature in this vein seeks to understand practices of mutual recognition around a set of shared norms that mediate between differences and provide for the integrity of a polity.[6] These common values may be thought of as "thin" values, in that they are loosely defined to accommodate diversity without encroaching upon strong (thick) attachments like national, ethnic, or religious identities.[7] Cosmopolitan democracy is built on commitment to such thin values: creating transnational communities governed by dialogue and consent,[8] inclusion and receptivity of the Other, and the recognition of our common humanity by virtue of our Otherness.[9] Despite this flourishing literature, however, cosmopolitanism continues to be challenged on the grounds that it can generate neither spheres of political action/social solidarity for a cosmopolitan democracy nor deep attachments that mobilize.[10]

The need to live with difference nonetheless makes cosmopolitanism appealing in an increasingly transnational world in which demands for accommodating diversity, deepening democracy, and improving inclusion make cosmopolitan democracy a significant political project. Scholars can observe, after all, the actions of "rooted cosmopolitans" who move between local and transnational spheres of action and are "embedded in transnational, multiple, changing, nonterritorial, as well as territorial—and thereby inclusive communities."[11] As Beck has suggested, such realities mean cosmopolitanism is no longer an aspirational project but rather one whose conditions have become banal and everyday. The inexorable reality of global risks (like financial, ecological, or security crises), generate the recognition that others are also affected by common worries.[12] The recognition that "we are all in the same boat"—the "cosmopolitan imperative"—becomes not an intellectual pursuit confined to elites but a sufficient basis of joint action.[13]

If there is indeed a cosmopolitan imperative, how do national/local communities relate to transnational spheres constituted around ecological risk? Environmental issues can create both common frames—the shared meanings, interpretations, and commitments necessary for joint political action—and environmental public spheres in which actors participate at the transnational level (albeit with differentiated responsibilities). What then are the mechanisms of cosmopolitan integration and infusion at work?

Changing Sites of Contention: Mobilizing against a Third Bridge in Istanbul

Although the new political cosmopolitanism is often envisaged as a nonterritorial, democratic project based on transnational public spheres and thin commitments, mobilization against Istanbul's third bridge was locally organized but potentially cosmopolitan in orientation. As a struggle framed around an environmental issue centered on the protection of Istanbul as a common value, the case of the third bridge can help to assess whether environmental concerns can create cosmopolitan attachments. These environmental concerns were, at the same time, embedded in particularistic attachments, such as opposition to the bridge because it would pass through the contenders' own neighborhood.

The mobilization against the construction of the third bridge emerged as a local initiative within the larger environmental movement in Turkey, which broadly seeks conservation (of forests and water basins in the vicinity of the city) and sustainable urban development and transportation. It gained momentum when the government announced a new bridge project in the late 1990s to supplement the two existing bridges connecting the European and Asian sides of the city.[14] This mobilization shifted both spatially (as the government retracted and reintroduced routes) and in terms of the weight of actors involved and frames employed.[15] The arguments offered in favor of a third bridge centered on the city's seemingly intractable problem of transportation. Those who contest the bridge emphasize the irreversible ecological impact that the third bridge will have, the destruction of urban fabric as a result of rent-seeking pressures from finance capital, and the existence of more sustainable alternatives to the city's transportation problem.

The data in the following sections on the three phases of anti-bridge mobilization are taken from secondary research of relevant literature, reports, press releases, calls for action, and news items, as well as interviews with representatives of organizations involved, such as the Chamber of Forest Engineers, the Chamber of Urban Planners, and the Green Party of Turkey. The analysis is also informed by interviews with representatives of civil society actors that emerged in the aftermath of the 2013 Gezi Park protests to defend Istanbul and its ecological reserves against not only the third bridge but also other megaprojects such as the third airport and Canal Istanbul.[16]

The Initial Mobilization: The Arnavutköy Neighborhood Initiative

Objections to the construction of a third bridge across the Bosphorus were first made by the Arnavutköy community in Istanbul, the projected site of the European pillar of the bridge in the 1990s. The Arnavutköy Neigborhood Initiative (ASG), organized by the residents of Arnavutköy in 1998, launched a spirited campaign after the government announced plans to connect the two continents via Arnavutköy on the European side and Kandilli on the Asian side. Between 1998 and 2005, the residents of Arnavutköy rallied against the project through street protests, meetings, festivals, dances, and tea parties, as well as a website, a mailing list, and open discussions.[17] The campaign was supported by civil society organizations such as the Association for the Promotion and Protection of Environmental and Cultural Values (ÇEKÜL), the Association for the Protection of Natural Life (DHKD), and the Chamber of Architects, as well as artists, intellectuals, and individuals situated both nationally and transnationally.[18] Peak activity subsided when the decision to build the bridge was suspended.

Anti-bridge activists constructed multiple frames for their opposition. These included the environmental frame, which emphasized the ecological damage that the bridge would cause; the cultural frame, which situated Arnavutköy as a historically and culturally unique global heritage site; and the democratic participation frame, which highlighted policy making, democratization, and respect for human rights.[19] The ASG initiative was an explicitly environmental mobilization, relating its demands to air quality, natural beauty, and the sea, all of which would be degraded. Moreover, the initiative expanded the environmental frame to include damage from tanker crossings in the Bosphorus, air pollution caused by traffic on existing bridges, and measures to regenerate traditional fish. Sustainability was an important dimension of the environmental argument as well. Participants underscored the value of the neighborhood and the sea for future generations and advocated sustainable practices such as the use of public transportation.[20]

The ASG initiative also framed its contention in cultural terms, since the bridge would damage the historical architecture and a particular neighborhood (*mahalle*) way of life where face-to-face relations and support networks are prevalent. Environmental and cultural heritage arguments further informed demands for political participation. These claims emphasized the undemocratic nature of decisions taken in relation to the bridge and appealed to politicians, representatives of civil society, and broader publics to adopt the position of the ASG.

This global cultural heritage emphasis resonated with and was supported by the international links that ASG established. The Greek Fellowship of Mega Revma, founded by Christian residents of Arnavutköy who were either expelled or left of their own volition during the 1950s and 1960s, lent support to the contention, arguing that the neighborhood was "one of only a handful of neighborhoods where the cultural mosaic of Greek, Armenian and Turkish influence, once so much a part of Istanbul life, can still be seen and felt, both in the architecture and in the residents."[21] The neighborhood's famous wooden-house architecture from the nineteenth and early twentieth centuries, its functional Greek school and church, and the ruins of an ancient synagogue make Arnavutköy a site of cultural heritage. Emphasizing the lack of democratic process in pushing the bridge project through, the ASG described the plan to build the bridge as an "an assault on the cultural, historic and aesthetic sensitivities" of not only the residents, but also the city and the world.[22] In addition to support from the Fellowship of Mega Revma, the ASG was involved in an exchange with the organization Mediterranean Cities Organization and UNESCO. As a result of ASG lobbying, the International Council on Monuments and Sites (ICOMOS) listed Arnavutköy as "Heritage at Risk."

These international links and the cosmopolitan frames upon which they were based were crosscut by the particularistic attachments of ASG members. People mobilized because they were concerned about their own houses, neighborhood, and city. At the same time, they came together around thin commitments such as the protection of the environment, Istanbul as global heritage, and democratic participation. Recognizing the interplay of these dynamics—between the demand for protection of a particular urban locale in which people lived and its wider relevance as a site of global heritage or sustainability—can help us unpack the mechanisms of cosmopolitan democracy.

The Right to Habitat: Sarıyer-Beykoz Line

Following this mobilization, the plan to construct a third bridge lay dormant for a while, only to resurface around 2005 with the announcement of the new Sarıyer/Tarabya and Beykoz route. This moved the projected route of the bridge farther north of Istanbul. The route is farther from the city center than Arnavutköy and goes through the shantytowns in Sarıyer. The announcement sparked opposition from groups who lived in the shantytowns in this area and faced the threat of losing their homes. A professional organization, the Chamber of Forest Engineers, whose new management held a press conference on the issue, initiated the campaign against this route. It attracted the immediate and popular support of civil society organizations and political parties. In fact, the trigger in the second phase of the mobilization came from an urban focus on Istanbul, since the Chamber of Forest Engineers chose specifically to work on Istanbul-related issues. The initiative established itself formally as the Life Instead of the Third Bridge Platform (LTBP) and began working on information dissemination to increase public support. Support for the platform remained local at first, limited to the neighborhoods around Sarıyer. It then slowly expanded to include a variety of Istanbul neighborhoods and organizations.

As in the case of Arnavutköy, activists organized street protests, meetings, mini-concerts, press conferences, and street festivals, most intensively between the years 2008 and 2010.[23] Prominent national environmental organizations such as The Turkish Foundation for Combating Soil Erosion, for Reforestation and the Protection of Natural Habitats (TEMA), the Turkish Environmental and Woodlands Protection Society (TÜRÇEK), and the Doğa Association, as well as the environmentally oriented travel magazine *Atlas*, lent support by organizing a protest and press conference.[24]

Like its predecessor, the anti-bridge mobilization for the Sarıyer-Beykoz route employed multiple frames with slightly varied emphases. These frames included environmentalism, the right to habitat, democratic participation, the assertion of Istanbul as a common value, and political economy. The environmental frame underlined the ecological costs of the third bridge, which would destroy the last remaining forests, water basins, and wildlife situated in the north of Istanbul. Moreover, the new bridge would open up this space to new settlements, accelerating the ecological costs. These concerns were expressed in the following words: "Do not touch my forest, my water, my neighborhood" and "Life, not the bridge."[25]

The second phase of the mobilization claimed Istanbul as a common value, stressing the relevance of the issue for all Istanbul residents. Championing Istanbul "as their own," activists made constant references to "Istanbul, our city," "Istanbul is ours," and "we, the people of Istanbul." For instance, one banner in the March 2010 protest read: "These forests have been taken under the protection of the people of Istanbul."[26] One of the achievements attributed to the mobilization is also related to claiming Istanbul, in the sense that representatives of the platform feel that they have changed how residents perceive Istanbul.[27] In effect, activists and concerned citizens claimed the right to the city, contesting the financial gain and speculative rents that would enrich investors due to the size of the project. They also objected to the marketization of the environment in the neoliberal policy mind-set of the ruling party. Many labeled the bridge the "rent bridge," underscoring the rent-seeking process set into motion with the announcement of the project (supporters of the bridge were referred to as "rentiers" and "fat cats)."[28] A related frame was democratic participation. Those who opposed the bridge plan pointed out that planners never consulted the parties concerned, disregarding the residents of Istanbul.[29] The mobilization in this phase also had a strong "right to habitat" dimension, reflecting the fact that many people, especially in Sarıyer, contested the plan because they were threatened with the loss of their homes.[30] By arguing that people's right to habitat was being undermined, activists situated their cause within a broader framework of human rights.

In this second phase of mobilization, there was also clear cross-infusion of the particularistic commitments of the participants with cosmopolitan frames. Political action was driven by concerns for the environment, maintaining Istanbul as global heritage, and democratic participation that were crosscut by particularistic attachments to one's house and neighborhood. Yet these particularistic attachments also generated frames that could accommodate actors across interests and commitments. When people claimed Istanbul "as their own" as a city of global importance under threat, they defined it as an issue of interest to others beyond neighborhood borders and even of Istanbul and Turkey more broadly. Invocations of the ecological destruction in store for Istanbul, for example, resonated with others who mobilized to reduce ecological risk globally. Moreover, there were instances of cross-identification between political and social cleavages, as in the case of the Beykoz protest march and press conference in 2009, organized by the platform. On this occasion, they were joined by people who had come out of Friday prayer—an apparent endorsement from a group whose identities differed from the prosecularist orientation of the majority of the protestors.[31] The Sarıyer-Beykoz phase of the mobilization thus substantiates the argument that cosmopolitan commitments are shaped by local dynamics at the nexus of thick, particularistic and thin, universalistic commitments.

Two Million Istanbulites Campaign

In April 2010 the Turkish government announced yet another route for the third bridge—the very bridge that Erdoğan would flag in his speech on the eve of Gezi—triggering a new anti-bridge campaign. This time the site of contention moved farther north, into the heart of Istanbul's only remaining forests and water basins.[32] In response the Green Party of Turkey initiated a campaign under the rubric "two million Istanbulites" (*2 milyon İstanbullu*).[33] The slogan aimed for inclusivity in a bid to attract participants and organizations of diverse political orientations.[34] Hence the campaign's label did not explicitly reference the Green Party but rather claimed Istanbul as a comprehensive common value. As one party member explained: "Let's not take the issue as an anti-AKP problem; on the contrary, let's try to bring them in. . . . That's why from the first day we thought of doing something that would include the support of all institutions and organizations. . . . Since 2 million trees will be cut down, we will mobilize one resident of Istanbul to defend each one tree. So 2 million residents for 2 million trees. . . . Get out to defend a tree, no matter what your political affiliation is."[35] This quote illustrates both recognition of the exclusion created by particularistic political attachments (e.g., association with the Green Party) and an explicit effort to overcome it. The position thus underlined the interplay between particularistic attachments and cosmopolitan concerns. In this spirit, the Green Party organized protests and a large meeting in 2010 together with environmental organizations and previously affiliated groups such as the LTBP, Greenpeace Mediterranean, TEMA, and Global Action Group (*Küresel Eylem Grubu* [KEG]).[36] The ways—often heated—in which these groups negotiated solidarity shed light on the mechanisms and challenges that face cosmopolitan democracy. In this instance, cosmopolitan contestation took place between individuals with diverse political affiliations (e.g., supporters of the party in government—the AKP and the main opposition party, the Republican People's Party or CHP) committed to the cosmopolitan value of environmental protection.

The "*2 milyon İstanbullu*" platform used frames similar to those of the previous phases of mobilization, although the weight of each frame went through some shifts. The "right to habitat" frame lost steam as the route had relocated to a nonresidential area. The environmental and democratic participation frames claiming Istanbul as a common value remained central, however, to the mobilization. Even the trademark of the new campaign, "*2 milyon İstanbullu,*" reflects both environmental concerns and the view of Istanbul as a common value, since it envisaged two million residents of the city coming to the rescue of the two million trees that would be felled for the bridge. In framing the campaign around Istanbul and its trees as a common concern for all, there was a conscious effort on the part of the Green Party to transcend cleavages like party affiliation and organizational membership. The goal was to furnish a common trademark that the various groups involved could use whenever they planned a protest event.[37]

The frame of Istanbul as a common value was also noticeable in the campaign's emphasis on an alternative lifestyle based on public transportation and opposition to an "automobile civilization."[38] The argument suggested that the additional bridge, if constructed, would deteriorate quality of life for all Istanbul residents, not just those in the vicinity of the bridge route, by encouraging more car traffic, pollution, and unsustainable urban sprawl at the expense of the northern forests.

Finally, the campaign, like previous waves of mobilization, built its claims on the importance of democratic participation. As one Green Party member put it: "For us, for the Green Party, what is important is to make sure people participate in decision-making processes."[39] Once again, activism on the ground drew attention to processes of negotiation and solidarity building between conflictual positions, lobbying for the protection of Istanbul's trees as a common value and insisting on the participation of diverse actors as a basis for cosmopolitan democracy.

Situating Istanbul at the Crossroads of Local Mobilization, Environmental Commitments, and Cosmopolitanism

Do environmental concerns for Istanbul inspire cosmopolitan values and sensitivities? Are people propelled into action because they recognize, as Beck argues, a cosmopolitical imperative? Partial answers lie in the experience of the anti-bridge movement, which fused particularistic concerns like political affiliation or home ownership with cosmopolitan values such as environmental conservation, Istanbul as a common value and global heritage, and democratic participation.

At the same time, anti-bridge activism transcended particularistic positions and immediate concerns. This was possible through the construction of thin attachments that appealed to a diverse array of actors claiming Istanbul as a common value and global heritage, environmentalism, sustainability, endorsement of a certain way of life, and democratic participation. Hence, in the process of contention, cosmopolitan frames were constructed and crosscutting identifications were built even as they were embedded in local dynamics of solidarity, conflict, and negotiation.

The claim, for example, of Istanbul as common value and global heritage starts out from a thick attachment to a particular city. Yet at the same time, it reshapes this particularistic position into a concern for residents beyond the neighborhoods immediately on the planned routes. The city's future is even relevant to the world as global heritage, as the ASG underlined. On the one hand, people were acutely aware of the threat to their homes, which they did not want to leave, expressed in the words "we left our villages; we don't want to leave our cemeteries (once more)."[40] On the other hand, they emphasized that the bridge would be detrimental to life in general in Istanbul, including its ecology, regardless of the location of neighborhoods in relation to planned routes.[41] This is why people from Istanbul neighborhoods not directly affected by the construction joined the mobilization.

This study suggests that environmental concerns for Istanbul can be infused with a "cosmopolitan imperative" in which all of humanity is vulnerable to the ecological crisis. Yet these concerns are crosscut by the political affiliation of some of the actors who supported the mobilization. For example, some CHP members who voiced their support disclosed that they were "politically opposed" to the bridge. This meant that they were opposed simply because it was the project of the ruling party (AKP) and that they might have endorsed it had they been in power.[42]

Many actors across the three stages of the mobilization against the bridge recognized these political cleavages as explicit challenges to the more cosmopolitan frames employed by the movement. Hence, they looked for ways of negotiating solidarity. Also, those who were initially "politically opposed" came to realize the broader environmental costs to Istanbul and its residents and began to advocate also in the name of environmental conservation, the city, and democratic participation. Framing the most recent campaign as "*2 milyon İstanbullu*" was yet another conscious effort on the part of organizers to transcend cleavages. It was negotiated as an inclusive campaign that everybody could join regardless of ideological or organizational affiliation.

A final point important in the analysis of how cosmopolitan frames have bridged embedded political and social positions is that a not-in-my-backyard (NIMBY) position—in which residents oppose an infrastructural proposal because of negative consequences for the locality but do not necessarily oppose the project's implementation elsewhere—was avoided in the case of the antibridge mobilization in Istanbul.[43] This was achieved by maintaining links between various groups and endorsing references to a certain way of life. Environmental networks and concerns transcended the immediate (proposed) location of the bridge for each of the three sites. In fact, groups that were active in various stages of the mobilization maintained links throughout the protests. For example, the ASG opposed the construction of the bridge not only in Arnavutköy but also in the north of Istanbul and gave support to subsequent contentions.[44] Similarly, the Green Party was part of the LTBP and organized joint meetings and protests with its main actors, such as the Chamber of Forest Engineers and the Chamber of Urban Planners, even when the plan to build the bridge on the Sarıyer-Beykoz route was changed.[45]

A NIMBY position also was avoided by expanding the frame of the contention from a local point (neighborhood or city) to more generalized references of an alternative way of life, one built on sustainability. These references consisted of advocating sustainable transportation, defending human life instead of the third bridge, and emphasizing that life cannot be tendered for a contract.[46] One press release with a cosmopolitan orientation read: "It is the natural right of all of us to live in an Istanbul planned for humane living areas for the working people, not capital. Defending the forests which are the most important part of this humane living is to defend Istanbul and our future."[47] These references to thin values in addition to the intra-links forged among civil society actors and urban localities underline the non-NIMBY nature of the waves of mobilization, a crucial point in establishing the cosmopolitan frames of the anti-bridge mobilization in Istanbul.

The anti-bridge mobilization constructed cosmopolitan frames in a specific locality but lacked the wider cross-border networks of transnational activists, seen as an essential part of global city dynamics.[48] Istanbul may be seen as an aspiring global city insofar as the government courts, through its neoliberal policies (e.g., megaprojects such as the third bridge, third airport, and Canal Istanbul), those industries that produce services for the implementation and management of the global economy. However, the networks of solidarity among transnational environmental actors linking various global cities are missing in Istanbul. The potential to build those links exists in the cosmopolitan frames but is constrained by the political context, in which the state imposes a top-down project of integration into the global neoliberal economy. This disregards the grassroots demands arising from local cosmopolitan concerns in an aspiring global city.

Conclusion

The case of Istanbul's third bridge enables us to unpack relations of solidarity and conflict that shape political action at the nexus of particularistic attachments and cosmopolitan concerns. As the story of the third bridge movement shows, cosmopolitan values are crosscut by particularistic positions, while at the same time particularistic attachments can transform into cosmopolitan frames. This creates a concrete set of relations and networks of action within which cosmopolitan democracy can be grounded.

It should be noted that despite these mobilizations, the construction of the bridge at the third proposed location has been completed. This study has not sought to explain the success or failure of a social mobilization, because outcomes, as well as factors that explain them, are multiple. It notes, however, that there is a general sense among the movement participants that effective mobilization led to the retraction of the chosen routes, first in Arnavutköy and then in Sarıyer-Beykoz. The fact that the mobilization failed to stop the bridge altogether is not central to understanding how cosmopolitan frames are shaped locally, which is the main concern of this chapter. This is because there were other outcomes, like the creation of networks that spilled over into further mobilization, the organization of forums, and the experience of cross-identification, all of which laid the groundwork for activists to embrace cosmopolitan frames.[49] The anti-third-bridge movement thus illustrates that cosmopolitan attachments are submerged in local dynamics.

On a final note, the common ground built on the environment, the city, and democratic participation was an early basis of the Gezi Park protests, which likewise can be read within the framework of cosmopolitan democracy (see chapter 10 in this volume). The concerns raised and frames employed in the contention against the third bridge were appropriated and deployed during the Gezi protests. The perceived challenge to democratic participation, for example, was a primary concern for Gezi participants[50] and to a certain extent explains the widespread support for the defense of the park. Environmental concerns initially triggered the protests, coupled with discontent with mega-infrastructural and urban transformation projects.

Thus, local environmental mobilizations can generate a common space of political action constituted by cosmopolitan commitments. However, this common space, as I have argued throughout the chapter, is not constructed smoothly, but rather builds on existing tensions and is largely shaped by them. The struggle for Istanbul's environmental future suggests that we need to look for the cosmopolitan within the local.

ACKNOWLEDGMENTS

I am grateful to Fikret Adaman, Nora Fisher-Onar, Gaye İlhan Demiryol, Zeynep Kadirbeyoğlu, and Baran Alp Uncu for their constructive criticisms, which much improved this chapter.

NOTES

1. "3. Boğaz Köprüsünün temeli atıldı," http://www.sabah.com.tr/Ekonomi/2013/05/29/3-bogaz-koprusunun-temeli-atiliyor.

2. Murat Arsel, Fikret Adaman, and Bengi Akbulut, "Türkiye'de Kalkınmacılığı Yeniden Okumak: HES'ler ve Dönüşen Devlet-Toplum-Doğa İlişkileri," in *Sudan Sebepler: Kalkınma ve Çevrecilik Kıskacında Hidro-Enerji ve HES Karşıtı Mücadelenin Ekoloji-Politiği*, ed. Erdem Evren, Sinan Erensu, and Cemil Aksu (Istanbul: İletişim, 2016), 291–312.

3. Seyla Benhabib, "Democratic Exclusions and Democratic Iterations," *European Journal of Political Theory* 6 (2007): 445–462.

4. Saskia Sassen, "The Global City: Introducing a Concept," *The Brown Journal of World Affairs* 11, no. 2 (2005): 27–43; and Saskia Sassen, "Global Cities and Survival Circuits," in *Global Woman*, ed. Barbara Ehrenreich and Arlie R. Hochschild (New York: Holt Paperbacks, 2002), 254–274.

5. See, for example, Craig Calhoun, "The Class Consciousness of Frequent Travelers: Toward a Critique of Actually Existing Cosmopolitanism," *South Atlantic Quarterly*. 101, no. 4 (2002): 869–897; and chapter 1 in this volume.

6. Ulrich Beck, *The Cosmopolitan Vision*, trans. Ciaran Cronin (Cambridge, UK: Polity Press, 2006); and Feyzi Baban and Fuat Keyman, "Turkey and Postnational Europe: Challenges for the Cosmopolitan Political Community," *European Journal of Social Theory* 11, no. 1 (2008): 107–124.

7. Nora Fisher-Onar and Hande Paker, "Towards Cosmopolitan Citizenship? Women's Rights in Divided Turkey," *Theory and Society* 41, no. 4 (2012): 375–394.

8. Andrew Linklater, "Cosmopolitan Citizenship," *Citizenship Studies* 2, no. 1 (1998): 23–41.

9. Robert Fine and Vivienne Boon, "Cosmopolitanism: Between Past and Future," *European Journal of Social Theory* 10, no. 1 (2007): 5–16; and Benhabib, "Democratic Exclusions."

10. Andrew Dobson, *Citizenship and the Environment* (Oxford: Oxford University Press, 2003); Craig Calhoun, "Imagining Solidarity: Cosmopolitanism, Constitutional Patriotism, and the Public Sphere," *Public Culture* 14, no. 1 (2002): 141–171; and Calhoun, "The Class Consciousness."

11. Sidney Tarrow, *The New Transnational Activism* (Cambridge, UK: Cambridge University Press, 2005); and Toni Erskine, "'Citizen of Nowhere' or 'The Point Where Circles Intersect'? Impartialist and Embedded Cosmopolitanisms," *Review of International Studies* 28 (2002): 457–478.

12. Beck, *The Cosmopolitan Vision*; and Ulrich Beck, "Cosmopolitanism as Imagined Communities of Global Risk," *American Behavioral Scientist* 55, no. 10 (2011): 1346–1361.

13. Beck, "Cosmopolitanism as Imagined Communities."

14. The first bridge was built in 1973 and the second in 1988, expanding the urban sprawl toward the north of Istanbul. The fact that the second bridge increased the population and unplanned urbanization toward unsustainable levels is one of the arguments used by the opposition to show that the third bridge would trigger similar trends, this time exceeding sustainable thresholds in terms of population, natural resources, and infrastructure (author interviews).

15. The government in office was a center-right and center-left coalition government in the first phase of the mobilization and AKP during the second and third phases.

16. For a detailed analysis of how megaprojects are used by the AKP to strengthen its hegemony in a framework of neoliberal developmentalism, see Hande Paker, "The 'Politics of Serving' and Neoliberal Developmentalism: The Megaprojects of the AKP as Tools of Hegemony Building," in *Neoliberal Turkey and Its Discontents: Economic Policy and the Environment Under Erdoğan*, ed. Fikret Adaman, Bengi Akbulut, and Murat Arsel (London: I. B. Tauris, 2017), 103–119.

17. Günham Danışman and İsmail Üstün, "Contentious Politics at a Bosphorus Neighborhood: Perspectives on Conflict and Solidarity During the 20th Century," in *Contested Mediterranean Spaces: Ethnographic Essays in Honour of Charles Tilly*, ed. Maria Kousis, Tom Selwyn and David Clark (London: Berghahn Books, 2011), 178–194; and Aimilia Voulvouli, "Transenvironmental Protest: the Arnavutköy Anti-Bridge Campaign in Istanbul," *Environmental Politics* 20, no. 6 (2011): 861–878.

18. Both ÇEKÜL and DHKD are national environmental organizations, while the Chamber of Architects is a professional association. Additional support came from the alumni of Robert College, which launched an anti-bridge signature campaign. Robert College is an elite high school in Istanbul whose graduates have become national and international leaders in arts, literature, academia, and politics. The campaign was also supported by national icons such as the pop singer Sezen Aksu. Moreover, the campaign received coverage in the international media in outlets such as the *Washington Post*, the *LA Times*, and *Le Monde*. Such alliances have provided global elite support to the movement, turning it into a high-profile and highly legitimate campaign.

19. Voulvouli, "Transenvironmental Protest."

20. Ibid.; and Danışman and Üstün, "Contentious Politics."

21. www.megarevma.net.

22. Ibid.

23. Interview with representative of the *Life Instead of the Third Bridge Platform*, http://www.sendika.org/2008/06/sariyer-ve-beykoz-halki-3-kopru-istemiyor; http://kentvedemiryolu.com/icerik.php?id=432; and http://sariyerhalkevleri.blogspot.com/2010/03/istanbullu-3cinayet-koprusune-hayr-dedi.html.

24. http://www.kadikoygazetesi.com/6380-sariyer-beykoz-arasina-yapilacak-kopruye-tepkiler-suruyor.

25. http://www.genel-is.org.tr/diger_incele.php?id=NDcy; see also http://www.sendika.org/2008/06/sariyer-ve-beykoz-halki-3-kopru-istemiyor; http://kentvedemiryolu.com/icerik.php?id=432; and http://sariyerhalkevleri.blogspot.com/2010/03/istanbullu-3cinayet-koprusune-hayr-dedi.html.

26. http://sariyerhalkevleri.blogspot.com/2010/03/istanbullu-3cinayet-koprusune-hayr-dedi.html. The president of the Urban Planners Association wrote in an opinion-editorial in 2010 that deciding to build the bridge would be tantamount to giving up on Istanbul. Demirdizen, "3. Köprü mü, İstanbul mu?," *Radikal 2*, February 14, 2010. See also http://www.genel-is.org.tr/diger_incele.php?id=NDcy.

27. Interview with representative of the Life Instead of the Third Bridge Platform.

28. Ibid.; press release, March 27, 2012, http://sthp.org/, http://kentvedemiryolu.com/icerik.php?id=432; http://www.mimdap.org/?p=21886; and http://sariyerhalkevleri.blogspot.com/2010/03/istanbullu-3cinayet-koprusune-hayr-dedi.html.

29. Interview with representatives of the Green Party of Turkey; http://www.genel-is.org.tr/diger_incele.php?id=NDcy; and http://sariyerhalkevleri.blogspot.com/2010/03/istanbullu-3cinayet-koprusune-hayr-dedi.html.

30. Interview with representative of the Life Instead of the Third Bridge Platform, June 28, 2012; interview with representative of the Green Party of Turkey, November 29, 2010; and http://kentvedemiryolu.com/icerik.php?id=432, http://www.mimdap.org/?p=21886.

31. Interview with representative of the Life Instead of the Third Bridge Platform, June 28, 2012.

32. http://www.istanbultimes.com.tr/guncel/sariyer-belediyesinden-3-kopruye-hayir-h4325.html.

33. The slogan used the term *İstanbullu*, which translates as "resident of Istanbul."

34. The Green Party of Turkey merged with the Equality and Democracy Party (EDP) in November 2012 and became the Greens and the Left Future. However, as the campaign took place before this merge, the party is referred to as the Green Party throughout this chapter.

35. Interview with representative of the Green Party, November 29, 2010.

36. Ibid.; "Istanbul Residents Protest against Construction of '"Third Bridge,'" http://www.greenhorizon-online.com/index.php/Turkey/istanbul-residents-protest-against-construction-of-third-bridge.html; and "İki milyon İstanbullu Galata köprüsünde," http://yesilgazete.org/2010/11/07/iki-milyon-istanbullu-galata-koprusunde/. The meeting in Kadıköy was initiated by the Life Instead of the Third Bridge Platform but was attended by all participants in the *2 milyon İstanbullu* campaign.

37. Interview with representative of the Green Party, November 29, 2010.

38. Interviews with members of the Green Party. It was not just the most recent campaign that emphasized that their contention was about defending a way of life. Hence, the ASG brought forth the neighborhood (*mahalle*) way of life that would be destroyed by the bridge, while the Life Instead of the Third Bridge Platform underlined "humane life," which could not be sustained if the bridge was built.

39. Interview with representative of the Green Party, November 29, 2010.

40. Interview with representative of the Life Instead of the Third Bridge Platform, June 28, 2012. This comment was made with regard to the possibility that if they had to leave their homes because of the bridge, they would have to move elsewhere once more.

41. This emphasis can be seen in all the references to the inevitable destruction of forests and water basins of the city and increased settlement, congestion, and air pollution. http://www.mimdap.org/?p=21886; http://sariyerhalkevleri.blogspot.com/2010/03/istanbullu-3cinayet-koprusune-hayr-dedi.html; and http://www.yesilgazete.org/blog/2012/01/10/yesiller-3-kopru-icin-hukumeti-uyardi/.

42. Interview with representative of the Life Instead of the Third Bridge Platform, June 28, 2012; and interview with representative of the Chamber of Urban Planners, July 25, 2012.

43. NIMBYism refers to contention at the local level when residents oppose the site of a proposed infrastructural or energy project in the vicinity of their habitat; however, it is prevalently associated with parochialism, narrow interests, and selfish behavior because the opposed project may have beneficial value for the broader public. Maarten Wolsink, "Invalid Theory Impedes Our Understanding: A Critique on the Persistence of the Language of NIMBY," *Transactions of the Institute of British Geographers* 31, no. 1 (2006): 85–91.

44. Although ASG built its contention around Arnavutköy, the residents of Arnavutköy also gave support to the demonstrations against the construction of a public building in the middle of a park in Kuzguncuk and the construction of a coastal highway in Moda, respectively. Danışman and Üstün, "Contentious Politics." ASG emphasized the relevance of the contention not only to the current residents of Arnavutköy but also to its former residents and the world.

45. "Çözüm Köprüden Vazgeçmek ve Toplu Ulaşım," *Bianet*, October 26, 2005, http://m.bianet.org/bianet/print/69418-cozum-kopruden-vazgecmek-ve-toplu-ulasim; interview with members of the Green Party; interview with representative of the Life Instead of the Third Bridge Platform, June 28, 2012.

46. "Çözüm Köprüden Vazgeçmek ve Toplu Ulaşım"; http://sariyerhalkevleri.blogspot.com/2010/03/istanbullu-3cinayet-koprusune-hayr-dedi.html; http://kentvedemiryolu.com/icerik.php?id=432; and http://www.sendika.org/2008/06/sariyer-ve-beykoz-halki-3-kopru-istemiyor.

47http://sariyerhalkevleri.blogspot.com/2010/03/istanbullu-3cinayet-koprusune-hayr-dedi.html. Studies have shown that local mobilizations are able to and do transcend the concerns of conserving immediate habitat, combining a sense of locality and belonging with broader sensitivities expressed in a "view of the good life" and human health. Christopher Rootes, "A Limited Transnationalization? The British Environmental Movement," in *Transnational Protest and Global Activism*, ed. Donatella Della Porta and Sidney Tarrow (Lanham, MD: Rowman and Littlefield, 2005), 21–43; Mark Garavan, "Resisting the Costs of 'Development': Local Environmental Activism in Ireland," in *Acting Locally, Local Environmental Mobilizations and Campaigns*, ed. Christopher Rootes (London and New York: Routledge, 2008), 124–143; and Donatella Della Porta and Gianni Piazza, "Local Contention, Global Framing: The Protest Campaigns against the TAV in Val di Susa and the Bridge on the Messina Straits," in *Acting Locally, Local Environmental Mobilizations and Campaigns*, ed. Christopher Rootes (London and New York, Routledge, 2008), 144–162.

48. Sassen, "The Global City."

49. The analysis of other environmental movements in Turkey has also identified multiple outcomes. A case in point is the anti-gold-mining movement of the peasants of Bergama, which is the longest standing and the best known environmental movement in Turkey, both nationally and transnationally. It failed to stop the extraction of gold, which was the acknowledged goal of the mobilization, but succeeded in creating an unprecedented level of environmental awareness and public support. Baran Alp Uncu, "*Within Borders, Beyond Borders: The Bergama Movement at the Junction of Local, National, and Transnational Practices*" (PhD diss., London School of Economics and Political Science, 2012).

50. Gaye İlhan Demiryol, "Rebirth of the Political" (unpublished manuscript, 2014).

CHAPTER 10

Performing Pride in a Summer of Dissent

ISTANBUL'S LGBT PARADES

Susan C. Pearce

Istanbul presents a unique historical geography of built and accidental environments. These spaces have grounded centuries of cosmopolitan encounters—both peaceful and contentious—between cultures. The city's diversity continues to be salient in the twenty-first century, not least because like other global cities, Istanbul has emerged as a site of growing lesbian, gay, bisexual, and transgender (LGBT) activism and political performance.[1] As LGBT activist communities proliferate in Istanbul and other Turkish cities, their presence—and their insistence on the right to be present—interact with the ethnic and religious social identities of other urban denizens. Such encounters shed light on the modalities by which gendered and sexual "others" pursue inclusion, especially within and across culturally conservative polities.

In this chapter I examine the expansion of Pride parades and their intersections with other cultural identities in Istanbul. I read LGBT identities and their politicization in Istanbul as a site of "cosmopolitics": local practices and encounters between communities that seek to challenge entrenched social and political divisions.[2] This intervention is situated at the nexus of cosmopolitan theory, social movement theory, cultural sociology, and gender and sexuality studies. It seeks to contribute to our understanding of what Ulrich Beck labels "cosmopolitization" or social-scientifically observable processes (as opposed to the theory of cosmopolitanism, which in its predominant Western form has roots in Kant's philosophical ideal).[3] The chapter accordingly brings sociological methods and perspectives such as ethnographic participant observation to bear on cosmopolitan theory, a need identified by scholars like Delanty.[4] Analysis emanates from a study on gender and sexuality, social movements, and migration in Turkey and Southeast Europe, based on interviews with regional activists; it also draws on participant observation of Istanbul's 2013 LGBT Pride parade.[5] I argue that LGBT activists' cosmopolitical performances through a public event can help catapult a social movement from marginal to legitimate in the eyes of other groups in a polity.

LGBT Movements, Extraordinary Encounters

If global cities are spaces of cross-cultural encounters that potentially result in mutual recognition and respect for difference, the arena of sexual and gender diversity warrants particular scrutiny. Decades of global activism to counter gay- and trans-bashing, to press for the political and scientific will to end HIV/AIDS, and to secure human rights protections have only recently penetrated mainstream political agendas in most parts of the globe. Communities of coexistence that recognize gender and sexual diversity remain a utopic vision today. This is especially the case in countries such as Turkey, where conservative values predominate and have helped to legitimize a ruling political party.

Among the reasons for public conflict over LGBT rights is that boundary maintenance by ethnic and national groups is commonly infused with heteronormative, pronatalist agendas.[6] Heteronormativity—a set of cultural and institutional patterns that promote and support heterosexual relationships—is the presumed natural family formation across most societies. Public policies to increase birthrates, and thus the size of a nation, grounded in heteronormativity, are dubbed "pronatalist." Pronatalism inflects many forms of policy making, including ethnic cleansing. It defines social roles for women, since their bodies are constructed in pronatalist discourses as sites of reproduction. Pronatalist policies similarly have consequences for individuals who appear to defy heteronormative family relations such as the expectation to reproduce. Religious leaders who promote these norms as divinely ordained amplify ethno-national boundary maintenance. As a result, gender and sexuality have become prime arenas of contestation in conflicts over cultural identities and claims to autonomy, land, power, and rights in every region of the world.[7] Such tensions have led to violence against LGBT people, and Turkey is not immune to this experience.[8]

These realities are reminders that neither nationalism nor cosmopolitan coexistence is gender or sexuality neutral. At first glance, one would assume that alliances between groups rooted in nonconformist sexuality and groups based on inherited traditions would be among the least likely of coalitions to emerge in a society. When the June 2013 Istanbul Pride parade experienced a dramatic increase in scale and ally diversity, skepticism about the possibility of LBGT alliances with heteronormative groups informed the wonder of a participant in the 2013 LGBT Pride parade who declared: "We haven't seen this kind of unity in Turkey before."[9] The unexpected solidarities were due in part to the unfolding, in the same period, of massive antigovernment protests whose participants interacted with LGBT activists and vice versa. The complex city of Istanbul and its culturally contested neighborhood of Beyoğlu offered the site for such collusion. The 2013 parade enables us to investigate one of the more difficult knots of cosmopolitan theories: the question of how mutual recognition of the other across "thick identities" transpires in practice.[10]

Istanbul's LGBT Movement and Cosmopolitan Sensibilities

Istanbul's LGBT activism exemplifies two distinct meanings of "cosmopolitan" discernible in recent literature: that of the "boundariless politics of belonging" and "as a participatory mode in supranational polity."[11] In the first, individuals view themselves as rootless citizens of the world; in the second, people are rooted locally but engage with some form of international "cosmopolitics."[12] This might include the quest to secure human rights by invoking transnational treaties, courts, and allies. Although researchers often ground their work in one of these two meanings rather than both, they potentially work together in the case at hand.

Local LGBT movements in Turkey and beyond participate in transnational alliances for sexual and gender diversity and rights. Such movements share terminology ("LGBT," "*gej*" ("gay"), "pride," "trans," etc.) and symbols (the rainbow flag and the annual Pride parade). As one of the "new social movements" that characterize post–World War II activism—especially since the last quarter of the twentieth century—the LGBT movement has coalesced around an identity (or set of identities) that transcends the boundaries of a particular nation-state.[13]

A further way in which LGBT activism exemplifies transnational "cosmopolitics" is in the way that activists consult across borders, collaborate to effect change that targets international bodies, and share or borrow strategies—activities the social movements literature calls "repertoires."[14] Specifically, Turkish gay rights activists have solicited external assistance and human rights instruments to pursue their goals[15]—employing a "boomerang" approach, a term introduced by Keck and Sikkink to describe how locally based activists can expand their influence and power by using transnational interventions, whether governmental or nongovernmental.[16] Turkish activism has been bolstered by observer groups such as Amnesty International, Human Rights Watch, Human Rights Campaign, and Freedom House, which have criticized Turkey's record on human rights and specifically referenced gender and sexual minorities.

More generally, treatment of LGBT people is receiving growing scrutiny across transnational governmental and nongovernmental bodies.[17] Turkey's candidacy for the EU has subjected the country to more detailed surveillance to protect the rights of sexual minorities, including their safety during Pride events. Cosmopolitics infuses this process as EU conditions are increasingly incorporating LGBT rights into human rights bundles.[18] Turkish LGBT activists have used this as an opportunity to make, in effect, a cosmopolitan point: that the "West" should take Turkey to task. As one Turkish activist bluntly implored the EU: "We, as lesbian, gay, bisexual, trans and intersex people, demand that you stand up for us, . . . against those who try to cover up discrimination in the name of morality, culture, and traditions and conceal hate crimes, hate speeches and even hate murders."[19]

Mutual Recognition, Place, and Space

Just as a parade performs a transnational "boundariless politics of belonging," it simultaneously affirms a deeply visceral local identity, which theorists label "rooted cosmopolitanism" or "trans-local."[20] Global cities, Sassia Sasken observes, host practices that are simultaneously transnational, or "hypermobile," and rooted locally.[21] Istanbul's LGBT movement and local performances illustrate this reality: they embody their own indigenous manifestations of economic, cultural, and political globalization. Spatial location matters in both a cultural and a physical sense. In fact, even though cultural diffusion from a West-East direction has clearly influenced the LGBT movement and subculture, this is only one dynamic of the Istanbul and Turkish LGBT experience. As İbrahim Kaya and other scholars put it, Turkey underwent its own process of "inventive modernization" with indigenous roots.[22] The practice of alternative, nonconforming sexualities has a rich non-Western cultural history, including in Turkey,[23] albeit one that also echoes patterns of suppression, repression, and villainization found in Western cultural traditions.[24] The Ottoman Empire, for one, decriminalized homosexuality in 1858, more than a century before Western countries began to do the same.[25] And although the LGBT movement has only coalesced into a nationwide movement in Turkey quite recently, the popular culture scene has for decades included successful figures who are not gender conforming, such as the singer Bülent Ersoy.

Researchers have mapped similar cultural histories globally, including other non-Western cities. In fact, as Richard Aldrich has documented, from ancient Athens onward the city has represented a haven from the constraints of the provinces and a site for homosexual relationships.[26] In work on queer spaces and cosmopolitanism in Shanghai, for example, Hongwei Bao identified Chinese queer spaces that predated the contemporary LGBT movement, predominantly in the theaters where Chinese opera was performed.[27] Today, global cities from Asia to North America continue to provide the same functions, offering spaces where freedom from convention is possible, perhaps because they are in some ways disconnected from other geographical spaces and cultural practices within the nation-state, as Sassen has observed.[28]

Across the world's cities, the Pride parade form has evolved as a hybrid of the annual festival or procession and the sporadic street protest. Among the many cities offering Pride parades are New York, Hong Kong, Delhi, Tel Aviv, Berlin, Johannesburg, Tokyo, Paris, Athens, Mexico City, and Sao Paulo. The list includes the key global cities that are cross-networked in other aspects (economic, political, and cultural). These Pride parades are city-to-city conversations that resemble one another while maintaining their own local cultural stamps, by exposing locally experienced and culture-specific homophobia. Mirroring the transgressive attitude of the medieval carnival, which Mikhail Bakhtin described as a playful performance that temporarily reverses and ridicules community norms and hierarchies of power relations,[29] Pride similarly turns conventional social relations on their heads for a day. In Istanbul, for example, the Turkish state is a clear target audience for the parade and the larger movement's cosmopolitical demands for protection as citizens. These have most recently been directed toward the ruling Justice and Development Party (AKP).

The Turkish LGBT movement and Istanbul Pride further claim their rootedness by performing in cultural and physical space. Municipal pride is stamped into the logo of the lesbian, gay, bisexual, transgender, and intersex (LGBT/LGBTI) parade organization, İstanbul LGBTİ Onur Haftası. Ownership of that city space has become critical to the LGBT community. The 2013 Pride parade, and its ability to create a mass spectacle with little contention, exemplified what Begonya Enguix has documented in other countries: that Pride events help the LGBT community to carve out "a space for vindication, [visibility], and commemoration."[30] Lynda Johnston concurs, arguing that the events help sexual minorities to claim physical access to heteronormative public space, at least momentarily.[31] In Istanbul, this applies to Beyoğlu, a particular public space that the LGBT community has imbued with its stamp.

Beyoğlu is the neighborhood where the 2013 Gezi protests and Pride parade unfolded and is the city's most comfortable area for LGBT people. It is a main tourist destination, alongside the historic Sultanahmet district. Beyoğlu, although host to a vibrant club and restaurant district, commands one of the city's oldest built environments. Architecturally, it blends historic styles, but is dominated by nineteenth-century buildings, especially foreign consulates housed in earlier *Belle Époque* embassies. The neighborhood sports a cosmopolitan flavor, with rooftop terrace bars, dance venues, English-language bookshops, and souvenir shops. Taksim Square, at the heart of the district, represents secular space, home to a prominent military statue symbolizing the birth of the modern Turkish Republic, as well as the modernization of the city's center. The neighborhood is not a uniformly secular space, however, with two prominent and many discreet Christian churches and an active Sufi lodge.

Despite its cosmopolitan secularity and boundariless, multireligious character, Beyoğlu entails a contradiction in that it is simultaneously inclusive and exclusive (see also chapter 8 in this volume). As some critics note, Istanbul and other modern cities create European-inspired cosmopolitan spaces that favor certain national and religious identities. In the words of Amy Mills: "So-called cosmopolitan spaces represent European identity and are culturally and economically exclusive, as they leave out many others, be they religious, rural,

Kurdish, or otherwise not secular, upper class, and Turkish."[32] Beyoğlu displays this inclusive/exclusive character, particularly in its recent built history following the birth of the secular Turkish Republic in 1922.

Today, Beyoğlu is a site of mass, often spontaneous protests. Yet it is also where authorized protests take place. This makes it both a countercultural and an officially protected space. Its spirit contrasts clearly with conservative neighborhoods nearby and across Istanbul, as Beyoğlu is where both heterosexual and same-sex couples feel more free to kiss publicly. Gezi Park, for one, was a meeting place for romantic and sexual encounters between men, and the district's clubs regularly attract gay tourism. During the day the neighborhood is packed with tourists from conservative and progressive societies across the Middle East, Europe, and beyond. This ambivalent place of mutual influence, if not always recognition, is the stage on which the 2013 Pride parade was performed.

The Gezi Park Protests

As spring waned in 2013, an unassuming group of green activists staged a peaceful sit-in to protest government-steered urban development that threatened a rare remaining park in Istanbul's historic center: Gezi Park. In response to heavy-handed police intervention, the protests escalated to become the "Gezi Park" demonstrations, bringing together a multi-issue, multigenerational resistance movement. Two annual and already planned Pride parades (trans and LGBT) were scheduled for the same period. This resulted in unprecedented convergence between the LGBT and other protest movements, not least in response to the shared experience of police crackdown.

The unlikely assemblage of green activists, antigentrification groups, ethnic minority representatives, musicians and dancers, LGBT people, and others in the Gezi protests was based in a shared defiance of a common adversary: Turkey's ruling party, the AKP, and then prime minister (PM), Recep Tayyip Erdoğan. Erdoğan in particular was increasingly perceived to be micromanaging public spaces and personal habits. Government measures endorsed by the PM included a plan to build in Gezi Park's stead a replica of a late Ottoman period military barracks (which would serve as a shopping mall) as well as proposed curbs on alcohol consumption and on women's reproductive decisions.

Activists responded to the initial police crackdown by flocking to the Gezi protest site—across the larger adjacent space of Taksim Square—in the name of multiple political claims.[33] Visible among the many young people who reappeared day after day and camped overnight in late May and June 2013 were environmentalists to be sure, but there were also nationalists, merchants, musicians, ethnic subcultures, university students, feminists, and other identity groups. Some groups brought their own identity-based victim narratives. Others declared themselves allies of one or another constituency and defenders of public space, parks, and freedoms from top-down state interference. Occurring just two years after Arab activists occupied Cairo's Tahrir Square, the eruption of intrepid protestors drew the city of Istanbul into the center of global media attention. Eventually the protests would swell to 2.5 million people across seventy-nine Turkish cities.[34]

The 2013 LGBT and Trans Parades

Against this background, on June 30, 2013, Istanbul commenced its eleventh annual Lesbian, Gay, and Bisexual Pride parade. Istanbul had been the site of Turkey's first legal Pride parade in 2003, the first in a majority Muslim country. In 2003 there were thirty participants. By 2011, however, the parade's 10,000 marchers made it the largest in Eastern Europe, and in 2012 the numbers had doubled to 20,000. Ankara has likewise hosted a growing number of LGBT events in recent years, including university-based International Day Against Homophobia (IDAHO) events. In 2011 LGBT Iranian refugees and asylum seekers living in Turkey due to the criminalization of sexual diversity at home also organized their first Pride parade.

Istanbul holds two separate parades. In 2013 the trans community parade, which had also grown annually despite its smaller size, was held on June 23. LGB activists organized a second, larger event on June 30 (notably labeled "LGBT" so as to incorporate trans claims). The practice of holding distinct parades stems from divisions between LGB and trans activists, such as the concern of many trans people that they are less visible in the larger movement and as such want to assert their public presence separately. That said, efforts were under way in the 2010s to broker bridges between the groups, such as joint events and activist campaigns.

In the weeks leading up to the 2013 parade, LGBT activists had been highly active in the Gezi Park protests, forming an "LGBT *Blok*" and making themselves known with signs and emblems, as did other subcommunities, including football (soccer) clubs with their team banners. Collaborations among these radically divergent groups had been rare in Turkey to this point. The notion of cosmopolitics clearly fits these locally entrenched encounters; a sense of common purpose—opposition to the ruling party—rallied these individuals and groups to a politically shared place. Young activists outside of the LGBT community would have observed the gay bashing in which the police engaged, in tandem with aggressive dispersal tactics aimed at all protestors, involving tear gas, water hoses, and other measures. Observers reported that these daily encounters across identities may have forged a bridge across an LGBT/straight divide. Turkish trans activist Şevval Kılıç commented on the unique cosmopolitan encounters of the experience: "Anti-capitalist Muslims, queers, radical socialists, feminists, even the nationalists, the MHP, all of us were there at the same. It was like a fairy tale. I was lucky to experience it. This wasn't some group or some demonstration, this wasn't a kind of action. This was a public movement, a public awakening, you know. Whoever was outside that day, they knew, 'You're not alone.'"[35]

As the summer's Pride parades would demonstrate, other Gezi activists were grateful for the LGBT movement's strong, continuous contribution. They reciprocated in kind by joining the parades that traversed the same territory in the weeks to come. Thus, the summer's cosmopolitics was characterized by reciprocity as different groups' energies cross-infused.

Preceding the June 30 LGBT parade was a week of Pride events, including discussions, panels, and artistic performances.[36] Similarly reflecting the mood—indeed the hashtag—of the Gezi protests, Pride week organizers adopted the theme "Resistance" for 2013. As the ongoing Gezi protests unfolded, both the (fourth annual) trans parade on June 23 and the (tenth annual) LGBT parade on June 30 took place replete with gestures of sympathy for the Gezi Park occupiers. In this regard, the trans parade served as a precursor to the larger LGBT parade that followed, while both events complemented the simultaneous Gezi demonstrations. For example, trans parade marchers on June 23 chanted, "Everywhere is Taksim, everywhere is resistance," and "We don't want a transphobic state." Several parliamentary deputies representing the opposition secularist party, CHP (Republican People's Party), publicly participated in the march.[37] This signaled both an emerging public legitimacy for the movement and an outlet for the political opposition to express resistance to the ruling party. Notably, the trans parade swelled as a result. It grew from 500 participants just one year earlier to an estimated 10,000 in 2013. In 2013 the trans parade also enjoyed its first year without violent attacks on paraders.

It was the larger, June 30 LGBT Pride parade that I was able to witness firsthand. The parade started at Taksim Square, the epicenter of the antigovernment protests. Due to the unprecedented turnout, I waited with several hundred marchers at the back of the crowd for an hour for space to clear to file onto the pedestrian boulevard, İstiklal Caddesi. Despite the wait, a carnivalesque atmosphere was evident, with drumming and jubilant noisemakers. In contrast to the notable police presence in the square during the previous month, police lined up quietly shoulder to shoulder just behind the parade's back end. Conspicuously absent was the riot gear with which they had been fitted throughout the recent uprisings. Entertaining the waiting marchers and passersby was a burly man in a white wedding gown with a full puffed skirt, lace veil, tiara, and heavy makeup. Striking campy poses for photos with anyone who asked, he was bombarded with requests. Street vendors were on hand. They sold products that had become symbolic staples in the recent protests, such as Guy Fawkes masks and Turkish flags with the image of Mustafa Kemal Atatürk. A group of approximately fifteen or twenty LGBT socialist marchers formed their own subcontingent.

Participants' performance of a boundariless cosmopolitan diversity, in turn, clearly attracted individuals across international and intercommunal boundaries. For example, a youthful character was evident among marchers, but multiple generations also peppered the crowds. Shoppers and tourists *en route* to their destinations squeezed nonconfrontationally between the parade edges and the

Figure 10.1. 2013 LGBT Pride parade. Photo credit: Susan C. Pearce.

buildings lining the streets. Onlookers of diverse backgrounds seemed genuinely entertained by the spectacle of cross-dressers and a sea of crisply multicolored rainbow objects, costumes, and musical performances. To the casual observer, the parade resembled those in the West: it was a collective display of gaiety, solidarity, music, spectacle, fashion, and bawdiness. An occasional head-scarved woman danced to the revelry, and at least one photographed herself with a transvestite. The grim politics of the summer did not dissuade the marchers from silliness, which seemed infectious. Nevertheless, the march clearly performed sentiments and messages that struck a serious tone. Despite the spreading out of the trans and LGBT parades across two weekends, for example, in the latter many trans marchers made their presence known through signage such as one declaring "Trans people do exist" in Turkish.

Estimates of the 2013 parade's crowd size ranged from 40,000 to 100,000, easily doubling the 2012 parade count of 20,000. As for the trans parade, observers attributed the increase to Gezi allies. This Pride parade visibly echoed and attempted to advance the summer's broader protest action as a cosmopolitical gesture. Crowds booed as they passed all three Starbucks restaurants and a Mado ice cream store, franchises that had a reputation of refusing to harbor protestors escaping police violence. A pink banner stretched across the avenue on the ground read "Lesbian, Gay, Bisexual, and Trans RESISTANCE," with an image on it of one of the Gezi movement's symbols: the outline of a gas mask that recalls the stenciled "danger" symbol usually stamped on electrical boxes. Marchers carried at least one banner with the cartoon image of a penguin, also shorthand for the Gezi movement (due to the initial unwillingness of mainstream media to cover the protests; one channel instead broadcast a documentary about penguins). Many paraders also displayed "Gezi-wear" (my term) of gas masks, helmets, and Guy Fawkes masks.

Among the more striking representatives of cosmopolitan boundarilessness was the multilingual signage. A sprinkling of proud parents, for example, held signs that declared, "My Child is Gay"[38] in the Turkish, Arabic, and Kurdish languages. Observers took note of this unusually peaceful participation from diverse populations that generally are at odds in Turkey. Other polyglot appearances were paraders' placards calling for peace in Arabic, Armenian, Kurdish, and Turkish.[39] Visible also were politicians, representing the CHP (opposition) party and the Kurdish Peace and Democracy Party (BDP), as well as the European Union and the German Green Party. Their presence may have contributed to a growing sense of legitimacy among some sectors of Turkish society, regarding not only the parade but also the notion of rights for Turkish LGBT citizens. Other indicators of this trend had been the growing salience of LGBT issues and visibility in Turkish popular culture, with new feature and documentary films and Turkey's first LGBT film festival the previous year.

If the parades seemed almost idyllic in their celebration of diversity, reminders of stark challenges facing the movement also punctuated the route. The most clear-cut contrast to the cosmopolitan revelry was apparent at the parade's halfway point, the Galatasaray area. Lining the route on its left side were about twenty young men with stoic, defiant expressions standing in silent protest against the march. Hoisting a version of the Turkish flag motif with a sky-blue background rather than red, their counterprotest illustrated the persistent challenge to a fully cosmopolitan scenario of mutual recognition across identity groups. Each counterprotester pointed toward the parade with an extended index and pinky finger, a symbol of the ultraright Nationalist Action Party (MHP), which opposes Kurdish rights and EU membership. Though at odds with the AKP, in part due to the government's favorable gestures in that period toward both the Kurds and the EU, the stance was clearly directed at marchers, who smiled and flashed peace signs in response. Police officers created a human barrier between this group and the parade, and for the duration of the event no violent incidents were reported. However, the mutual recognition of difference in defiance of the present government among protesters clearly was not sufficient to ally at least one identity group (the MHP) with the LGBT movement. "The enemy of my enemy" is not always "my friend."

A further example of the darker side of these proceedings was the commemoration of community members whose sexual orientation had cost them their lives. One victim who was honored by name was gay rights activist Ahmet Yıldız, a twenty-six-year-old university student whose life was chronicled in a

2012 documentary five years after his father allegedly killed him for his sexual orientation. These reminders delimit the Turkish LGBT movement's apparent cosmopolitical breakthroughs.

As the parade reached its destination at the end of the boulevard, Tünel Square, there was peaceful if sonorous dispersal of crowds. A casual group of participants watched as a handful of young paraders climbed a monumental sculpture to hoist a massive rainbow flag, posing for photo ops and celebratory shouts. A little later, however, it became clear that the conflict-free possession of this central Istanbul space had been a parenthesis from the summer's uprising, as several marchers returned to Taksim and began heckling the police, resuming the contentious relationship that had been momentarily interrupted.

In sum, while the Pride parades of 2013 had been planned before the Gezi protests erupted, the events became infused with an unexpected development: the emergence of an imminent threat to LGBT urban spaces due to the government's renovation plans, and an alliance with other defiant constituencies. These cosmopolitan encounters were forged through the physical occupation of the streets. Thus while the Beyoğlu streetscape served as an *agora*—a politically sanctioned place of acceptable expressions of the people's will—the 2013 performances also revealed the boundaries that prevent full mutual recognition.

Forward to 2014

The year 2013 may have signaled a forward leap for LGBT activism in Istanbul and Turkey more generally. The June 30 LGBT parade was the largest Pride parade in Turkey to date. Two new parades were born that same day in the Turkish cities of İzmir and Antalya, and the aftereffects seemed to linger long past June. Later in the summer, a retired engineer painted outdoor stairs in rainbow colors on a prominent, visible hillside in Istanbul, reportedly simply to "make people smile" (though authorities immediately ordered the steps repainted in gray). This response only spurred further action; mimicking the hashtag #ResistGeziPark, #ResistStairs became another signal of the summer's reciprocal cosmopolitics. Stairways across Turkey were suddenly emblazoned in copycat rainbow colors.[40]

A particular cosmopolitan transnationality was evident in the presence of Iranian LGBT people in the parades and in their own events organized in Ankara: testimony to the queer spaces that cities allow. While Turkey is a country with a rich migrant history and present (see, for example, chapters 4 and 8 in this volume), these Iranians were fleeing a regime that criminalizes gay, lesbian, trans, or bisexual identities. Seeking a safe haven in Turkey or beyond, the Iranians' cosmopolitanism was unintended or even forced, but nevertheless brought together multiple "thick" identities in the common experience of gender-based oppression.[41] Together, Iranian and Turkish activists invoked transnational cosmopolitics as they demonstrated the boundarilessness of the LGBT community.

Istanbul Pride 2013 bore some resemblance to a parallel moment in US LGBT activism. In the late 1970s, as the San Francisco, California Pride parade similarly mushroomed and acquired ever greater respectability, a similar cosmopolitan air had prevailed. As with Gezi decades later, marchers came together under their respective identity banners, defined by religious affiliation, ethnicity, and professions.[42] This is not to imply that the Istanbul parade had sacrificed an edgy, transgressive character, as evidenced by its defiant moment (nor did the San Francisco parade, which was just beginning to confront the AIDS crisis).

There were other signs that the 2013 cosmopolitical protests and parades emboldened the LGBT movement, as some activists rode the wave of buoyed aspirations by entering electoral politics. In September 2013 Turkey's first openly gay mayoral candidate, Can Çavuşoğlu, an Istanbul native, unsuccessfully ran for office in a small Black Sea coastal town.[43] In 2014 four gay men entered the race for political office from their respective Istanbul districts; they did not win. Openly gay candidates on the Kurdish party ticket did win parliamentary seats in the June 2015 parliamentary polls, although the results were overturned by new elections in November.

Cosmopolitics may have been more salient for the LGBT movement than for the general antigovernment movement. By the summer of 2014 the visible Gezi Park movement had been largely suppressed. Due to arrests and intensive surveillance, few ventured into the streets. Nevertheless, a Gezi spirit continued to infuse Istanbul's summer 2014 LGBT Pride parade, which swelled to more than 100,000. Observers of this parade remarked on its resemblance to the 2013 procession, including the same emotions and causes, and in particular the Gezi movement-inspired resistance motifs. The wedding-gown-attired cross-dresser made a repeat appearance. A new Istanbul-based protest culture had clearly been born, manifest in the symbolic remnants within the 2014 parade, which vaunted the collective memory of Gezi and Pride from 2013.

Following the 2014 parade, I interviewed an LGBT activist about events since 2013. He reflected on the 2013 parade as a definite turning point toward greater legitimacy in the Turkish public sphere. Although he listed the many challenges that still faced his community in Turkey, he had also noted that the Gezi movement and the 2013 parade had propelled LGBT activism in an unprecedented way. The new domestic alliances and visibility that the movement enjoyed in 2013 and 2014 signaled that the interrelated, parallel street protests (Gezi Park and the parades) had at least emboldened the movement and galvanized unlikely allies to contribute. By all appearances, a novel protest culture had evolved and taken its place in a history of Istanbul social movement activism. Potential signals of cultural change—cross-identity alliances and Turkish LGBT visibility—illustrate how societal change is sometimes propelled forward: through a series of dialectical encounters across cultural difference, played out in such regular or sporadic rituals.

Cosmopolitan Apex?

Despite contentious and often violent past intergroup relations in Istanbul and Turkey more generally, the summer of 2013 offered a stage for omnibus causes and identity-based claims. These entailed a boundariless cosmopolitan flavor, whether at Gezi Park or on the Pride parade route. Due to the reach of media in the twenty-first century, these displays also went global. The mediatized nature of the movements in turn enhanced participants' capacity for collective learning: a phenomenon attested to by diverse identity-group interactions between those who were face to face in the park, in the square, and on the boulevard traversing the Beyoğlu neighborhood. As such, the digital age and social media platforms that helped to escalate the Gezi Park protests may have been critical ingredients in the LGBT mobilization. Cosmopolitan alliances were generated by these embodied encounters and the frenzy, fear, exuberance, and gratitude of collaborating in the face of the unknown and potential danger.

Such cosmopolitan encounters emerged unintentionally from the dynamics of social movement participation. Social movement scholars note that "sit-ins and encampments . . . can also serve to increase levels of commitment and solidarity among participants because of the intense and prolonged levels of face-to-face interaction involved in these tactics."[44] These outcomes may be intended or unintended and both external or internal to the movements in question.[45]

While the cross-fusion of identities at Gezi Park imbued an unprecedented vigor into the LGBT movement, it is difficult to predict whether these new cosmopolitan alliances will lead to enduring political and cultural convergences in Turkey. The years 2013 and 2014 are clearly memorable as unique moments with the potential for deep influence on Turkish society and intergroup relations. Given the oppositional presence of a nationalist group, it is clear also that backlash will continue to affect the movement, and that cosmopolitan encounters will remain incomplete, at least for the time being, especially in light of the ongoing authoritarian turn in Turkish politics to which Gezi was a response. In fact, in July 2016 the Istanbul resident and asylum seeker Muhammad Wisam Sankari, a gay man, was brutally murdered as Turkey continued to host Syrians escaping civil war.[46] National and local government resistance to Istanbul Pride, including the cancellation of subsequent parades since 2014, suggests that such Istanbul street action is now viewed as a political threat as well as a cultural offense. In fact, despite the successful 2014 parades and the 2015 trans parade held during the Ramadan season, on June 28, 2015, the annual LGBT parade was closed down just as it commenced by aggressive policing, following the AKP party's loss of a parliamentary majority in the summer elections. One explanation for the crackdown was that it should not be held during Ramadan. The shutdown was repeated for the 2016 and 2017 trans and LGBT parades.

The 2013 parades, I contend, nevertheless marked a momentary surge toward new forms of cosmopolitan encounters for Istanbul and for Turkey's LGBT movement.

They provided unique platforms for presentations of self at a moment of spontaneous grassroots opposition to the government and the coalescing of the Turkish LGBT movement. The cross-fusion of energies resulted in public performance of identities and unprecedented displays of empathy. This cosmopolitan collaboration surprised observers and participants, given entrenched divisions in Turkey. By all appearances, this cross-fusion has had consequences: its momentary intensity forwarded the project of gender and sexuality inclusion and melted divisions, even if the sitting government remained in power. Without claiming that Turkish society now fully embraces the project of gender and sexuality inclusion, this chapter has examined the possibility that the 2013 event represented a public leap forward on the issue, in part because of a new coalition of allies. Far from being a cosmopolitan patina over a canvas of historically entrenched ethnic, gendered, and religious divisions, Istanbul Pride helped to reveal the city's cultural complexity.

NOTES

1. Hongwei Bao, "Queering/Querying Cosmopolitanism: Queer Spaces in Shanghai," *Culture Unbound* 4 (2012): 97–120; Lynda Johnston, *Queering Tourism: Paradoxical Performances of Gay Pride Parades* (London: Routledge, 2005); and Susan C. Pearce, "'*Gej*' (Gay) in Southeast Europe: LGBTI Rights in a European-Global Corner" (The Global Europe Program of the Woodrow Wilson International Center for Scholars, 2014).

2. Pheng Cheah and Bruce Robbins, eds., *Cosmopolitics: Thinking and Feeling Beyond the Nation,* vol. 14 (Minneapolis: University of Minnesota Press, 1998); and Nira Yuval-Davis, *The Politics of Belonging: Intersectional Contestations* (Thousand Oaks, CA: Sage, 2011).

3. Ulrich Beck, *The Cosmopolitan Vision,* trans. Ciaran Cronin (Cambridge, UK: Polity Press, 2006).

4. Gerard Delanty, "The Cosmopolitan Imagination: Critical Cosmopolitanism and Social Theory," *The British Journal of Sociology* 57 (2006): 25–47.

5. I am deeply grateful to Cihan Hüroğlu for invaluable information about Turkish LGBT activism.

6. Sabrina P. Ramet and Branka Magaš, eds., *Gender Politics in the Western Balkans* (University Park: The Pennsylvania State University Press, 1999); and Metin Yeğenoğlu and Simten Coşar, "The AKP and the Gender Issue: Shuttling Between Neoliberalism and Patriarchy," in *Silent Violence: Neoliberalism, Islamist Politics and the AKP Years in Turkey*, ed. Simten Coşar and Gamze Yücesan-Özdemir (Ottawa: Red Quill Press, 2012), 179–209.

7. Seyla Benhabib, *Another Cosmopolitanism,* The Berkeley Tanner Lectures (Oxford: Oxford University Press, 2006), 51.

8. Pearce, "'*Gej*' (Gay) in Southeast," 6.

9. Erin Browner, "Istanbul Protests Help Build Unity for LGBT Pride," *Women's eNews*, July 11, 2013, http://womensenews.org/story/lesbian-and-transgender/130710/istanbul-protests-help-build-unity-lgbt-pride.

10. Nora Fisher-Onar and Hande Paker, "Towards Cosmopolitan Citizenship? Women's Rights in Divided Turkey," *Theory and Society* 41, no. 4 (2012): 375–394.

11. Yuval-Davis, *The Politics of Belonging*, 5.

12. Ibid.; and Pheng Cheah and Bruce Robbins, eds., *Cosmopolitics: Thinking and Feeling Beyond the Nation,* vol. 14 (Minneapolis: University of Minnesota Press, 1998).

13. Jean L. Cohen, "Strategy or Identity: New Theoretical Paradigms and Contemporary Social Movements," *Social Research* 53 (1985): 663–716.

14. Charles Tilly and Lesley J. Wood, Social Movements, 1768–2012 (Boulder, CO: Paradigm Publishers, 2012).

15. ILGA-Europe, "A Turkey and Europe with No LGBTIs. Till When Exactly?" 2013, http://old.ilga-europe.org/home/guide_europe/country_by_country/turkey/A-Turkey-and-Europe-with-no-LGBTIs.-Till-when-exactly.

16. Margaret E. Keck and Kathryn Sikkink, *Activists Beyond Borders: Advocacy Networks in International Politics* (Ithaca, NY: Cornell University Press, 1998).

17. This includes the United Nations, US federal agencies that operate internationally, the European Union, and others. See Pearce, "'*Gej*' (Gay) in Southeast."

18. ILGA-Europe, "A Turkey and Europe."

19. Ibid.

20. Pnina Werbner, *Anthropology and the New Cosmopolitanism: Rooted, Feminist and Vernacular Perspectives*, vol. 45 (Oxford: Berg, 2008).

21. Saskia Sassen, *The Global City: New York, London, Tokyo* (Princeton, NJ: Princeton University Press, 2001).

22. İbrahim Kaya, *Social Theory and Later Modernities* (Liverpool, UK: Liverpool University Press, 2004).

23. Dror Ze'evi, "Hiding Sexuality: The Disappearance of Sexual Discourse in the Late Ottoman Middle East," *Social Analysis* 49, no. 2 (2005): 34–53.

24. Michel Foucault, *The History of Sexuality: An Introduction* (New York: Knopf Doubleday, 2012); and Corinne Lennox and Matthew Waites, "Human Rights, Sexual Orientation and Gender Identity in the Commonwealth: From History and Law to Developing Activism and Transnational Dialogues," in *Human Rights, Sexual Orientation and Gender Identity in the Commonwealth: Struggles for Decriminalisation and Change*, ed. Corinne Lennox and Matthew Waites (London: Institute of Commonwealth Studies, Institute of Historical Research, Human Rights Consortium, University of London, 2013), 1–59.

25. Ishtiaq Hussain, "The Tanzimat: Secular Reforms in the Ottoman Empire," Faith Matters, February 15, 2011, http://faith-matters.org/images/stories/fm-publications/the-tanzimat-final-web.pdf.

26. Richard Aldrich, "Homosexuality and the City: An Historical Overview," *Urban Studies* 41, no. 9 (2004): 1719–1737.

27. Bao, "Queering/Querying Cosmopolitanism," 104.

28. Sassen, *The Global City*.

29. Mikhail Bakhtin, *Rabelais and His World* (Bloomington: Indiana University Press, 1984).

30. Begonya Enguix, "Identities, Sexualities and Commemorations: Pride Parades, Public Space and Sexual Dissidence," *Anthropological Notebooks* 15 (2009): 15–33.

31. Johnston, *Queering Tourism*.

32. Amy Mills, *Streets of Memory: Landscape, Tolerance, and National Identity in Istanbul* (Athens: University of Georgia Press, 2010), 31.

33. Vefa Saygın Öğütle and Emrah Göker, eds., *Gezi ve Sosyoloji: Nesneyle Yüzleşmek, Nesneyi Kurmak* [Gezi and sociology: Facing the object, constructing the object] (Istanbul: Ayrıntı Yayınları, 2014).

34. "2.5 million People Attended Gezi Protests across Turkey: Interior Ministry," *Hürriyet Daily News*, June 23, 2013, http://www.hurriyetdailynews.com/25-million-people-attended-gezi-protests-across-turkey-interior-ministry-.aspx?pageID=238&nid=49292&NewsCatID=341.

35. Piotr Zalewski, "A Curse to Be a Woman," Bülent: A Journal of Contemporary Turkey (July 2013), https://web.archive.org/web/20140122171950/http://bulentjournal.com:80/a-curse-to-be-a-woman/.

36. "21st LGBT Pride Week," 2013, http://prideistanbul.tumblr.com.

37. Axcella Zed, "Istanbul Trans Pride Parade Turns into Gezi Park Protest," June 24, 2013, *images on concrete words on paper* [blog], https://imagesonconcretewordsonpaper.wordpress.com/2013/06/24/istanbul-trans-pride-parade-turns-into-gezi-park-protest/

38. Erin Browner, "Istanbul Protests Help Build Unity for LGBT Pride," *Women's eNews*, July 11, 2013, http://womensenews.org/story/lesbian-and-transgender/130710/istanbul-protests-help-build-unity-lgbt-pride.

39. "Taksim Stages Exuberant Gay Pride March Joined by Gezi Protesters," *Hürriyet Daily News*, June 30, 2013, http://www.hurriyetdailynews.com/taksim-stages-exuberant-gay-pride-march-joined-by-gezi-protesters.aspx?pageID=238&nID=49779&NewsCatID=339.

40. Kendra S., "Rainbow Stairs in Istanbul," *Rusty Travel Trunk* [blog], September 12, 2014, http://rustytraveltrunk.com/2014/09/12/rainbow-stairs/.

41. Fisher-Onar and Paker, "Towards Cosmopolitan Citizenship?"

42. Randy Shils, *And the Band Played On* (New York: St. Martin's Press, [1987] 1988).

43. "Turkey's First Ever Openly Gay Mayor Candidate Announces Bid," *Hürriyet Daily News*, September 12, 2013, http://www.hurriyetdailynews.com/turkeys-first-ever-openly-gay-mayor-candidate-announces-bid.aspx?PageID=238&NID=54344&NewsCatID=341.

44. David A. Snow and Sarah A. Soule, *A Primer on Social Movements* (New York: W. W. Norton, 2010), 206.

45. Ibid.

46. "Gay Syrian Man Beheaded and Mutilated in Turkey," *BBC News*, August 4, 2016, http://www.bbc.com/news/world-europe-36973314.

Acknowledgments

First and foremost, we are grateful to the contributors to this volume for their patience and brilliance.

We would also like to thank all of the original speakers in the symposium series that launched this project through the support of the Istanbul European City of Culture 2010 and the hospitality of Bahçeşehir University. Special thanks in the context of the symposia are owed to Anna Maria Beylunioğlu Atlı, Selma Bardakçı, Ayşe Kadıoğlu, Kalypso Nicolaidis, Yeşim Pekiner, and Sabri Sayarı.

Susan Pearce would like to thank the Department of Sociology, East Carolina University, and the chair of the department, Dr. Bob Edwards, for support of this project. She is also highly grateful to the Woodrow Wilson Center for Scholars for the grant that supported some phases of this research. And she would like to extend her deep appreciation for the excellent work of Kathleen Basile in the final work of manuscript completion.

Nora Fisher-Onar is indebted to the National Humanities Center and her fellow fellows in 2013–2014 whose feedback on earlier iterations of the project was critical to its seeing fruition. She is especially grateful to participants in the Cities reading group, including Christian de Pee for comments on an earlier draft of the prospectus, and the immense generosity of Cemil Aydın, Sarah Shields, and Jocelyn Olcott, among many others in the Duke and UNC Chapel Hill communities. Similarly, she thanks the organizers and participants at the Reasonable Accommodations workshop, convened by Duke's Council for European Studies, the Duke Islamic Studies Center, the Council for North American Studies, the Kenan Institute for Ethics, and the Center for Jewish Studies at Duke on March 19, 2015.

Fisher-Onar is deeply grateful, moreover, to the Transatlantic Academy of the German Marshall Fund of the United States and the Program for Middle East Political Science (POMEPS) at George Washington University's Institute for Middle East Studies (IMES), especially Stephen Szabo, Michael Barnett, Nathan

Brown, and Marc Lynch, who provided multiple forms of support that enabled this volume to progress.

For the final stages of the process, Fisher-Onar owes much to Çağlar Keyder, Meriç Özgünes, and Jeremy Walton for incisive comments on the introduction. Seray Pulluk also provided exceptionally good assistance with the final manuscript and images.

Finally, this book is commended to the loving memory of Alan Fisher, Ataman Onar, and Ferdane Keyman.

Recommended Further Reading

Barkey, Karen. *Empire of Difference: The Ottomans in Comparative Perspective*. Cambridge, UK: Cambridge University Press, 2008.

Bryant, Rebecca, ed. *Post-Ottoman Coexistence: Sharing Space in the Shadow of Conflict*. New York and Oxford: Berghahn, 2016.

Çağatay, Soner. *Islam, Secularism and Nationalism in Modern Turkey: Who Is a Turk?* New York: Routledge, 2006.

Çınar, Alev. *Modernity, Islam, and Secularism in Turkey: Bodies, Places, and Time*. Minneapolis: University of Minnesota Press, 2005.

Göktürk, Deniz, Levent Soysal, and İpek Türeli. eds. *Orienting Istanbul: Cultural Capital of Europe?* London: Routledge, 2010.

Hanioğlu, Şükrü. *A Brief History of the Late Ottoman Empire*. Princeton, NJ: Princeton University Press, 2008.

Hintz, Lisel, *Identity Politics Inside Out: National Identity Contestation and Foreign Policy in Turkey*. Oxford: Oxford University Press, forthcoming.

Kadıoğlu, Ayşe, and E. Fuat Keyman. *Symbiotic Antagonisms: Competing Nationalisms in Turkey*. Salt Lake City: University of Utah Press, 2011.

Keyder, Çağlar. *Istanbul Between the Local and the Global*. New York: Rowman and Littlefield, 1999.

King, Charles. *Midnight at the Pera Palace: The Birth of Modern Istanbul*. New York: W. W. Norton, 2014.

Nicolaidis, Kalypso S., Berny Sebe, and Gabrielle Maas, eds. *Echoes of Empire: Memory, Identity and the Legacy of Imperialism*. London: I. B. Tauris, 2015.

Mills, Amy. *Streets of Memory: Landscape, Tolerance, and National Identity in Istanbul*. Athens: University of Georgia Press, 2010.

Örs, İlay Romain. *Diaspora of the City: Stories of Cosmopolitanism from Istanbul and Athens*. New York: Palgrave Macmillan, 2018.

Özyürek, Esra. *Nostalgia for the Modern: State Secularism and Everyday Politics in Turkey*. Durham, NC: Duke University Press, 2006.

Pamuk, Orhan. *Istanbul: Memories and the City*. New York: Vintage, 2006.

Tambar, Kabir. *The Reckoning of Pluralism: Political Belonging and the Demands of History in Turkey*. Palo Alto, CA: Stanford University Press, 2014.

Tanju, Bülent. "Public Space (I)." In *Becoming Istanbul: An Encyclopedia*, ed. Pelin Derviş, Bülent Tanju, and Uğur Tanyeli, 272–274. Istanbul: Garanti Gallery, 2008.

Tuğal, Cihan. *Passive Revolution: Absorbing the Islamic Challenge to Capitalism*. Palo Alto, CA: Stanford University Press, 2009.

Turam, Berna. *Gaining Freedoms: Claiming Space in Istanbul and Berlin*. Palo Alto, CA: Stanford University Press, 2015.

Walton, Jeremy F. *Muslim Civil Society and the Politics of Religious Freedom in Turkey*. New York: Oxford University Press, 2017.

White, Jenny. *Muslim Nationalism and the New Turks*. Princeton, NJ: Princeton University Press, 2014.

Web Resources

MUSIC, TELEVISION, AND FILM

Crossing the Bridge—the Sound of Istanbul: For a review of a feature-length documentary about Istanbul's vibrant music scene by award-winning director Fatih Akın, see http://www.nytimes.com/2006/06/09/movies/09brid.html.

Fetih 1453 (*Conquest 1453*): For a review of a blockbuster film about the conquest of Constantinople by Mehmet the Conqueror, see https://www.theguardian.com/world/2012/apr/12/turkish-fetih-1453.

Kedi (*Cat*): For a documentary that evokes a quintessentially Istanbulite humanism and aesthetics via the lives of seven cats and their caregivers, see https://www.kedifilm.com/.

MuhteşemYüzyıl (*The Magnificent Century*): For an analysis of the popular soap opera about the life, times, and harem politics of Süleyman the Magnificent, see http://www.newyorker.com/magazine/2014/02/17/ottomania.

MAPS

For a digital humanities database that allows one to trace the evolution of the city in interactive maps, see http://www.istanbulurbandatabase.com.

For historical maps showcasing the demographic diversity of various parts of the city, see a fine collection in the 1922 Pathfinder guide to Istanbul, see Clarence R. Johnson, *Constantinople Today or The Pathfinder Survey of Constantinople: A Study in Oriental Life*(London: Macmillan, 1922), esp. 18 and 150. https://archive.org/details/constantinopleto1922john.

For a map of Istanbul's evolving metro system, including interactive animated features, see http://www.metro.istanbul/passenger-services/network-maps.aspx.

PHOTOGRAPHY

For the work of iconic chronicler of the city Ara Güler in images, seehttp://www.araguler.com.tr.

For compelling contemporary images of Istanbul, among other places, see the work of Alison Lyons at http://www.alisonlyonsphotography.com.

GENERAL INTEREST

For an overview of Istanbul's history, see https://www.britannica.com/place/Istanbul.

For a list of Ottoman sultans with images, see http://www.turkishculture.org/general/ottoman-sultans-433.htm.

For the website of Nobel Prize–winning novelist Orhan Pamuk, who writes about Istanbul, see http://www.orhanpamuk.net/.

Notes on Contributors

FEYZI BABAN is a professor of political studies and international development at Trent University. His research interests include international relations theory, critical theory, cosmopolitanism, citizenship studies, Turkish politics, and Turkey-EU relations. He has written for journals such as *Postcolonial Transitions in Europe*, the *Journal of Ethnic and Migration Studies, Citizenship Studies, European Journal of Social Theory*, and *Global Society*.

KRISTEN SARAH BIEHL is an anthropologist who specializes in migration research in Turkey. For the past decade she has been involved in both academic and policy research on migration and asylum in Turkey, working with a number of migrant and refugee communities, NGOs, and public institutions. Such work includes the EU's comprehensive needs assessment of the situation of Syrian refugees in Turkey. Her research interests range from exploring the everyday lived experiences of asylum seekers in Turkey to understanding how urban society and space are transformed through migration and diversification processes. Kristen is currently completing her doctorate in anthropology at the University of Oxford. Her doctoral research entailed ethnographic fieldwork in Istanbul's Kumkapı district, in which she examined how differences are socially and spatially experienced, which she theorizes through the notion of dwelling. Kristen joined Istanbul Policy Center of Sabancı University as a 2016/17 Mercator-IPC Fellow.

ANNA BIGELOW is associate professor of Islamic studies in the Department of Philosophy and Religious Studies at NC State University. She received her MA from Columbia University (1995) and PhD in religious studies from UC Santa Barbara (2004) with a focus on South Asian Islam. Her book, *Sharing the Sacred: Practicing Pluralism in Muslim North India*, is a study of a Muslim majority community in Indian Punjab and the shared sacred and civic spaces in that community. Bigelow speaks and writes frequently on religious extremism, religion and conflict, and the role of Islam in the world today. Her current research involves further study of contested yet shared sacred sites in South Asia and the Middle East.

NORA FISHER-ONAR is assistant professor in global politics at Coastal Carolina University. She serves as research associate of the Centre for International Studies (CIS) at Oxford University and as a nonresidential fellow of the German Marshall Fund (GMF). Her research interests include international relations, political and social theory, comparative area studies, gender, history/memory, and foreign policy analysis. She received her doctorate from Oxford and holds master's and undergraduate degrees from Johns Hopkins (SAIS) and Georgetown Universities, respectively. She lived in Istanbul for over a decade and speaks five languages, including fluent Turkish. Fisher-Onar has published extensively in academic journals including *Theory and Society*, *Women's Studies International Forum*, *Conflict and Cooperation*, *and Millennium*. She also regularly contributes to policy fora such as the GMF, Brookings Institution, and Carnegie Endowment, and platforms such as *Foreign Affairs*, the *Guardian*, and *OpenDemocracy*.

ÇAĞLAR KEYDER is professor of sociology at Binghamton University. Author of *State and Class in Turkey* and editor of *Istanbul: Between the Local and the Global*, most of his work has been on Turkey, covering historical sociology and political economy of the Ottoman Empire and modern Turkey, urbanization and globalization of Istanbul, and agrarian transformations in Anatolia.

E. FUAT KEYMAN is professor of international relations at Sabancı University. He is also the director of Istanbul Policy Center (IPC) at Sabancı University. He works on democratization, globalization, international relations, civil society, Turkish politics and foreign policy, and Turkey-EU relations. Keyman is a member of the Turkish Science Academy, as well as of respected international academic and journal boards. He served as a member of the Wise People Commission as part of the peace process with the Kurdish movement. Keyman's many publications in English and Turkish include *Democracy, Identity, and Foreign Policy in Turkey: Hegemony Through Transformation*; *Symbiotic Antagonisms: Contending Discourses of Nationalism in Turkey*; and *Remaking Turkey: Globalization, Alternative Modernities, and Democracies*.

CHARLES KING is professor of international affairs and government, chair of the Department of Government, and former faculty chair of the Edmund A. Walsh School of Foreign Service at Georgetown University. He is the author of *Midnight at the Pera Palace: The Birth of Modern Istanbul*, which was awarded the French Prix de Voyage Urbain Le Figaro-Peninsula Paris; *Odessa: Genius and Death in a City of Dreams*, which received the National Jewish Book Award; *The Ghost of Freedom: A History of the Caucasus*; and other books.

AMY MILLS (MA Middle East studies; PhD geography, University of Texas at Austin) is an associate professor of geography at the University of South Carolina.

Her research engages with conversations in critical human geography, urban studies, and interdisciplinary Middle Eastern studies. Her first book, *Streets of Memory: Landscape, Tolerance, and National Identity in Istanbul*, explored cultural memories of Istanbul's non-Muslim minority pasts. Dr. Mills's current research examines the cultural geopolitics of urbanism in Istanbul after World War I. Her work has been published in venues including *Comparative Studies of South Africa, Asia, and the Middle East*; *Cultural Geographies*; the *International Journal of Middle East Studies*; and *Gender, Place and Culture*. Dr. Mills serves on the international advisory boards of *fe dergisi/fe journal*, the *Turkish Journal of Human Geography*, and the *International Journal of Middle East Studies*. She has held leadership positions in the Turkish Studies Association and in the Association of American Geographers and supports interdisciplinary scholarship in geography and Middle East studies.

İLAY ROMAIN ÖRS is associate professor of social anthropology and a faculty member at Istanbul Bilgi University. She completed her PhD in anthropology and Middle Eastern studies at Harvard University, following her master's studies at University College London and her two BA degrees in sociology and political science at Boğaziçi University Istanbul. A Turkish citizen born in Istanbul, ÖRS is competent in English, German, and modern Greek. She recently revised her dissertation fieldwork on the Rum Polites into a book entitled *Diaspora of the City: Stories of Cosmopolitanism from Istanbul and Athens*. Her further research and publications are concentrated on topics including migration, mobility, minorities, political movements, and urban studies in Greece, Turkey, and the Mediterranean.

HANDE PAKER, a political sociologist, works on civil society, the state, the transformation of citizenship, and political ecology. She has carried out research and published on modes of civil society-state relations, politics of the environment at the local-global nexus, and grounded cosmopolitan citizenship, with a particular focus on environmental struggles and women's rights. Her articles have appeared in *Environmental Politics, Theory and Society, and Middle Eastern Studies*. Her research as a 2015/16 Mercator-IPC fellow focuses on local and transnational environmental spaces of action to analyze how environmental civil society actors engage the issue of climate change to mobilize publics. Paker holds a PhD and an MA from McGill University, and a BA from Boğaziçi University. She is based at the Faculty of Economics, Administrative and Social Sciences, at Bahçeşehir University.

SUSAN C. PEARCE is associate professor of sociology at East Carolina University in North Carolina. She conducts research on the cultural contexts of politics, particularly concerning ethnicity, migration, gender, and social movements. She is coauthor of the monograph *Immigration and Women: Understanding the American Experience*, with Elizabeth Clifford and Reena Tandon; coeditor of *Reformulations: Markets, Policy, and Identities in Central and Eastern Europe*, with Sławomir Kapralski; and coeditor of *Mosaics of Change: The First Decade of Life in the New Eastern Europe*, with Eugenia Sojka. Her PhD in sociology is from the New School for Social Research in New York. She has also served on the sociology faculties of Gettysburg College, West Virginia University, University of Gdańsk (Poland), and Central European University (Poland).

SAMI ZUBAIDA is emeritus professor of politics and sociology at Birkbeck, University of London, a fellow of Birkbeck College, a research associate of the London Middle East Institute, and a professorial research associate of the Food Studies Centre, both at SOAS. He has held visiting positions in Cairo, Istanbul, Beirut, Aix-en-Provence, Paris, Berkeley, California, and New York. He has written and lectured widely on themes of religion, culture, law, and politics in the Middle East, with particular attention to Egypt, Iran, Iraq, and Turkey. His other work is on food history and culture. Zubaida's books include *Islam, the People and the State: Political Ideas and Movements in the Middle East* (translated into Arabic, Hebrew, Italian, and Turkish); *A Taste of Thyme: Culinary Cultures of the Middle East* (edited, with R. Tapper, translated into Arabic and Turkish); *Law and Power in the Islamic World* (translated into Arabic, Danish, and Turkish); *Beyond Islam: A New Understanding of the Middle East*; and the forthcoming book *Food, Politics and Society* (with A. Colas, J. Edwards, and J. Levi).

Index

AVAILABLE TITLES IN THE NEW DIRECTIONS IN INTERNATIONAL STUDIES SERIES:

Niki Akhavan, *Electronic Iran: The Cultural Politics of an Online Evolution*

A. Aneesh, Lane Hall, and Patrice Petro, eds., *Beyond Globalization: Making New Worlds in Media, Art, and Social Practices*

Dora Apel, *War Culture and the Contest of Images*

Daniel Leonard Bernardi, Pauline Hope Cheong, Chris Lundry, and Scott W. Ruston, *Narrative Landmines: Rumors, Islamist Extremism, and the Struggle for Strategic Influence*

Mark Philip Bradley and Patrice Petro, eds., *Truth Claims: Representation and Human Rights*

Hye Seung Chung and David Scott Diffrient, *Movie Migrations: Transnational Genre Flows and South Korean Cinema*

Kennan Ferguson and Patrice Petro, eds., *After Capitalism: Horizons of Finance, Culture, and Citizenship*

Nora Fisher-Onar, Susan C. Pearce, and E. Fuat Keyman, eds., *Istanbul: Living with Difference in a Global City*

Melissa A. Fitch, *Side Dishes: Latina American Women, Sex, and Cultural Production*

Elizabeth Swanson Goldberg, *Beyond Terror: Gender, Narrative, Human Rights*

Linda Krause, ed., *Sustaining Cities: Urban Policies, Practices, and Perceptions*

Linda Krause and Patrice Petro, eds., *Global Cities: Cinema, Architecture, and Urbanism in a Digital Age*

Andrew Martin and Patrice Petro, eds., *Rethinking Global Security: Media, Popular Culture, and the "War on Terror"*

Tasha G. Oren and Patrice Petro, eds., *Global Currents: Media and Technology Now*

Peter Paik and Marcus Bullock, eds., *Aftermaths: Exile, Migration, and Diaspora Reconsidered*

Lisa Parks and James Schwoch, eds., *Down to Earth: Satellite Technologies, Industries, and Cultures*

Rebecca Prime, *Hollywood Exiles in Europe: Blacklisted Filmmakers in Postwar Europe*

Freya Schiwy, *Indianizing Film: Decolonization, the Andes, and the Question of Technology*

Cristina Venegas, *Digital Dilemmas: The State, the Individual, and Digital Media in Cuba*

